Deviant Interpretations

EDITED BY

David Downes
Paul Rock

1979

LAW IN SOCIETY SERIES

edited by

C. M. C. Campbell and P. N. P. Wiles

Martin Robertson

First published in 1979 by Martin Robertson & Co. 108 Cowley Road, Oxford OX4 1JF.

ISBN 0 85520 265 3 (case edition)
ISBN 0 85520 264 5 (paperback)

Typeset by Pioneer Associates, East Sussex.
Printed and bound in Britain by
Richard Clay (The Chaucer Press) Ltd, Bungay, Suffolk

Contents

Preface

Largely in the space of two decades, criminology and the sociology of deviance have come to incorporate almost all the theories of social systems and action which exist in mainstream sociology. The division of labour in both main and subsidiary fields roughly matches. But this process has also been more jagged and discontinuous than such a description might imply. The special features of crime, delinquency, deviance and control — the inherent attributes of deviousness, covert practices, the departure of much deviant behaviour (and control) from the canons of 'rationality' — have led theorists to draw more heavily on certain traditions, or on certain aspects of those traditions, than others. Thus, symbolic interactionism, with its injunction to attend to the subjective interpretation of meaning, and to do so by ethnographic work based on participant observation, has been thought to yield more systematic glimpses 'beneath the surface' than quantitative methods allow. The recent resurgence of interest in Marxist analysis has partly derived from its apparent capacity to 'decode' deviant phenomena as responses to the 'normalised repression' of modern capitalism.

These and other approaches vie for attention and also for ascendancy (as they do in other fields) in both philosophical and theoretical terms. The days when their practitioners were more united than divided by the common aim to eradicate positivism are now past. A host of theoretical problems have been raised by the succession of attempts to supplant previous perspectives with more comprehensive and rigorous alternatives. The common bid in these essays is to forestall the premature burial of some of these problems; otherwise, as in some Poe-like fantasy, they will surely return to haunt us.

The themes include the limitations of according too central a role to praxis in criminology (Downes); the dangers of presuming to demystify (Cohen); the pitfalls of the search for 'total' explanations of deviance (Rock); the rise and 'fall' of labelling theory (Plummer); the much-invoked but largely unexplored issue of determinism and its alternatives (Beyleveld and Wiles); and the difficulties to be surmounted in attributing motive and meaning to 'deviant' subjects (Taylor). These by no means exhaust the themes available, but they represent some of the most urgent problems left by the debates of the past decade.

There have been clear transformations in the sociology of deviance which have received scant public discussion but which, conversely, arouse the most animated arguments in teaching settings. It was to amplify some of the informally developed arguments that the authors of these papers decided to collaborate, not least to prevent new orthodoxies from arising for want of the informed debate we hope to stimulate.

Praxis Makes Perfect
A Critique of Critical Criminology[1*]

David Downes

For the past fifteen years or so, the trend has been for the dominant 'model' of sociological thought — composed of a more or less deterministic, explanatory and quantitatively researched set of assumptions — to give way before the attacks mounted against it by sociologists of a more or less voluntaristic, interpretative and qualitatively minded persuasion. Three articles signalled the decisive break as far as American sociology was concerned: Dennis Wrong's 'The Over-socialised Conception of Man' (1961), George Homans's 'Bringing Men Back In' (1964) and Everett Hughes's 'Race Relations and the Sociological Imagination' (1963).† In substance, these articles were less radical in the alternatives they preferred than in the dramatic challenge to orthodoxy implied by their titles. Wrong's trenchant attack on the 'over-socialised' conception of man as a counterpart to the 'over-integrated' view of society led to a plea for the reinstatement of Freud in sociological theorising. Homans's dissection of the incongruity of structural-functionalism and historical change must be seen in the context of the limitations of his own brand of social behaviourism. And Hughes, in his laying of the blame for American sociology's failure to foresee a sharp deterioration in race relations at the door of 'abstract empiricism', did little more than echo C. Wright Mills.[2] But all these papers were addressed to the American Sociological Association: all duly appeared in the *American Sociological Review* between 1961 and 1964. In sum, they were an acknowledgement, from the most senior platform in the discipline, that sociological theory was ill-equipped to cope with the most pressing social and intellectual problems. Gouldner's 'coming crisis' (Gouldner, 1970),[3]

*Notes on the text will be found at the end of each paper.
†A consolidated bibliography is provided at the end of the book.

1

announced somewhat late in the day, had already come, and it is clearly still with us.

Ultimately, two attempts at resolving the crisis have attracted most following (though even now it is doubtful whether more than a minority of sociologists on either side of the Atlantic subscribe — in any thorough-going sense — to either; they either lack any firm theoretical anchorage or opt for a safe Weberian harbour.) These attempts emanate from Mead and the symbolic interactionist tradition,[4] and from Marx — and the 'humanistic' early Marx in particular.[5] For a time an uneasy alliance between the two prevailed. The case was made anew for regarding man as a subject rather than an object: for causality as mediated through men as active agents, rather than as passive receptors; and, more tentatively, for sociology as a practice attuned to social conflicts and the open advocacy of radical means of resolving them, rather than as an upholder of the *status quo,* with a veiled advisory role in the making of social adjustments. But this compromise proved provisional only. For if the most penetrating work in sociology in the sixties went on at the micro-sociological level, it was because the issue of determinism at the level of the individual and interpersonal relations was pursued at the expense of the issue of deter-minateness at the institutional and macro-sociological level. The pull to Marx has been a move to 'bring society (or political economy) back in'. And events which shook American society in the late 1960s and 1970s prised the two approaches even further apart.

In criminology these developments were more dramatic, chiefly because the initial gap between the mode of explanation favoured in criminology and the revived aspirations for a more humanistic sociology of deviance was even greater than in sociology in general. The dominance of the medico-legal approach to explanations cast in terms of structural and cultural 'forces' and 'patterns' had given criminology a marginal status as far as sociologists were concerned. Even so, the vogue for regarding criminology as a sort of unique backwater in the social sciences has been overdone. In the sociology of education, in demography, in political sociology and in industrial sociology, similar rigidities prevailed. What gave peculiar force to the trend away from positivism in criminology was the conjunction between the more general reassertion of the claims of interpretative sociology and an unusually forceful rejection of the philo-sophical grounds for the existence of criminology as a subject in its own right.

The grounds on which criminology existed as a subject have never been adequately appraised or even satisfactorily outlined, but **the distinctiveness** of the criminal sanction is implicitly assumed to lend credence to the study of those found guilty of legal infraction. As it evolved, criminology paid little attention to how and why the criminal sanction came to be invoked against certain kinds of behaviour and not others, or against certain individuals and not others who engaged in similar infractions. This omission was seen as crucial by those who preferred a different and more inclusive deviancy framework for the study of crime and delinquency. Because the law is the outcome of processes of definition which emanate primarily from the powerful, and as a result is so cast as both to secure their interests and minimise the likelihood of their incrimination, it cannot be taken for granted as a neutral arbiter of conforming and aberrant behaviour. Moreover, many laws are almost wholly declaratory, 'more honoured in the breach than the observance', e.g. the 30 m.p.h. speed limit in built-up areas; by contrast, many quite legal activities are both viewed as morally opprobrious and arouse an intense emotionality and hostility of response, e.g. homosexual exhibitionism. The assumption that the criminal sanction is somehow unique palls before the sheer variability of its definition and enforcement. In criminology, as a result, Becker's publication of *Outsiders* (1963) was an event of much greater significance than the articles by Wrong, Hughes and Homans in sociology. His central organising principle — 'Deviant behaviour is that which is so labelled' — superficially a banal and even trivial assertion, caused an explosion in the petrified forest of criminology. It signalled a major reorientation from a position which assumed the virtual unchallengeability of studies which took the legal code and the manner of its enforcement for granted to one which treated these processes as problematic. The scope of enquiry was widened from law infraction to rule- and norm-infraction. The mode of inquiry was shifted from the statistical to the interpretative. The social reaction to deviance became as central to inquiry as the deviance itself. In the process, the sociologist was required to take account, as never before, of the deviant's view of himself and the world. One aspect of this concern was a redefinition of praxis: the sociologist was to be partisan in his defence of the underdog (deviant) in the face of the attack mounted against him by social controllers (police, social workers, welfare bureaucrats). Arguments for decriminalisation and an active reassertion of liberal pluralism followed in train.

It was primarily to this aspect of the new sociology of deviance that Gouldner addressed himself in his critique of Becker and others in 1968. Donning the mantle of C. Wright Mills, Gouldner was at pains to point out that, to mix mythological metaphors, having helped to slay the

minotaurs of objectivity and structural-functionalism in sociology, he did
not intend standing idly by whilst new dragon's teeth were sown in the
shape of subjectivism and relativism which lacked all semblance of regard
for social structure. In a by now hallowed phrase in the annals of critical
criminology, he stated: 'Becker's school of deviance thus views the underdog as someone who is being mismanaged, not as someone who suffers or
fights back . . . [It] is directed at the caretaking institutions who do the
mopping up job, rather than at the master institutions that produce the
deviant's suffering' (Gouldner, 1968, p. 39). To Gouldner, the deviant's
version of events and himself, ironically, can only reproduce that of the
master institutions whose definition of reality has been stamped upon him.
While this is in itself questionable, the way forward for radical, as distinct
from liberal, sociologists is to be the study of the deviance of 'overdogs',
whose power not only to grasp but to *shape* the machinery of control also
enables them to shape the worlds in which both deviants and caretakers
move and interact. 'The Sociologist as Partisan' provided the point of
departure for those who sought to differentiate a radical criminology from
a liberal sociology of deviance. It is in this spirit that *The New Criminology*
(Taylor et al, 1973a) and *Critical Criminology* (Taylor et al, 1975a), as
well as *Crime of the Powerful* (Pearce, 1976) should be approached.

As critical criminologists lay great emphasis on purposes, my own
should be alluded to. Since the appearance of *The New Criminology,* but
especially since that of its successor volume, *Critical Criminology,* teaching
the subject to a wide variety of students in higher education, further
education and training courses has had to take account of a challenging
new approach. Long moribund, Marxist criminology has been revitalised
by these books (whatever the Althusserians might say). Some effects have
been entirely to the good: students can now be directed (in the case of the
first of the books) to what is still the most comprehensive and succinct
coverage of virtually the entire criminological studies field; certain issues
— for example, the contribution of Durkheim to the study of crime and
deviance — have been freshly explored, and the 'crimes of the powerful'
issue has been rediscovered. But some effects have been more negative:
notably, the difficulties encountered, in my own case at any rate, in
examining the issue of just what the 'new' or 'critical' criminology is *for.*

This may seem obtuse, in that the authors concerned have stated their
aims with great apparent clarity as being 'to argue for a criminology which
is normatively committed to the abolition of inequalities of wealth and
power' and 'to attempt to create the kind of society in which the facts of
human diversity are not subject to the power to criminalise' (Taylor et al,

1975a, p. 44). Where, then, is the difficulty?

The core of the problem lies in their relation of theory and practice (praxis), and it is best conveyed by quotation:

> The point about theoretical praxis, for us, is that it is concerned to encourage the changes specified by the precepts of its own radical theory, and to develop research procedures relevant to that project . . . It has to develop methodologies for the realisation of the societies its own critique would necessitate, for, as David Harvey puts it, 'a revolutionary theory . . . will gain acceptance only if the nature of the social relationships embodied in the theory are actualised in the real world.' (Taylor et al, 1975a, p. 24)[6]

In other words (a) the answers to the questions that matter are already known; (b) it is not, however, possible to specify what these answers amount to in advance of their actualisation.

In my view, these axioms serve ultimately to constrain rather than liberate, to fetter rather than free; because they commit their authors to precepts and purposes which are inherently self-confirming, their work seems to present insurmountable difficulties to sociologists who may otherwise be in sympathy with their aims.

One of the most striking criticisms that Gouldner makes of Becker's 'Whose Side are We On?' (1967) is that Becker never makes explicit his answer to this question. While in both that address (to the American Society for the Study of Social Problems) and in *Outsiders,* Becker implies throughout that we should be on the side of the underdog deviant who is 'more sinned against than sinning', nowhere can Gouldner find an explicit assertion to that effect, a discovery that leads him to some dark reflections on the difficulty that liberals would find themselves in both professionally and financially if they had the courage of their convictions.

In a similar spirit, the collected writings of radical criminologists can be searched in vain for what one might take to be the central premise on which their project rests: a statement of the properties which a truly socialist (and crime-free) society would possess. Now this omission is of a far more fundamental character than that attributed by Gouldner to Becker, for, in the latter case, whether or not Becker made an explicit personal commitment to the underdog makes not one jot of difference to the intellectual strengths and weaknesses of his position. But in the case, as it has so far been stated, of critical or radical criminology, the entire intellectual construction rests on the postulates that capitalist society is essentially criminogenic, and that only by the total repudiation of the ethic of possessive individualism on which it rests can 'true' equality and 'socialist diversity' — the prerequisites for a 'crime-free' society — be attained. As it may be argued that these propositions are quite independent, that is, that we may accept the one without *ipso facto* needing to accept the other, the authors concerned might appear to be making things unnecessarily hard for themselves by linking the two. Yet this is what they appear to do. .

> The processes involved in crime-creation are bound up in the final analysis with the *material* basis of contemporary capitalism and its structures of law . . . Critically, we would assert that it *is* possible to envisage societies free of any material necessity to criminalise deviance. Other controls on 'anti-social' behaviour (and other definitions of what that might constitute) can be imagined, and, from the point of view of a socialist diversity, would be essential. (Taylor et al, 1975a, p. 20)

On this last point, the reader is then referred to Young's essay, 'Working-class Criminology', (1975) which asserts the need for working-class control of deviance in working-class communities (on which, see below). This aside, nowhere is any attempt made to lay bare for analytical inspection the properties which would characterise a truly socialist society. Frequently invoked, it serves as a rhetorical foil against which to highlight the evils of capitalism. This kind of argument by affirmation reaches a pitch of absurdity in the statement 'A socialist conception of man would insist on the unlimited nature of human potential in a *human* society' (Taylor et al, 1975a, p. 23), where the italics are in some fashion intended to carry the full weight of philosophical argument to sustain the assertion.[7]

Were this simply a matter of parenthesis, of a stylistic flourish or embellishment to the major issues at stake, it would hardly be worth pursuing. But all the indications are that, far from serving merely to decorate the argument, the invocation of a crime-free socialist diversity is the very core of the argument. It enables the authors to dismiss all or almost all that has gone before as so much 'conservative' or 'liberal' mystification, the former (knaves) actively supporting, the latter (fools) indirectly reinforcing, the structures of capitalist political economy. The sharpest analysis and the deadliest invective are indeed applied to mere 'social-democrat reformism', particularly of the Fabian variety. Any attempt to reform capitalism from within, by recourse to the institutions of bourgeois democracy, is to be rejected. The idea that considerable variations exist *between* capitalist societies, in the extent to which the welfare state, for example, has made inroads upon the market economy, is held in particular scorn. By definition, such interventionism can only serve to prop up the essentially exploitative nature of capitalism. That state socialist

societies have not only found it necessary to develop a welfare state
apparatus, but have also experienced a set of social problems comparable to
those in social democratic societies is not regarded as much of an obstacle
to this line of argument, though a growing literature attest to this — *The
Case-Worker* by George Konrad (1975) is the most impressive recent
example from Eastern Europe.[8] In common with the New Left, the answer
to this would doubtless be that these societies are not truly socialist, but
rather state capitalist. As to how it came about that state capitalism was
the outcome of socialist praxis, there is a massive apologetic literature
concerning the 'wrong road' or whatever taken by the socialist societies in
the main. But the twin themes that recur in that literature, betrayal from
within and capitalist encirclement, are increasingly threadbare. Socialists
would greet with derision the argument that capitalism had taken the
wrong road because its leaders had betrayed it, or because of feudal or
precapitalist encirclement. The sad truth is that, as increasing proportions
of the world's population come to experience one or other variations of the
state socialist theme, the relevance of Marx diminishes and that of Weber
increases in almost geometric progression. But the authors of *Critical
Criminology,* and the New Left in general, rarely feel obliged to resolve
these questions. Next time, they say, it will be different.

Now the conception of praxis which is brought into play at this stage has
several crucial functions. It enables the 'radicals' to postpone indefinitely
the need to examine analytically the nature of the socialist alternative to
the capitalist system; to insist that, because the future is unknowable, no
time need be wasted on the likely institutional configuration that would
render socialist diversity more than a nominal possibility; to ignore the
substantial differences and variations that exist between capitalist societies
in the light of the experience gained of different 'mixtures' of private and
public sectors of the economy and welfare services; and, finally, to minimise
the relevance of the experience of state socialism in resolving the very
problems they discern as essentially bound up with capitalism. Praxis
becomes a means for suspending awkward theoretical issues and stubborn
historical constraints. The ideal of freeing men from the tyranny of
causality by endowing them with knowledge gained by sociological
theorising is undermined by the insistence that its tentative and ambiguous
character should be rejected in favour of clear-cut Marxist presuppositions
about the world. Attempts to translate the latter into practice have,
moreover, a familiar authoritarian ring to them (see Stan Cohen's 'It's All
Right for You to Talk' (1975)) 'We Know Best' is not the only possible
outcome of this epistemology but it is the one historically shown to be

most likely, especially when concepts like 'false consciousness' can be employed to bridge any gaps between theory and actuality.

The search for what in *The New Criminology* was described as the 'total interconnectedness' between crime and the political economy of capitalism too easily leads to a revival of the 'seamless web' approach to social phenomena. An example of the latter is Jock Young's argument that

> Cultures which threaten work discipline, sexual behaviour which undermines the nuclear family, adolescent hedonism are all subject to legal prosecution and distorted coverage in the mass media. Thus when the state of California spends $73 million in 1968 on marihuana control, when more is spent on Social Security prosecutions than has even been obtained illegally from the State, when supposedly scarce police resources are utilised in the persecution of gays, and when legislation denies women the right to choose whether to give birth or not — all this seeming ruling-class irrationality contributes enormously to the maintenance of bourgeois institutions. (Foreword to Pearce, 1976, p. 18)

Doubtful as it is whether or not such 'irrationality' does indeed contribute to the 'maintenance of bourgeois institutions', the point about this argument is its circularity. If marihuana use is prosecuted, then that is because it threatens capitalism. If the penalties are drastically reduced, or if they are abolished altogether (as is in prospect in several U.S. states), then that is presumably because capitalism no longer fears it. (This is not, however, the case with Greenwood and Young's study of abortion (1976), where more careful consideration is given to the 'ruling-class interests' variable.) None of which should detract from the importance of seeking to establish what connections obtain between crime and its control and the 'master institutions' of any society, capitalism included. But it is even more important to forestall a resurgence of functionalism in the process, even if it is linked with humanistic Marxism. As Sklair concluded in his review of Parsonian functionalism: 'It is essential to evaluate the functionalistic method, in the sense that it suggests to us where to look, in isolation from the functionalist doctrine, that tells us what we will find there' (Sklair, 1970, p. 40).

The most depressing accompaniment of this form of praxis is the foreclosure it threatens on theorising. The premise that crime derives from the material facts of life in propertied societies rests on a set of unexamined assumptions about crime and its control, assumptions which have been subjected to the most searching criticism over the past decade. Not that such a premise lacks plausibility: just that it begs all the most fruitful methodological, analytic and theoretical questions raised by the critics of positivist and consensual approaches in criminology. Praxis brings the wheel of consensus full circle, back to an unproblematic view of the world. The premise ignores the possibilities that alternative sources of crime exist which are not reducible to propertied inequalities: notably, that the division of labour in advanced industrial societies of both capitalist and socialist societies of various kinds may play a causal role. Neither does the premise begin to make sense of the vast differences of crime and its control in societies with rough equivalence in properties inequality; for example, such differences hardly account for the variation in homicide rates that exist between the U.S.A. and Britain. In one society, China, there is a correspondence between the absence of propertied inequality and a (from all accounts) negligible crime rate, but the fate of political deviants, and the possibility of diversity (the phrase is never expanded upon) must await further documentation than has so far been available even to sympathetic Western observers. This is not to say that the present range of human societies exhausts the full range of human possibility. But the experiences of the post-1917 period should be enough to be going on with, without acting as if socialist praxis has never been tried before. Theorising may not have to end with what exists, but should at least take it into account. As it is, critical criminologists too often write as if imperialism was monopolised by capitalist societies, as if the tanks had never rolled into Prague or Budapest, as if people in capitalist societies were utterly dehumanised (except where they are struggling heroically against the bosses).

Such comments may seem invidious, particularly when the authors elsewhere clearly display an acute consciousness of the repression endemic in state socialist regimes — as in Ian Taylor's review of Connor's book on crime in Russia (1973a), and Young's reference to Soviet labelling of political dissidents as mentally ill (Foreword to Pearce, 1976, p. 12) (though the Soviet regime goes far beyond mere labelling in the last case). However, the comments do seem appropriate in the context of such absolutist statements as: 'It is not that man behaves as an animal because of his "nature" (under capitalism): it is that he is not fundamentally allowed by virtue of the social arrangements of production to do otherwise' (Taylor et al, 1975a, p. 23). Such a statement is simply bizarre when set beside such a record as *The Gulag Archipelago* on the one hand, and against the humanistic achievements of Western societies ('under capitalism') on the other. In general, however, it is not that they are asking unimportant or wrong questions about capitalism: it is that they allow such questions to *stop* at capitalism, as if oppression and corruption, of a systematic and regularised nature, did not present issues of any great analytic interest when they occur under nominally socialist systems. In one passage only (Taylor et al, 1973b, p. 401) do they state that crime is not specific to capitalism, i.e. that capitalism is distinctively criminogenic, not uniquely so. The issue is treated as 'true' (but 'obvious'): no more need be said than a reference back to the incompatibility of criminalisation with socialist diversity.

The usual reply to this kind of criticism is that existing forms of state socialist society are not to be equated with *true* socialism, that it is ludicrous to expect a blueprint for a truly socialist society, when its possibilities have only ever been glimpsed, and when praxis is by definition a process of open-ended struggle, rather than the ushering in of a preformulated framework. It is certainly the case that a blueprint is the last thing we want. The ideal of a perfectly planned Utopia has proved as abhorrent to twentieth-century writers in the dystopian tradition — particularly Zamyatin and Huxley — as it was to Marx. But avoiding prediction at all costs is no solution to the Utopian dilemma. What is needed is not a blueprint, but an ideal-typical sketch of the kind of society summoned up by the phrase 'socialist diversity'. How is it envisaged that we move away from a society based on propertied inequality without becoming a state capitalist society? How would people be allocated to jobs — by merit, by rota, or what? How will political life be conducted? These questions could be postponed in the not-too-remote past, when a capitalist ruling class was unquestionably dominant, when class differences resembled a caste-like massification, and before any substantial attempt had been made to remove basic industries and services from the private to the public sector. The first can hardly retain credibility when a Tory government has been trounced from office after a humiliating confrontation with the miners. The second has given way to a far more complex structure in which class inequalities still obtain but are increasingly measurable only by resort to relative rather than absolute indicators of difference. The third has reached the point where approaching one-third of productive industry and two-thirds of all transfer payments are state owned and managed. In other words, we have reached the point at which the days of modern consumer capitalism *could* be numbered, in Britain at any rate, if the political will to despatch it matched the evident and already mobilised strength of the forces which oppose it ideologically, yet actually operate to keep it in existence. (Its days are ultimately numbered anyway, since — as *The Limits to Growth* spelt out, with data that may be problematic but on principles that surely aren't — the constant fostering of the propensity to consume, by which capitalism has sustained itself these last fifty years, cannot outlast the limits on that consumption set by the eco-system; see Meadows et al, 1972, and Hirsch, 1977.) But the system is still actively kept in existence, if only in a negative and inert way, by the very movements which oppose it, in part at least because no specifiable alternative to it has been shown to exist, or has been adequately proposed as a potential alternative by the various groups on the Left. A few exceptions should be noted. The work on workers' control by Ken Coates is one; the writings of André Gorz on political democracy are another (see Coates, Gorz in Anderson and Blackburn, 1965). But in the main, the Left has concentrated on sheerly polemical fulmination against the existing system or endless analyses of the contradictions of capitalism, with all of which we are by now wearisomely familiar.

It is to this impasse that the conception of praxis which appears in the work of radical criminologists and others on the Left has helped bring us. By equating specifiable and documented proposals for change with 'mere' reformism, by — indeed — dismissing the ideal of gradual and therefore reversible change as contemptible, they may convey the *grounds* on which the socialist diversity they invoke is preferable or superior to the liberal capitalist-cum-social democratic society they reject, but we are left without any clue as to what practices might constitute its character (see, for example, Titmuss, 1970). In seeking to transcend *all* aspects of contemporary practice, in asserting the need to change the *status quo out of recognition,* they create a vacuum which is to be filled by . . . what? Since they not only fail but make a positive virtue of *refusing* to specify those institutional features which might serve as the basis for socialist diversity, they should not be too surprised if the response is guarded caution.[9] As Orwell pointed out even thirty years ago, the British people have a great deal more to lose than their chains.

In one instance, though, an attempt has been made to outline an alternative to present institutional practice. In his 'Working-class Criminology' (1975), Jock Young asserts the need for the working class to wrest control of its own communities from 'external policing agencies'. The implications of this position (which lacks any accompanying strategy) can at least be subjected to some sort of sociological scrutiny, in sharp contrast to the foreclosure of any possibility of validation that characterises the critical perspective in other respects. This said, Young's brief allusion to this issue is more remarkable for what it leaves unexplored than for what it actually states. It rests on the assumption that external policing agencies simply or mainly act to enforce the law of the bourgeoisie, in a manner and on principles which are at odds with working-class interests. (Needless to say, this is quite different from the Fabian position, which is broadly that considerable consensus exists about the law, but structured inequalities exist in relation to its mobilisation on behalf of those — still the majority — who lack the means to afford its practitioners' services.) It assumes that the working class overwhelmingly resides in homogeneous communities which share a distinctive consensus, at odds with the middle class, about the scope, range, aims and methods of policing. It implies that working-class communities would benefit from internal policing, in the face of the considerable conflicts and fissures that exist *within* such communities. It implies that working-class deviants would fare better under class-specific rather than constitutional safeguards — but no differentiation is made between types of justice, which run the gamut of possibility from authoritarian and arbitrary lynch law to the most subtle forms of mutual aid. All the dilemmas of due process vs. executive, legalistic vs. welfare and restitutive vs. deterrent forms of justice and control are ignored. In sum, it raises the most important issues only to duck them. The most likely result of implementing Young's ideas would be a reversion to the chaos that prevailed in London before the Metropolitan Police Act of 1829. It would leave the poorer and more vulnerable sections of the working class far worse off than now, reproducing a state of affairs that already prevails in the worst American ghettoes. It would herald the rapid expansion of private security forces, the costs of which would be heaped regressively on the poor — unless, of course, all this hinges on the prior attainment of a state of 'socialist diversity'. In which case, the adoption of a class-based form of control will be redundant.

Linked with Young's argument is the view that the criminal statistics are most fruitfully interpreted as an index of 'the credibility of a propertied society at particular periods of its development — the extent to which the distribution of property is latently accepted or rejected amongst certain sections of the working population' (Taylor et al, 1975a, p. 42). The fact that we *can* 'read' them this way, by extension reading into the rise in crimes against property a growing rejection of the ethic of possessive individualism, in no way overcomes the formidable problems involved in 'reading' the criminal statistics any way at all, or of choosing between this 'reading' and the equally plausible alternative that a rise in propertied crime entails an *increase* in attachment to possessive individualism. For one of the striking findings of the recent rash of studies of victimisation has been the extent to which the victims of crimes against property are those people without any (relatively speaking, that is). For example, field studies carried out for the 1967 President's Commission on Law Enforcement and the Administration of Justice in the U.S.A. were summarised as showing that 'the risk of victimisation is highest among the lower-income groups for all Index offences except homicide, larceny and vehicle theft; it weighs most heavily on the non-whites for all Index offences except larceny' (Ennis, *Challenge of Crime in a Free Society,* 1967 p. 39). Moreover, even the larceny finding relates only to sums of $50 or more: if all larcenies had been included, that finding too may have tallied with the other offences in its distribution of victims, since the lower one's income, the less one is likely, presumably, to be in possession of sums of over $50. Indeed, this is partially borne out by figures showing median net property losses by income group, which for whites shows the average for those whose incomes were under $6,000 was $34, while for those whose income exceeded that sum it was $30, a result that could have occurred only if the lower-income group experienced a far higher rate of larceny of sums under $50 than the higher income group (see Ennis, 1967, tables 8 and 14). The point, however, is that only by the most tortuous reasoning can a rejection of the ethic of possessive individualism and the current distribution of property be culled from such evidence. For what such figures show is not a Robin Hood-like robbing of the rich to serve the poor, but a massive infliction of misery on those least able to protect themselves. These results hardly tally with the often-quoted denial of local victimisation by delinquent boys; though the most fiercely held loyalties may be respected, this does not necessarily protect those of the same status living on the next block. What this evidence points to is an affirmation of possessive individualism *come what may,* what Robert Merton some forty years ago termed 'innovation', as opposed to its alternative, 'rebellion'. It may well be that such predatory activity represents the final, seedy triumph of 'bourgeois' culture: but it is possible to test this proposition against the resurgence of similar forms of victimisation in non-capitalist societies only if we abandon approaches which limit analysis to capitalism alone.

All the issues debated here are of ancient lineage. Their reinscription, their resurfacing at this stage is perhaps a sign that sociology has come full circle, that its potential as an escape route from time-worn philosophical constraints is at an end. I would prefer to believe that those constraints are illuminated and modified by sociological theorising and research, that the grounds on which certain positions are advanced can be clarified by sociological work, but that such a perspective bears fruit only if certain ground rules are respected. As Giddens has argued, '. . . those conditions in which human beings appear as objects to themselves . . . may be altered by "self-knowledge" which is false just as much by that which is valid (Giddens, 1976, p. 154). To foreclose the issue at the outset, on the strength of a world view that takes in only half the world, can only pre empt all possibility of criteria that hold the terms of the debate open. If, on the other hand, you choose to operate on the view that capitalism is the source of nothing but evil, that no accommodation with it can be reached short of revolutionary action, that state socialist societies are really state capitalist societies and thus are not admissible as models of the likely outcomes of socialist praxis — a species of 'convergence' theory just as unacceptable as the orthodox kind — then you can indeed reel off the connections between crime, delinquency and capitalism as the central causal matrix.

Ironically, the adoption of this form of socialist praxis makes the advocacy of socialist diversity unnecessarily difficult. For the intellectual 'self denying ordinance' that true socialism can be known only by negation, dialectically, rather than empirico-deductively, by tangible documentation, removes debate altogether from the realm of the known or knowable to that of sheer speculation. Not that such an alternative is easy, but it at least offers certain safeguards against absolutist conceptions, such as the comparative assessment of one system against another in terms of certain agreed-upon criteria, rather than resisting such scepticism as incompatible with immaculate theoretical conceptions. It is the mode of analysis shared by both social-democratic reformism, whose record is hardly as contemptible as critical criminologists make out, and latter-day anarchists, whose mauling at the hands of the state in both capitalist and socialist societies has lent a certain defiant modesty to their proposals. The most significant of these is an insistence that freedom, equality and justice are not remote abstractions to be realised only in some future and essentially unknowable society, but tangible realities to be grasped here and now in the many-sided forms of praxis that exist in education, housing, industry and family relations. It is the difference between a specifiable mode of praxis, in which it is possible to document the more from the less human, and a transcendental form of praxis, in which the contrast is made between an utterly inhuman and deformed present and an immaculate future and unknowable Utopia.

Marxists, especially those of the New Left, are fond of referring to social democratic theory in disparaging terms connoting theoretical vacuity, emptiness, intellectual void, etc. Most typically, Perry Anderson's diagnosis of British culture as 'bourgeois' culture was based on his view that intellectual life in Britain lacked the centre that in other European societies was formed by Marxism and the dialogue with Marxism (Anderson, 1968). Yet this notion of the 'absent centre' seems to apply with equal force to Marxist theory itself, for at the very centre of Marxist theory there is indeed a void: the nature of the 'classless' society. That that void has since been filled in by two major possible structures, Stalinism and Maoism, is no great comfort, since we know far too much about the former and far too little about the latter to be able to take them as corresponding to what theorists might mean when they invoke the classless society as their ideal. What is missing is any developed analytic treatment of the distribution of power and the division of labour that would match the attainment of 'classlessness' in an advanced industrial society. For, as Parkin and Giddens have made clear, it is upon the power relations that ensue from the *fusion* of control over the polity and the economy that the most oppressive features of state socialist societies are built (Parkin, 1972, especially ch. 6; Giddens, 1973, especially ch. 15).[10] In this perspective, even the deformed split between these two bases of power under modern capitalism afford their citizens some measure of freedom from total 'dehumanisation'.

NOTES

1. My thanks to Ernest Gellner, Paul Rock, Stan Cohen and Laurie Taylor for helpful comments on an earlier draft of this paper.
2. Mills's classic onslaught against 'grand theory' and 'abstracted empiricism' in *The Sociological Imagination* (1959) began what these and a host of other writers later consolidated.
3. The ultimate consolidation of Mills's critique.
4. See Matza (1959) for the most elegant summary of this tradition.
5. See Gouldner (1970) for a summary of these developments in the sixties. The most influential exponents in Britain were to be found in the New Left.
6. Their reference here was to Harvey (1973), p. 125.
7. The references are to *Critical Criminology* (Taylor et al, 1975a), in which these issues loom distinctly larger than in *The New Criminology* (Taylor et al, 1973a). The passage quoted is aptly met by Passmore's argument that:

   > One ought to regard with an initial suspicion such expressions as 'truly human' and 'dehumanising' . . . Cruelty and envy are peculiarly human forms of behaviour; to assert of someone who is cruel or envious that he is not 'truly human' is undeservedly to compliment the human species. It takes a human being to be a Marquis de Sade, to construct the concentration camps at Auschwitz, to wage war, to lie, to betray, to hate. Man is never less an animal than in the depths of his depravity. To describe a state of society as 'dehumanising' merely because it encourages men to deceive, to lie, to be cruel is, on the face of it, arbitrarily to admit as human only what is good. (Passmore, 1970, p. 279-280.)

8. This novel is both by, and portrays the life of, a social worker in Budapest.
9. The work of Thomas Mathiesen is of special relevance here, particularly his *The Politics of Abolition* (1974). One critic of the 'critical criminologists', Stan Cohen (in Bailey and Brake, 1975), finds Mathiesen's strategy of the 'unfinished'

preferable to one recipe for praxis floated by Ian Taylor. The strategy of Mathiesen, however, which is basically to avoid incorporation at all costs (whilst taking his role as an academic sufficiently seriously to struggle for abolition long-term and general reforms short-term) by means of a refusal to specify alternatives, is difficult to distinguish from sheer pragmatism. It is a pragmatism inspired by a passionately real commitment to work for a (wholly unspecified) socialist society, but that does not rescue us from the impasse of being asked to work for a future about which we are not allowed to theorise (at least in public). For an astringent view of the consequences of abolition in practice in the USA, see Scull, *Decarceration* (1977).

10. Both of these authors argue for the continuing relevance of Marx's concepts of class and class conflict as essential for an understanding of societies based on market economies. But the importance of their work is their avoidance of an acceptance *a priori* of the Marxist mode of analysis, their subjection of Marx's theories to the critical perspectives offered by other modes of analysis and their extension of the scope of inquiry to a comparative assessment of neo-capitalist and state socialist societies. It is this kind of approach, which seemed immanent in *The New Criminology*, from which *Critical Criminology* represents a turning away.

Guilt, Justice and Tolerance: Some Old Concepts for a New Criminology [1]

Stanley Cohen

It is not the business of writers to accuse or prosecute, but to take the part even of guilty men once they have been condemned and are undergoing punishment. You will say: what about politics? What about the interests of the State? But great writers and artists must engage in politics only so far as it is necessary to defend oneself against it. There are plenty of accusers, prosecutors and gendarmes without them; and anyway the role of Paul suits them better than the role of Saul. (Anton Chekov)

If by 'writers' we are to understand novelists, poets or dramatists, then perhaps Chekov had some sort of point. Substitute, though, 'sociologists of deviance' or 'criminologists' for 'writers' and we find that different parts of his statement lead us in quite opposite directions. The recommendation not to accuse or prosecute looks acceptable enough, but the warning against politics is obviously less so. It is the split between these two directions that I want to examine in this paper.

The new sociologies of deviance of the sixties and the emergent radical/new/critical/Marxist criminologies of the seventies certainly followed the injunction not to accuse or prosecute — or not (as we would have put it) to 'side with the agents of social control'. And the specific injunction 'to take the part even of guilty men' was exactly the principle articulated in the writers who shaped our ideas in the sixties and whose quotes littered our lectures and publications: Polsky on the need to suspend conventional moral judgements, Becker's 'Whose Side Are We On?' and — most eloquently and imaginatively — Matza's advocacy of appreciation as against correctionalism. Any comparisons of sociological naturalism with naturalism in the novel (or 'social realism' in another tradition) were

17

quite deliberate and indeed most sociologists working in this vein began t
see themselves as novelists *manqués*. Sociology of deviance booklists wer
(and still are) full of those works of fiction which we told our student
would give a more realistic view of the world than our own research: *Las
Exit to Brooklyn, Junkie, Our Lady of the Flowers, One Flew Over th
Cuckoo's Nest* . . . these would tell it like it is. (Curiously, we forgot tha
most such 'realistic' works were also profoundly moralistic in intent.)

The methodological and theoretical problems in this position have bee
pursued relentlessly enough — and most of the warnings against the dri
towards an ahistorical subjectivism are surely justified. But one set c
problems, the moral ones to which this paper is addressed, were brushe
aside. It is not that we were unaware of them: intellectual autobiographie
always make us sound dumber in the past than we really were in order t
give the illusion of continual cerebral progression. In fact, few were dum
enough to think that naturalism and appreciation were without certai
moral inconsistencies — to say the least. Matza, with his usual sense c
irony, covered himself: 'To appreciate the variety of deviant enterprise
requires a temporary or permanent suspension of conventional moralit
and thus by usual standards inescapable elements of irresponsibility an
absurdity are implicit in the appreciative stance' (Matza, 1969, p. 17).

Both in this early naturalistic phase and its later more romanti
deviations such irresponsibility and absurdity were obvious enough in th
heady world of seminar rooms, but they could not be readily translated int
the public world of social policy. Indeed, their existence there could nc
even easily be admitted. If — so one of the public's questions ran –
deviants were not pathological beings driven by forces beyond their contro
then surely as rational, responsible beings they should be punished *mor*
severely? Ah no, that's not *quite* what we meant. And when we talke
about being on the side of the deviant, did this mean we were actually i
favour of what he did? Here, our answers were really tortuous. Faced wit
behaviour like vandalism or football hooliganism which we couldn't openl
approve of (in the sense of advocating tolerance or non-punishment), the
our main message was that actually there was much *less* of this than th
public thought (because of moral panics, selective perception, stereotyping
scapegoating, etc.). Simultaneously, of course, to other audiences, w
welcomed such behaviour and pointed to the evidence which showed tha
if society didn't Radically Change, then indeed the public's fears woul
materialise and more of the behaviour would occur. With other forms c
deviance easier to support openly within the liberal consensus — abortior
the gay movement, dope smoking — we happily advocated tolerance, eve

in public. And this time we would say that there was not less, but far, far *more* of such behaviour than anyone could imagine through their stereotypes. Confusion indeed.

Already apparent in these stances was the vacillation between the image of the deviant as mismanaged victim and the deviant as cultural hero — images which Young (1975) later correctly identified as associated with *laissez-faire* liberalism and a more full-blown ideological romanticism. The moral mixture persisted. Towards most forms of deviance an exceedingly low-minded moral nihilism seemed the order of the day — but this stance was hardly consistent. Towards other forms of deviance a high-minded moral absolutism prevailed — crimes of the powerful were condemned with puritanical zeal. Appreciative studies of polluters, exploiters and manipulators (all highly morally loaded words) were not, to my knowledge, advocated. And who today would dare to embark on an appreciative study of rapists in the face of the consensus between radicals of both sexes that these offenders must be immediately and strictly punished? But appreciation is not the same as *conversion,* and a suspended morality operated all along in the choice of subjects and groups which were suitable candidates for the new theories. It was less a question of consistent moral nihilism — which is, at least, an established philosophical position — than of selective morality. Refusing to support conservative values, we operated only just a fraction outside the liberal consensus. 'Radicalism' was liberalism with a loud mouth — and on subjects like paedophilia, not a very loud mouth either.

The further we got drawn into the world of criminal justice policy (on which this paper focuses), the more evident these confusions became.[2] Correctly, I believe, the solution to this was seen as the need to move to more macro-political theory and strategy. The precise direction which this move took (towards developing a political economy of law and crime and worrying about meta-theoretical issues) might be defensible in itself. It does not, however, really answer the confusions left behind by the faltering attempts to translate an earlier unstated morality into policy.[3] It was as if we had drafted the blueprint for a new bomb, even constructed bits of it, left it lying around — and then run rapidly in other directions. In this last year or so the running has stopped, and in a number of important statements, such as Young's 'Working Class Criminology' (1975), we are at last back to the scene of the intended crime.

'What about politics? What about the interests of the state?' Now, while there might be something to be said in favour of Chekov's injunction simply to defend oneself against the interests of the state, this was obviously not the direction the new criminologies took. Libertarian and Marxist principles, though inarticulated, unseparated and usually submerged under a simpler underdog sympathy, were always there. When the Marxist elements became more explicit, the problem was not that criminology became too politicised (whatever that may mean) but that the crucial political question about the interest of the state — the question central to libertarian and anarchist writing — was never properly asked. Matza made a beginning with his baroque philosophical contemplation of Leviathan, but the preoccupations of Marxist criminology — with the political economy of law and the theory of capitalism as criminogenic — never came to grips with the concrete political and moral dimensions to which think Chekov refers. The interests of the state lie in prohibiting certain actions and punishing those responsible for these actions. The questions these interests raise (and always have) — are only now being considered in the new criminologies. I believe that it is only by putting them firmly on the agenda that the connections with criminal politics can be made.

In suggesting this agenda I am not really concerned whether anyone has got Marx right (as Rock is in his contribution to this volume) or with the bridge between these theories and the rest of sociology. It is the bridge to criminal justice policy which is the more precarious. Beyond filling in the picture of the system as repressive, the impact of the new theories has been slight. And while it would be politically naive to assume that our writing in themselves could have much power, it is important to construct an agenda which does not leave the debate to the Right.[4]

ON REDISCOVERING MORAL JUDGEMENTS

In classical criminology, the moral fit between the image of the criminal and the nature of criminal policy was reasonably close. And the moral judgements in the debates about what the law should prohibit and how individual offenders should be punished were open and transparent. With the positivist introduction of determinism and its consequent inversion of the notion of personal responsibility, the potential for a new fit between image and policy began. All historians have exaggerated the impact of the positivist revolution: not so much in the world of academic theory, where it was profound, but in criminal policy, where it was extremely uneven. The gap between image and policy never closed; as *The New Criminology* (Taylor et al, 1973a) correctly pointed out, the conflict between the free will, classical, legal model and the deterministic, scientific paradigm of positivism was resolved by the extremely awkward compromise of neo-classicism — 'a qualitative distinction is made between the majority who are seen as capable of free choice and the minority of deviants who are determined' (Taylor et al, 1973a, p. 37). It is not clear whether this 'minority of deviants' refers to *all* the deviants compared with the conformists, or a minority *within* the deviant population. In either case, though, while the compromise might have been theoretically clumsy, it was ideologically quite sound.

In some areas, most notably juvenile justice, the fit looked a bit closer, though even here the classical model was undermined more in theory than in practice. Instead of one policy replacing another, the rhetoric of treatment and the rhetoric of punishment were used simultaneously in the same courts and the same custodial institutions. But the impression of a genuine fit between theory and policy was sustained in public. Hence it is more obviously in regard to juveniles that the current attack from radicals (in the name of justice) and conservatives (in the name of law and order) is the most aggressive.[5] In adult criminal policy it has been more transparently business as usual — and to blame the failures of the criminal justice system on the doctrine of positivism is much like blaming structural inequality on the doctrine of functionalism. In retrospect: our attacks on positivism should have been more discriminating and should have identified more clearly the special ways in which 'positivism' appeared under such guises as extenuating circumstances, diminished responsibility, probation, parole — all within a neo-classical system. And all these developments (even comparing just England with America, let alone the rest of the world) were extremely uneven from one society to another. Positivism was, indeed, a massive theoretical con-trick — the separation of crime from the state — but we were also conned into thinking that the change had happened in criminal policy as well. The separation indeed went along: but so did the state.

At this point — the assault on positivism — there was some potential for the moral position of neo-classicism (some should be punished, others should not) to be positively confronted. But in its initial stages, the assault was only a job of demystification. As Pearson describes it well, it was medicine and technology defrocked. The effect of the new sociologies was to dereify the technical and professional screen behind which welfare and medicine operated. This was supposedly to lay bare the morality underneath to reveal that deviance is a moral matter: a matter about what sort of society we are to live in (Pearson, 1975).

But this defrocking and undermining was not nearly as effective as

Pearson and others suggest — partly because the original sin of mystification had never been committed in the first place. More important, the effect was lost because the implicit substitute — the emperor underneath the tacky clothes of positivism — was revealed not in his full moral nakedness, but in his new underwear of naturalism and appreciation — with the absurdities I earlier suggested. Our first glimpse in the dressing room was of the mismanaged, stigmatised, underdog — or so he looked to some. This was quickly deemed inadequate (not a 'fully social' picture of man) but once again, instead of a glimpse of moral nakedness, a new (albeit short-lived) disguise was tried on: the 'fully social', rational, crypto-political deviant.

Here, with so many outfits being tried before so many fitting-room mirrors, is where our problem starts. Though few were irresponsible or silly enough to promote these disguises in their pure forms, these two new images remained in the mirrors: the underdog and the hero. And whatever the differences between them, these images suggested a common suspension of conventional morality. Deviants are troublesome or disruptive, but we should still try to appreciate them. This could and did lead to a giddy irresponsibility and although these successive images were always accompanied by careful qualifications and later were repudiated altogether, their reflections remained in the mirror. In the texts of this period, delinquents are busy redistributing private property and schizophrenics are attacking the double-bind concentration camp of the nuclear family.

I want to repeat that these images were both qualified at the time and rejected later. This rejection was most explicit in Young's argument that the new theories merely inverted positivist images: either man's possibilities were pictured as infinite, or he was naturally good and interfered with by the state busybodies, or (in the voyeuristic version) he was the existentially superior deviant poised on society's margins (Young, 1975, pp. 68-71).[6] So while deviancy theory was applauded for demystifying positivism, it was condemned for doing so at the expense of erecting '. . . a rational Frankenstein constructed out of the inverted conceptual debris of its positivist opponents' (Young, 1975, p. 71).

Unfortunately these rejections came too late and — as I will suggest — they still need filling out with some sort of alternative. To vary my earlier metaphor: we flashed around the plans for a new bomb, and then said, 'That's not what we really meant. Back to the drawing board.' In the meantime, despite the dire warnings, the old images remained. The new sociologies were stranded in positions which lacked credibility. The reaction to all this — which as Pearson (1975, p. 105) suggests was partly an embarrassed reaction to the excesses of the counter-culture — has been interesting enough, but it bears on a different set of questions. The emerging political critique of criminology — right or wrong — simply did not address itself to the criminal policy questions raised by the initial defrocking.

Such a critique was understandable in the light of the harder political realities of the seventies compared with the softer subjectivism of the heady sixties. Worries about subjective idealism, irresponsible hipsterism, moral voyeurism, zoo keeping, liberal cop-outs — though by now surely sounding a little tired and hysterical — are understandable. It must be right to correct a theory which suggests (to the theoretically unsophisticated, at least) that people make their own history in conditions of their own choosing. But my complaint remains. This critique leaves us either contemplating men who have no motives, no subjective lives, or else with the vacuous rhetoric in which, as forty earnest students tell me each year, 'Matza's view of man' (or something like that) is 'inadequate' and has to be replaced by a 'fully social' picture. Either way we remain frozen in the old gestures of demystification. And either way moral nihilism is close at hand. We are locked in the same stances that Matza warned us would result from the temporary suspension of correctionalist interests and of the common-sense view that criminals should be punished.

These stances — as we are now realising to our cost — are extremely difficult to emerge from. The current justice debate (which I will later examine) is a major breakthrough, and there are two other roads within critical criminology now which offer routes back to the moral dimensions of criminal politics (though the authors of these routes might not agree with my signposting them this way). The one lies in the view more prominent in the American strands of critical criminology (Schwendinger and Schwendinger, 1975, and Platt, 1975): to extend the definition of crime. To me this has always seemed little more than a muckraking and moralistic exercise — in the best sense. This position attacks the state definition of crime and tries to redefine and extend criminology's subject matter in terms of violations of politically defined human rights (such as food, shelter, dignity). Thus imperialism, racism, sexism, colonialism, capitalism and exploitation are all to fall within the rubric of criminology. This is, of course, no mere plea for demarcating new academic subject lines, drawing up new book lists and asking different exam questions (though, curiously, from such a group of radicals it usually looks to be just this). It announces a moral stance: not just that we should 'study' (and certainly not 'appreciate') all these evils, but that we should *condemn* them — condemn them as if they were like or worse than the crimes which fill our current textbooks and our criminal justice system. It is not always too clear whether we are being asked to condemn these evils *instead of* conventionally defined crime or *in addition* to these crimes. But in either case the moral element is right in the open. Indeed, this element appears with such naive and evangelical fervour in some American adherents of radical criminology that one wonders what they were doing in the sixties and what sort of sociology they have ever read. For them the debate is cast as a quixotic onslaught against Value Freedom and is not only openly moralistic but also extravagantly partisan.[7] Here is Quinney:

> . . . I find it difficult to support the position that the criminal law can be stripped of its moral judgements. To the contrary the very stuff of the criminal law is moral. The criminal law is moralistic if for no other reason than it takes the position that any human action should be limited. The assumption that either society or the individual should be regulated is a moral one. And certainly the decision to regulate specific substantive actions is moralistic. A moral decision is taken when it is decided to protect others by means of the criminal law. Legal reform or even legal revolutions cannot be achieved by taking morality out of the law. (Quinney, 1972, p. 24)

Leaving aside the embarrassing possibility that such statements could be interpreted as saying anything 'radical' — it would be difficult to find anyone who has thought about the criminal law for more than two minutes who could disagree with a word — the importance of all this is that it carries the simple recognition that the regulation of human behaviour is on the radical agenda and involves moral judgements. Hardly a startling insight — but an important one to come from the radical camp which sometimes (as I will discuss later) comes close to the assertion that in the good society the eventual regulation of human behaviour through the criminal law will become an irrelevant matter. This Utopia is a crime-free society, where apparently the troublesome and difficult business of making judgements about regulating and limiting behaviour will not take up too much time.

The other route back to what I see as the relevant debate about the state is potentially more fruitful than the concern with changing the definition of crime. This lies in the recognition (Young, 1975, pp. 71-5) of two simple matters: (1) on the public side: the existence of some moral consensus, however much the product of bourgeois ideology, which condemns certain crimes. The working class also suffers from crime and their objective class interests here coincide with certain features of bourgeois ideology — for example, the stress on justice; (2) on the criminal side: there are internal contradictions and problems of guilt and irrationality. There is no monolithic criminal consciousness.

I'm not sure that all of Young's analysis of these matters help — particularly the circular reference back to the content of bourgeois ideology to 'explain' working-class politics and crime. The notion, though, that the effect of brutalisation by the system might make men become determined creatures is important in developing what is in effect a new typology of crime. Crime *could* be brutalisation by the system; it *could* arise from voluntaristic action within an ethos of competitive individualism; it *could* indicate a primitive political consciousness. Whether we accept such a typology or not (and this one is more illuminating than most), the mere recognition of such possibilities must, as Young sees, change the game and in just the directions I think it should change: 'If we confuse these categories we are unable to discriminate in our attitudes to crime — i.e. we either condemn it out of hand or we romanticise it' (Young, 1975, p. 79). Young then goes on: 'Either way, we accept the legal categories at face value and neglect to study criminal phenomena from the perspective of class interests and socialist principles' (p. 79). This particular recommendation seems to me unhelpful, but at least by discriminating between categories of crime and (like the American radical criminologists) talking about categories of anti-social behaviour outside the criminal law, some ways are open to counter the conservative domination of the public debate on crime. This does not yet confront, though, the specific issue of punishment which I believe has been obscured by a careless and tendentious reading of the fit between criminological theory and policy.

For it is punishment — in both its dimensions of ban and enforcement — which is at the core of criminal politics and always has been. It is fatal that, until recently, radicals have ignored or fudged this question. Alongside the tendency to pretend a suspension of morality, there was the assumption — implicit in *The New Criminology* — that any sort of correctionalism, however liberal, must depend upon theories of pathology. In fact, correctionalism in its classical version made no such judgement of pathology: this was its whole point. And when the new deviancy theory tried to expel pathology (by arguing against determinism and in favour of rationality) what this did was to open up the route back to the older form of correctionalism. Responsible criminals were constructed, whose responsibility lay precisely in their right to be punished and not treated.[8]

Even in Matza's weaker rejection of pathology — weaker in the sense that 'deviance as diversity' is not as radical a break as 'deviance as rational' — no necessary elimination of correctional interests is implied. Pathology is an untenable variant or change; diversity may be tenable, but is nonetheless a variant which is prescribed, regulated and controlled. In the same way as common sense should lead us away from a romanticism which ignores pathos, dissatisfaction and weakness, so it should remind us about punishment. Despite having drawn attention themselves to the compromised position of neo-classicism on precisely this point, the new criminologies assumed a fit between theory and policy which was never present.

The other fit they assumed, is, as I have suggested, closer to the mark: the tendency for appreciation and subjectivism to lapse into moral relativism. But again this tendency was one which should have contained an in-built self-correcting mechanism:

> The appreciation of shift, ambiguity and pluralism need hardly imply the wholesale repudiation of the idea of common morality. Such an inference is the mistake of a rampant and mindless relativism. Plural evaluation, shifting standards and moral ambiguity may and do co-exist with a phenomenal realm that is commonly sensed as deviant. (Matza, 1969, p. 12)

Correctionalism interferes with appreciation, but it is hardly an absurd goal in itself: 'The correctional perspective is reasonable enough, perhaps even commendable, except that it makes empathy and understanding difficult and even impossible' (Matza, 1969, p. 17).

In fact, appreciation is not intrinsically connected with moral nihilism any more than (in a completely opposite version of the radical attack) it is simply a more liberal version of correctionalism. It was something recommended and adopted as a tactic, a temporary methodological stance. Criminologists no doubt *looked* as if they were transcending what Matza refers to as their earlier 'incapacity to separate standards of morality from actual description' (Matza, 1969, p. 17). And we might have *said*, with Chekov, ' "There are plenty of accusers, prosecutors and gendarmes' without us.' But all this shrill moral innocence struck a false note. Most of the time we were saying to 'our' deviants (who knew this quite well): 'We will study you *as if* we had no moral judgements whatsoever about your actions.' That we could get away with such dishonesty was no doubt a tribute to the prevailing intellectual climate, but sometimes it really was the product of innocence rather than bad faith. In our waking hours we were innocent; we simply never raised the question: did these people deserve to be punished in this way?

The connection between appreciation and relativism thus was, and is, no more an organic one than the connection between pathology and correctionalism. In any event my earlier problem remains: if pathology goes out of the window, and so does the underdog, the drifter and the rebel, then what is left? Young's 'typology' offers a way out, an unexpected one: the rediscovery of another sort of pathology, perhaps the kind Lukács had in mind when repudiating the romantic view of psychopathology:

> Life under capitalism is often rightly presented as a distortion (a petrification or paralysis) of the human substance. But to present psychopathology as a way of escape from this distortion is itseif a distortion. We are invited to measure one type of distortion against another and arrive, necessarily, at universal distortion. (Lukács, 1963, p. 33)

This is another version of Young's admission that the unreflexive attribution of rationality to all forms of deviance could lead to a denial of any consensual reality in the external world. His plaintive, not to say poignant, tone marks the possibility of emerging from the frozen moral positions left behind in the attack on positivism:

> . . . there is some standard somewhere, whereby one is able to talk of appropriate and, most importantly, inappropriate responses to problem situations. The spectre of normality and pathology, once exorcised, re-emerges. Only by holding to some standard of normality is it possible, indeed, to talk of lapses in rationality on the part of an individual, a group or even on the part of a total society. (Young, 1975, p. 75)

The re-emergence of the spectres of normality and pathology, of appropriate and inappropriate behaviour, of standards and of rationality all open the way to a more plausible criminology. As theorists such as Jaccoby have commented, positivism is often at least nearer the *appearance* of reality than pure idealism.

GUILT AND RESPONSIBILITY

'It is a failure of sociological theory that it has rarely examined concepts such as guilt and conscience' (Taylor et al, 1973a, p. 52). Indeed. Words like guilt, conscience and evil (especially evil) are not ones with which sociologists have ever been comfortable. A course in the sociology of evil would be laughed away in most departments — though it is no less respectable than many, and more so than some (for example, those analysing telephone conversations).

In criminology the fuzziness of the attack on positivism left the problem of guilt unresolved. Appreciation, as we saw, should not have implied conversion or the impossibility of condemnation. It should allow that what might have to be appreciated is whether and how the subject feels guilty. The common-sense conception of guilt — implied in Chekov's reference to 'guilty men' — refers probably to *legal* guilt: the simple judgement of whether the subject is responsible for the supposed offence. But determinism also allows for judgements of *moral* guilt: the action is caused by factors for which the subject is not responsible.

At its extreme — in the novelist's resolve to 'take the part even of guilty men once they have been condemned and punished' — the appreciative stance appears to urge a suspension of judgements of either sort of guilt. This is indeed the whole point of appreciation: one must try to understand the crime even if it is the actor's fault. There is no point in making such a fuss if the crime were not his fault — *anyone* could 'appreciate' it then.

But to move from all this to policy is another matter. It calls for making connections with the obvious literature in law, moral philosophy and jurisprudence which deals with the question of moral and legal guilt, the relationship between deterministic theories and the rationale of punishment. I would be the last to suggest that we abandon empirical sociology for philosophical speculation — we have already been colonised by philosophers — but in this case the connections between the pretensions of the new criminologies and standard philosophical concerns is absolutely intrinsic. The problem of individual responsibility is more relevant to the study of crime than it is to any other area of sociology — and in the particular sense that our theories have unstated implications for the rationale of punishment.

We have only dimly realised that these theories (and the criminal's own accounts — more of this later) obscured the question at the heart of criminal politics: in what sense is the criminal *guilty?* It was never thought necessary even to enter this debate on blameworthiness. In the hermetically sealed world of theory we performed elegant pirouettes around notions of freedom and determinism — and meantime let the state get on with its business of blaming and prosecuting. The quicksands to which such political irresponsibility leads might best be illustrated in the extreme but instructive case of war crimes. Even the most cursory examination of this subject[9] shows how problematic are the connections between theories ('they were just obeying orders', 'they were part of the system') and assessments of responsibility, culpability, blameworthiness or guilt. One of the best recent examples of the mess which radicals can get into because of not thinking through these problems is the reaction of part of the American Left to the series of trials of Calley, Medina and others for their alleged part in the My Lai massacres.

Mary McCarthy's superb account of Medina's trial (1972) should be required reading for criminologists. Her argument is that the deliberate massacre of over a hundred innocent villagers at My Lai was morally different — and seen to be so — from, on the one hand, the 'ordinary' prosecution of the war[10] and, on the other, the haphazard rapes and killings practised by ordinary soldiers. The earlier attempts by Nixon and the Right to whitewash Calley coincided with attempts by the Left to denounce the Calley prosecutions as 'scapegoating' (Calley was innocent; the army was the real criminal). Though — by most accounts — Medina (Calley's company commander) knew pretty well what was happening in the village, it was argued that it was liberal hypocrisy to blame such figures. But as McCarthy comments:

> Medina was a transition figure between the war makers and the 'animals' (as the airmen in Vietnam called the infantry) and his acquittal halted a process that might have gone up the ladder of responsibility. If Medina had been in jail, it would have been harder to acquit Colonel Henderson. With Henderson in jail . . . [the] finger would steadily have pointed upward. Had public pressure been maintained, it might not have been left to the Army to decide when enough was enough. If there was a conspiracy, it was a great nationwide breathing together of left, right and much of the middle to frustrate punishment of the guilty. (McCarthy, 1972, p. 168)

McCarthy's point is that from the North Vietnamese and Viet Cong positions it did not follow that if Johnson and General Westmoreland were war criminals, Calley, Medina and others directly responsible for the massacre were 'choiceless victims of the war machine'. The North Vietnamese could draw a distinction between the ordinary soldier shooting at troops and an infantry company butchering women, old men and children. Some of the Left and the counter-culture in America not only would not concede this distinction, but seemed to hold to a theory which denied all freedom of action. The notion was that those like Calley were pawns moved around from birth by 'the system'. But if Calley's social conditioning left him no option as to whether or not to 'open up' on the people of My Lai, how did other (presumably similarly conditioned) ordinary soldiers keep their rifles to the ground? And how did others express disbelief and shock about what was happening and eventually denounce the massacre to the authorities? Without some notion of individual responsibility, no credit or blame could be assigned to anybody. Masochistic indictments of the whole culture as 'guilty' — everyone is a war criminal — sound virtuous but are politically sterile. And they helped in producing a visibly devastating result:

Medina and Henderson off the hook, Calley's sentence reduced, others not tried, several identified and unidentified mass murderers welcomed back into the population. Now any member of the armed forces in Indo-china can, if he so desires, slaughter a reasonable number of babies, confident that the public will acquit him, (a) because they support the war or (b) because they don't. (McCarthy, 1972, p. 87)

The position is perhaps more complicated than McCarthy allows, in that it should be possible to theorise about the 'ultimate' or 'real' cause of the massacre, and still hold that individual participants exercised some real choices at a particular moment. I have, nevertheless, spent much time on this case because — without putting too fine a point on it — there are some parallels between the dissidents who championed Calley and Medina against the army and criminologists who champion 'their' criminals against society. It was not just that we didn't think too much (if at all) about the problem of legal guilt, but that the more we talked about the problems of determinism and individual responsibility, the cloudier we made the whole issue. One constant sociological impulse has been to shift account-ability for crime onto higher and higher levels of the social structure. Not just family, neighbourhood, social class position, but the whole system — capitalism in all its ways — was to blame. And — final irony — the very system of social control itself was fatefully implicated in the causal path to crime.

Each successive theory harboured its own particular implications for the question of guilt — but these never surfaced. In regard to juveniles, as I suggested earlier, the fit looked more transparent: the move to welfare, treatment and rehabilitation seemed to have happened. But even here, the specific implications for policy of theories of shifting accountability are open to dispute. Finestone's recent ambitious attempt to relate changes in the image of the delinquent — from 'potential pauper' to 'disaffiliated' to 'frustrated social climber' to 'aggrieved citizen' — to changes in American society and its juvenile justice system raises interesting problems here (Finestone, 1977). Note for example, his comment on labelling theory:

> Labelling theory fundamentally represents a crisis in the legitimacy of authority, a crisis that is quite inconsistent with the acceptance of legitimate authority in any form, even under the guise of professionally trained experts, for it attributes delinquency precisely to professionals and experts. (Finestone, 1977, p. 215)

Such statements vulgarise labelling theory (see Plummer's paper in this volume) and surely exaggerate its radical thrust. But leaving this aside, even if the theory hardly implied a 'crisis in the legitimacy of authority', some political consequences surely followed from the more sentimental (and, I believe, largely correct) thrust of the theory that most criminals have been pushed around and railroaded and have generally had a raw deal. We were elusive about these consequences; nor did we stop to analyse the fundamentally morally compromised position into which we had cast agents of social control. We were asking them to uphold a system whose very basis rested upon the notion of individual responsibility — and at the same time to subscribe to theories which cast them as partially responsible for delinquency.

As the My Lai case illustrates, causal theories, however aesthetically pleasing or even morally worthy, have to be translated into the real social settings where blame is allocated. At least this is a well charted intellectual enterprise and we could have followed (though we chose not to) the standard philosophical discussion; for example, about the extent to which determinism is compatible with talk of legal guilt and responsibility.[11] Aside from this intellectual parochialism, we made matters worse: for just when the constant sociological impulse to shift accountability upwards was gathering momentum, the new deviancy theory suddenly changed ground and mounted what looked like a massive critique of determinism in any form. Even more bewildering: accountability was shifted upwards and determinism attacked by the very same theorists. Just when the startling implications of anti-determinism were being digested, Marxist criminology appeared on the scene to announce an even more deterministic edifice than ever before contemplated.

The initial thrust of the new theories was indisputably against determinism in any form. In its earlier naturalist version (Matza's formula was: '. . . *anyone* can become a marijuana user and *no one* has to') and the later more 'radical' strands, the attack on determinism was accompanied by implicit exercise of decoding. A new semiology of meaning was constructed within the conceptual debris of positivism. If the deviant had previously been denied legitimacy, meaning, rationality, intentionality, authenticity, then (but by implication only) a correct decoding would restore these properties. Not only was this new semiology never made very explicit, however, but — as I have stressed repeatedly — its implications for policy were never made clear. Such implications should have been even more obvious at the historical point at which a self-conscious conflict was being staged between two rival conceptual discourses trying to establish hegemonic control over meanings.

When, at the beginning of the nineteenth century, an earlier such conflict took place (precisely the one which established the psychiatric version of positivism in the first place) it was clear enough what sort of policy consequences would follow. Foucault (1975) has used the startling case of Pierre Riviere to show how dramatic the alternatives were. Was Riviere's crime to be coded as rational and hence as grounds for executing him? Or was he to be diagnosed as mad and hence shut up for life in a mental hospital? The issue was clear: clumsy psychiatry, with its new epistemology and causal theories, was trying to *cheat* Riviere of his death.

Was this, in fact, the allegation against positivism that was being made some hundred and fifty years later: that it was trying to cheat deviants? But cheat them of what? From being punished properly as responsible, free human beings? Or from being seen as critics of society? Or was there, after all, in the attack on determinism, the equivalent sophistry that Pearson detects in the liberal treatment model: '. . . the misfit must at one and the same time be held accountable for his actions, which are judged wrong *and* treated with compassion?' (Pearson, 1975, p. 25).

But such questions were not only never posed; they were rendered surrealistic by the simultaneous presence of strident attacks on determinism *as well as* statements denouncing elements of voluntarism in everyone else's theories for being idealistic and individualistic. (It might, of course, be quite right to attack the extremes of both total voluntarism and total determinism, but not — in criminology, at least — unless some credible and not wholly rhetorical alternative is sketched out.) Anyway, just when readers were beginning to make sense of this dizzy double-bind, we were informed not that the original attack on positivism was to be recanted, but that because of romantic and Fanonist excesses, the new criminal man had been a mistaken creation. All criminals were not, after all, Weathermen. A Frankenstein had been constructed.

But, in truth, he was less a Frankenstein than a Jekyll and Hyde: rational in the morning, drifting in the afternoon and brutalised in the evening. How could all this confusion arise? My answer is breathtakingly simple and will doubtless be seen as simplistic: it lies in the nature of the sociological world view. What was being attacked all the time was not 'determinism' at all, but its psychological and psychiatric versions. The fight was against nasties like Lombroso and Eysenck. Accepted social facts, the brutal Marxist and Durkheimian contingencies of life — history, structure, inequality, power — were never questioned. And how could anyone question them and remain a sociologist?

To repeat: it was not that the new semiology had merely inverted the positivist image by replacing determinism with freedom. Only *some* forms of determinism were attacked; sociological determinism remained alive and well, the taken-for-granted backdrop against which the whole play was being enacted. This backdrop has now come alive by being filled out with a specifically Marxist appearance. *Both* the determinism of psychological positivism *and* the supposed voluntarism of new deviancy theory have been banished by a powerful new set of forces: material circumstances, subjective feelings, the persuasiveness of bourgeois ideology, the potential for biography to be ossified by the control apparatus. All this, together with Young's form of typology, resolved the double bind by a compromise parallel to that of neo-classicism. The crypto-political criminal is allowed *more* free choice, the brutalised criminal *less* — though the area of choice for everyone is whittled down. In one sense, our single Jekyll and Hyde monster disappears: there are, after all, different criminals, with different degrees of choice. But a tension remains, precisely the tension within Marxism between subjective choice and the forces of history. And because of its moral implications, criminology has registered this tension perhaps more sensitively than any other social science. On the one hand, it was assumed to be 'radical' to uncover those deterministic forces structurally most remote from the actor, while on the other, the influence of the early Marx and the residue of 1960s cultural voluntarism left behind the potentially free actor, struggling heroically against structure and the mystifications of bourgeois ideology:

> . . . the biographical characteristics that lead to psychic conflicts and resistance are ossified by the ongoing institutions of the social control apparatus and by the lack of any real moral or material alternatives. Choice occurs within a cage, whose bars are obscured and glimpsed with certainty only at the terminal points of the social control process. It is the role of the radical criminologist to demystify control and to join with those movements which seek to provide tangible alternatives and areas of choice. (Young, 1975, p. 90)

Putting aside any internal problems in this view of determinism, we are still left with the old policy questions. If people have no 'moral and material alternatives' (to crime?), how can anybody be held responsible or punished for his action at all? And what follows from seeing the 'cage' as more solid for some people than for others? Radical criminology cannot evade these questions by labelling them perjoratively as 'correctional' or 'moralistic'. Its own stance, even when it denies the value of exposé criminology, is both correctional and moralistic: openly so in regard to crimes of the powerful and tacitly so elsewhere. It might not look 'correctional' to call for ending the system which allows the powerful to exploit and damage others: but in the meantime, must they be left unpunished? And how about rapists? Or female criminals, whom we are being urged to see not as pathological but to be taken as seriously as we do male criminals — in other words, not to *cheat* them of their punishment?

There is one criminological debate which might be used to open up the question of guilt and responsibility to such policy considerations. This is the familiar 'technique of neutralisation' controversy (whose basis in theories of motivation is examined in Taylor's paper in this volume). A standard question is this: does the presence of certain motivational accounts really indicate a sense of guilt which has to be neutralised, or are these statements merely surface gestures, behind which may lie the shadow of an alternative value system or at least more self-consciousness than Sykes and Matza (1957) allow? This is, of course, an important question in itself to resolve, from the point of view of the competing casual theories of delinquency: but let us express the issue in a slightly different way. What degree of guilt has to be present or admitted by the criminal in order to fit a just and fair punishment for the offence?

Such a question raises that part of the Sykes and Matza argument which is usually ignored: the extent to which causally neutralising statements (moral guilt) actually rest upon or are coincidental with statements about legal guilt. An account such as 'I don't know what came over me' is at one and the same time subscription to a deterministic theory of causation *and* also (if honoured) not merely an extenuating circumstance but a method of evading legal guilt. My suggestion is that criminologists at all concerned with the consequences of their theories might begin to consider seriously the effects of the motivational accounts they accept or construct. There have only been a few speculations along these lines, such as Taylor's (1972) suggestion that if we are as sceptical as we claim to be about the total involuntarism common in sexual offenders' motivational accounts, then we should confront such offenders with their own responsibility. This might be psychologically more desirable as well as honest (though, Taylor does not ask what consequences this strategy might have in achieving goals of social justice). Following this tack: criminologists should be analysing such accounting systems as probation officer records and social enquiry reports to determine what sort of accounts might have particular consequences for the client. Probation officers are familiar enough with a model of social intervention which reverses the positivist sequence of diagnosis then treatment. One decides first on the best (by this I mean the most just) 'treatment' and then constructs the images accordingly.

If such programmes look too pragmatic and individualistic, there is a quite different line of analysis of guilt and responsibility which criminologists might follow. This is the type of comparative study which Downes suggests in his paper in this volume. When we examine other control systems, particularly those labelled as socialist, we might find that the systems often held up as desirable models (such as the Chinese) are precisely those in which the most massive sense of individual responsibility and guilt is engendered and built into the rationale of punishment. We need a typology of social control which relates dominant ideology and structure on the one hand to modes of allocating blame and responsibility to individual offenders on the other.

JUSTICE OR SOCIAL JUSTICE

The moral question, which positivism threatened to bury but only managed to disguise, and which radical theory rendered so confusing, has reappeared with startling force in criminal justice politics over the past few years. From the Right, the law-and-order lobby is saying more stridently and less apologetically what it has always been saying: the liberal treatment model is mistaken and we must go back to a hard-line, punitive approach based on strict classical lines. From the liberal Left there is much heart-searching and breast-beating: the ideals of treatment and rehabilitation have, alas, gone sour and we must go back to some sort of neo-classical position which stresses justice and fair play. And from the Marxist Left the debates about social justice and bourgeois versus socialist legality are beginning (at last) to mark out some position in this spectrum. I want to examine here some aspects of this debate, which I believe is the most promising possible one to rescue radical theory from some of its political stalemates and to find new answers to the old question: is it just to treat this offender this way?

The conservative position needs no exegesis — though it certainly needs more sustained attention than we have given it. The increasing plausibility of the law-and-order lobby and the resonant political chords it strikes have sometimes to be confronted in their own terms instead of always being evaded in a search for ideological roots. If, indeed, as radical criminologists now concede, such working-class interests as those for justice are real and not the product of false consciousness, then the coincidence of such interests with those of bourgeois ideology need exploration, not to say exploitation.

I would like to look, though, not at the conservative position but at one extremely radical version of the justice model. The Report of the Committee for the Study of Incarceration (von Hirsch, 1977) is radical not so much for its intrinsic content (which is hardly new) but for its emergence from the American Left-liberal disillusionment with the treatment ideology. Together with allied statements such as *Struggle For Justice,* this Report seems to me to announce an extraordinary landmark in criminal justice policy — again, for its context rather than its content.

Starting with the question of incarceration (and eventually suggesting some worthwhile policies to reduce incarceration) the Committee found itself arguing for a new rationale for punishment. Disenchantment is the dominant note: rehabilitation has failed and attempts to change people have been abused. Only a minimalist position is defensible, in the context not just of prisons, but of the whole criminal justice system. The state has to do less rather than more. This means '. . . a crucial shift in perspective from a commitment to do good to a commitment to do as little mischief as possible' (Gaylin and Rothman, preface to von Hirsch, 1977, p. xxxiv). What little should be done is to be guided not by the positivist notion of individuation, but by the principles of justice, equity, fairness and — above all — *just deserts,* a more palatable version of traditional retributivist principles. This marks a departure not just from the pure treatment ideal, but from any guiding utilitarian rationale. Intervention is not justified by prevention, deterrence or protection but the notion that 'certain things are simply wrong and ought to be punished'. The Report is all too aware of the ironies in liberal humanists arriving at this position today — and finding themselves so close to the conservatives. They abandon the therapeutic model with reluctance and despair — but it has not worked; it has often turned out more cruel and punitive than an overtly punitive system and it is hypocritical and unjust, especially in sentencing people guilty of similar crimes to different dispositions because of their 'background'. And finally, the treatment model has hardly furthered any goals of a more equal distribution of power and property (as if anyone thought it could).

Many details of the Committee's argument — against treatment, against attempts to predict dangerousness and against both individualism and utilitarian deterrence — are extremely persuasive and need sustained attention. I want to pay more attention, though, to their alternative, the key notion of commensurate deserts which invokes the quite explicit moral and common-sense rationale for punishment: people are punished because they deserve it and the seriousness of the offence (and the number and seriousness of prior offences) should determine the seriousness of the penalty.[12] Critically: *past* action and not predicted *future* action (as in the rehabilitation, deterrence or incapacitation models) is the criterion. More specifically: seriousness depends on the amount of *harm* done and the degree of the actor's *culpability* (in terms of the strict legal categories of intent, seriousness and negligence). Such considerations should have priority over all other overriding aims of punishment, such as crime control, deterrence, prevention or rehabilitation — and these need not all be juggled to achieve some hypothetical balance.

Let us begin consideration of the scheme by looking at some limitations acknowledged in the Report itself. It recognises, for example, that there might be problems in calculating the seriousness of offences, but then quotes public opinion surveys which suggest that some consensus on ratings can be found (with little race, occupational or educational variation). This suggests that some common-sense notion of seriousness exists — which sounds plausible enough, especially if we are thinking in such terms as a five- or six-point scale of judgement. But such measurements might only be reflecting a reified public opinion which is the product of the dominant ideology. And if the basis of this is unjust, public opinion surveys will hardly guarantee the objective of justice. An allied problem which the Committee acknowledges is that of harm: harm to whose interests? In an unequal society not all interests are comparable; simply taking what the Report refers to as the 'particular moral traditions of the culture' into account might again lead to an unjust result in trying to assess harm.

These, of course, are serious problems and not just examples of operational difficulties in putting the just deserts model into practice. They are related to the more fundamental flaws in the Kant-derived argument on punishment, which are conceded (in a footnote):

> The Kantian argument presupposes that what violators are being punished for is the infringement of rules that safeguard the rights of *all* members of a society including the violator's own rights. This raises a question . . . whether a desert-based justification of punishment, such as Kant's, can hold in a society whose penal system helps maintain a less than just social system. (von Hirsch, 1977, p. 47)

It is precisely when this flaw is explored — in the 'lingering questions' raised in the Report's last chapter, 'Just Deserts in an Unjust Society' — that we come to the criticisms from radical criminology of such versions of the justice model. For while it might be true that Marxism itself would suggest that the only morally acceptable grounds for punishment are that it is deserved (see Murphy, 1973) this principle only holds if the laws are fair and the society is equal. But if the laws (or even some of them) serve particular class or power interests, then it is not self-evident that all violations are moral wrongs which deserve to be condemned and punished along the lines of just deserts.

The Committee recognise this problem, but try not to let it disturb them too much. They concede that there might be social injustice, but there is also at least a partial acceptance of legal norms which allows violators to be considered deserving of punishment. The Committee will not accept that society (American society?) and its rules are fundamentally and irretrievably unjust. On the question of how *much* punishment is deserved, they concede only that the 'impoverished defendant' poses 'dilemmas' for the theory. If social deprivation is seen as a mitigating factor (thus allowing a plea of diminished culpability), this goes against the principled objection to the whole notion of individuation. It may not be feasible, anyway to treat social deprivation like this: '. . . the sentencing system may simply not be capable of compensating for the social ills of the wider society' (von Hirsch, 1977, p. 147).

There is obviously no question of 'may': clearly no sentencing system can possibly do this. The Report trivialises all these issues by referring simply to 'social ills' or 'impoverished defendants'. These are no mere isolated social pathologies: there are whole societies (such as South Africa) where the laws are fundamentally and irretrievably unjust, where the inequalities of privilege and power are so gross that even to suggest that the law can be fair or just is absurd.

The Committee must recognise something of this in their final, somewhat despairing concession: 'As long as a substantial segment of the population is denied adequate opportunities for a livelihood, any system of punishment will be morally flawed' (von Hirsch, 1977, p. 149). This is only a partial recognition of the problem, but even to allow a 'moral flaw' in an argument which rests so self-consciously on moral principles is almost to give the game away. Despite the obvious flaws in this version of the justice model, though, it confronts directly the hidden moral agenda of criminology and should be taken very seriously. In a reference to a paper by Greenberg advocating the justice model (if not the specific deserts version), Taylor and Young (1977) deride his 'collapse into the justice lobby' and they appear to be quite hostile to any radical sympathy with the back-to-justice movement on the grounds that this does not take into account the movement's origins and convergence with conservative interests.

It would seem to me more productive to confront the model in its own terms than mount only this sociology of knowledge critique. It might be true that the justice lobby is dominated by embittered liberals and shaped by the strains on corporate liberal reformism, and that any liberal influence can be easily absorbed into the most reactionary aims,[13] but these are not sufficient reasons for rejecting the model. It has enough problems in its own terms. As Marxist theory has itself always pointed out, it is the essence of bourgeois ideology that it will absorb contradictory elements. Where the radical critique is surely correct is in showing that the justice model is inadequate unless located in a broader critique and programme.

Such a critique is now beginning to emerge, though the programme is more opaque. Quinney and Wildeman, for example, despite their zeal to accept the moral elements of the law, argue that:

> To accept the principle of the rule of law, however, is to also run the risk of uncritically accepting the legal system and the political economy upon which the entire legal system rests. Therefore if we are to understand law and crime in the state we have to be aware of the ideological foundations of the legal order. (Quinney and Wildeman, 1977, p. 29)

This seems reasonably unobjectionable as a theoretical statement. It would be a pity, though, if the strategic implication of an awareness of the ideological foundations of the legal order was to abandon the struggle for justice to conservative interests. Taylor and Young's warnings about the danger of the struggle being co-opted into conservative goals might open up this risk: 'Greenberg's plea that radical criminology in America should work for justice is in danger of accommodation to the attempts made to restore order and legitimacy to American capitalist order in the midst of a crisis of hegemony' (Taylor and Young, 1977, p. 27). This is a legitimate political worry: the danger of lending oneself to struggles that make the social arrangements of capitalism appear to be just when patently they are not. And this is precisely the 'moral flaw' in the *Doing Justice* position. All this comes close, though, to the same potential problem which some of us (Cohen, 1975) found in the Marxist critique of social work: a theoretical critique, plausible or not, freezes the possibility of any sort of action at all.

Most radical criminologists seem aware of this problem and of the central strategic importance of the justice debate. Indeed, as one convincing argument about the historical evolution of penal and judicial systems indicates (Foucault, 1977), crime control is intimately related to questions of social control in other settings such as family, school and work. Far from being either a suitable target for piecemeal reform or a residual problem to be dealt with after the revolution, the question of justice must be near the top of the revolutionary agenda.

At the moment, the task of socialist criminologists has been seen as '. . . to work at the point of contradictions of law and justice' (Taylor and Young, 1977, p. 37). As I understand it, this implies pushing the justice model to the limits of its more political ramifications: showing, for example, that strict conformity to standards of justice would require massive structural change. (It would also point to an intermediate programme in which prison would be abolished for property offences and more upper-class criminals would be prosecuted.)

Two levels are distinguished in this Marxist version of the struggle for justice. At the first level one exposes the discrepancies between the ideals of the bourgeois legal code and the actual exercise of power in the penal system and in civil society generally. A real implementation of justice, it is argued, would raise political consciousness and reveal the class bias in the legal process. At the second level — once society has realised the connection between bourgeois legal standards and the creation of a just, classless society — the progression to socialist legality begins: 'The task is not merely to implement bourgeois legality nor either to ignore it . . . the task is to transcend the struggle for individual justice and to usher in a socialist legality' (Taylor and Young, 1977, p. 43). At this second level, the programme envisages such policies as the democratisation of the legal profession and the police force and the demand that the punishment for crime should be made proportionate to the amount of general harm caused to the community.[14]

This programme leaves a fair amount to the imagination — particularly the notion of moving from one 'level' to the other and the question of how exactly these new standards of justice and legality are to be implemented. How, for example, are assessments of 'general harm' and the 'context' of individual responsibility to be made? And who is to make them? Bland categories such as crimes 'against the state' or the 'general good' or whatever will not necessarily cover particular forms of harm or victimisation. And, in the transitional phase at least — where strict legality, we are told, will be ensured — how will such measures as the democratisation of the police force and legal profession actually guarantee the legal protection of the deprived and the powerless? I would also insist — at the risk of sounding sentimental — that both the new liberal and this Marxist version of the justice model are too determined to sound tough-minded and oh-so-*principled*. They forget that by the time many offenders get to this wonderful justice system, the damage has already been done. To set the standards of justice in terms of the principle of 'proportionate harm' is no less problematic than talking about 'commensurate deserts'. In both cases we lose sight of the humane and compassionate vision that positivism (and common sense) has allowed. Certainly the positivist ideal of reform and rehabilitation as being the *aim* of the criminal justice is fatal. But it is obvious also to anyone who has spent five minutes in a court or prison that it would be blatantly *unjust* to return — even as an intermediate tactic — to an undiluted classicism. The much-maligned humanitarianism which has been used to shield the otherwise unjustifiable positivist goal of 'treating' criminals should not itself be obliterated. Once upon a time it was 'radical' to attack law; then it became 'radical' to attack psychiatry. As we now rush back to the bewildered embrace of lawyers who always thought we were against them,[15] we should remind ourselves just what a tyranny the literal rule of law could turn out to be.

Socialist legality, we are assured, is another matter — and I turn to some aspects of this ideal in the next section. I would like to repeat, though, that however incomplete the 'two-level' radical programme might appear, the concentration on the question of justice is, from all perspectives, a welcome one.

TOLERANCE AND DIVERSITY

One of the more remarkable claims in the new criminologies — one that is now sometimes played down for being too Utopian — was that it is possible to envisage and work towards a crime-free society. This claim needs stating in full:

> Albeit by implication, the insistence in *The New Criminology* was that insofar as the crime-producing features of contemporary capitalism are bound up with the inequities and divisions in material production and ownership, then it must be possible via social transformations to create social and productive arrangements that would abolish crime. Critically we would assert that it is possible to envisage societies free of any material necessity to criminalise deviance. Other controls on 'anti-social behaviour' (and other definitions of what that might constitute) can be imagined and from the point of view of a socialist diversity would be essential . . . Additionally there are forms of human diversity which, under capitalism, are labelled and processed as criminal but which should not be subject to control in societies that proclaimed themselves to be socialist. In other words we were asserting that the 'withering away of the State' identified in orthodox Left discussions as a feature of

thorough-going socialist societies has to feature in the discussion of a socialist criminology. (Taylor et al, 1975a, p. 20)

The meaning is unambiguous: it is the structure of capitalist society which produces crime and a socially heterogeneous society is possible in which the powerful will not and need not criminalise human diversity. I said that this claim is remarkable; it also seems to me a most vulnerable and (at least as presently stated) implausible plank in the new criminology's programme. At the risk of being elliptical, let me briefly state some problems:

(1) The idea of a society which is free of crime but does contain human diversity is so vague as to defy imagination. Particularly vague is the notion of 'diversity' and whether or not this is the same as 'deviance'. What would be examples of 'human diversity', and would anti-social behaviour not appear in any system which could not be tolerated in the name of diversity and might have to be criminalised?

(2) A crime-free society, we are sometimes told, is one in which social control would be abolished. This makes complete sociological nonsense. A society implies rules and rules imply social control. One can certainly say that X type of society is more criminogenic than Y society, but one cannot talk about abolishing social control. And, as we are told at other times, if controls other than the criminal law are both imaginable and essential, just what forms will such controls take?

(3) When such claims are made so unambiguously, the onus is surely on those who make them to refer, even occasionally, to those known human societies which at least 'proclaim themselves to be socialist' in order to show how they are approaching the stated goal of being free of crime. The most cursory examination of societies that 'proclaim themselves to be socialist' — Russia, China, Cuba, the Eastern European satellites, Cambodia in its current transition to 'socialist legality' — can hardly be said to lend credibility to many theoretical claims about the possibility of a crime-free society. And even if such an examination were inconclusive (on the grounds that the theorist does not regard such societies as being truly socialist) it is disingenuous to refuse to embark on it at all.

(4) The struggle, we are told, is not for bourgeois legality but socialist legality. Whatever socialist legality might be — and some very well known and extremely unappealing policies have appeared under this name — it is not at all clear why a crime-free society should require *any* form of legality. A crime-free society is one thing; a society with a different legal system from that of capitalist social democracies is another. One cannot argue for

both at the same time. Any attempts to do so should be seen as nonsense — unless, that is (and this is by no means clear in the literature) 'socialist legality' is seen as merely the organising feature of the transitional rather than eventual regime.

(5) Finally — and this is the level which this paper is really most concerned with — it is not clear whether the immediate political strategy lies in either or both of the following: (a) an intellectual critique by which materialist criminology directs its efforts at erecting a political economy of crime and law. This would carry an implicit 'after the revolution' perspective about the actual policies of the transitional or eventual good society; or (b) as is suggested in the 'struggle for justice' programme, the identification of a recognisable set of policy objectives in the current social world.

Let us examine more closely the ideal of 'diversity', and the ways a society might attain this goal. In a sense — though this sense is not usually acknowledged — the argument here goes back to one of the oldest debates in political philosophy: what are the desirable limits of the state's intervention? The vision of diversity in earlier deviancy theory embodied an implicit *laissez-faire* position: the state should pull out and let deviants do their things. Of course, this stance was largely bogus, but reading it as a properly thought out theory of the state rather than as a well-meaning set of gestures about tolerance, radicalised criminology pointed to its obvious shortcomings. Some of the polemics about the culture of civility, zoo keeping and normative ghettoes were, I think, unfair but it was quite right to criticise the '. . . moralistic view of "tolerance" as a kind of free-floating sentiment to be mobilised irrespective of social context' (Young, 1975, p. 71). What *The New Criminology* proposed instead, most promisingly, was to 'substitute a conception of socialist diversity for the pluralism of the idealist tradition'. This substitute is spelt out as follows: '. . . a socialist culture which is diverse and expressive — that is, a culture which takes up the progressive elements in pluralism, whilst rejecting those activities which are directly the product of the brutalisations of existing society (however diverse, expressive or idiosyncratic their manifestations)' (Taylor et al, 1975a, p. 90).

At this point — I hope not unfairly — we have to ask for a certain concreteness. Critically: what does the word 'rejecting' mean? If it means 'punishing' or 'controlling' (and I cannot see any other conceivable meaning), then we are certainly not talking about a 'crime-free society' or the 'abolition of social control'. Nor is it clear just what action will be tolerated in the name of 'socialistic diversity' rather than 'idealist pluralism', or on what grounds certain elements will be judged as 'progressive' or who will make such judgements. At the risk of offending their liberal friends (surely a familiar occupational hazard), it is high time that Marxists came clean about these matters. If they would like to see an alternative model of social control in which offenders wearing sandwich-boards listing their crimes kneel before a crowd which shouts 'Down with the counter-revolutionaries!' and are then led away to be publicly shot, then let such alternatives be discussed. For it is something like this which socialist legality means to millions of people today. Its dubious history has been one of secret trials, the abandonment of the right to defence and criminalisation by analogy. And if different parameters of tolerance from those in traditionally valued bourgeois liberalism are envisaged, then let such criteria be made explicit. The issue is too important to be clouded by vague references to 'diversity'.

Clearly, it is some advance to acknowledge that even after the revolution, some forms of behaviour will need to be 'rejected'. And the re-emergence of the 'spectres of normality and pathology' gives us some basis for identifying what these forms might be. Indeed, it seems imminent in the notion of a truly socialist society that crime would not occur except for biological and psychological reasons. Paradoxically, then, correctionalist ideologies will be reproduced — buttressed by fully blown pathology theories which will look *more* rather than less tenable because the over-arching cause of structural inequality has been removed. The psychiatric labelling of political dissidents in the Soviet Union is the obvious perversion of this ideology.

Socialists will obviously want to dissociate themselves from such perversions. But in some form or another, a move is envisaged beyond the indiscriminate blame of pure classicism and the apparent amorality of early deviancy theory to distinguish between actions which are anti-social (and anti-socialist?), those which are justifiable (though primitive in conception) and others which are the products of brutalisation. But — to use Young's own example (1975, p. 91) in applying these distinctions — it is not clear what might follow from simply *distinguishing* between 'the positive and negative moments' in deviant sexuality. If, shall we say, the rape and murder of a small child is identified as one such 'negative moment', how can this 'moment' be rejected without it being criminalised?

The history of power (Foucault, 1977) has taught us one clear lesson here: that what appears in intellectual circles as a new sensibility or a paradigmatic change in the modality of social control (to make it more rational or more just) is invariably transformed into a base for exercising more power. Despite the references in the debate about crime-free societies to the withering away of the state, there is little evidence to suggest that 'socialist legality' as we know it will do anything other than increase the power of the state.

Actually radical criminology has been a lot more specific in its favoured models of control than I have so far allowed. One model which has correctly attracted much interest and support (both as an intermediate reform and as a model to be incorporated eventually into the good society) is the notion of decentralised self-control systems organised by the working-class community itself (when talking about 'community' it is sometimes forgotten that a middle class exists). In Young's version:

> We have to argue therefore, strategically, for the exercise of social control but also to argue that such control must be exercised within the working-class community and not by external policing agents. The control of crime on the streets, like the control of rate busting on the factory floor, can only be achieved effectively by the community actually involved. (Young, 1975, p. 89)

This is an attractive suggestion, though it is probably true that such visions can be traced to what Pearson calls the 'sociological pastoral'. It is assumed that the deviant question can only be resolved in the idealised *Gemeinschaft* village, in which people happily tolerate diversity and deal with their deviants through face-to-face social control. Much of the current radical preference for decentralised control comes from the standard critique about the dehumanising effects of urban life. In one criminological version:

> Urban America as we know it has become outmoded and, like the dinosaur, is threatened with extinction unless we radically restructure our urban institutions along truly humanitarian and socialist lines, free from alienation, competition, hierarchy and exploitation. Such restructuring, for example, would accord priority to decentralised power structures of community control over massive dehumanised and centralised power structures. (Quinney and Wildeman, 1977, pp. 149-50)

Some elements in these critiques of mass society are shared by conservatives and radicals alike. As anyone who has listened to magistrates or policemen will know, their vision of perfect social control is not a Nazi dictatorship, but a collection of simple rural communities in which the heroic village bobby (Dixon of Dock Green and not Kojak) deals with trouble by friendly cuffs on the ear and cosy chats with mum and dad. To point to certain similarities of interest between conservatives and radicals, is not — as I have said myself, in connection with the back-to-justice movement — to argue against these proposals. We should be wary though, of some versions of the decentralisation arguments (for example, those of Oscar Newman), which, under the banner of neighbourhood control, provide blueprints for paranoid fortress communities patrolled by local vigilante squads. And on the whole I would tend to be more suspicious than Marxist criminologists of putting such touching faith in the natural instincts of the working-class community on the streets and the factory floor to allow much human diversity. This might, admittedly, not be the most ideal of experiments to cite, but the contemporary example of self-policing in the 'no-go' areas of Belfast is hardly encouraging.

The more constructive criticisms I would like to make about these decentralisation proposals — and the overall programme for social change in which they are cast — are of very different kinds. In one sense, these proposals need to be more concrete and empirical; in another, they need to be more theoretical and Utopian. Concreteness is to be gained by looking at the levels of current systems at which changes might take place. There is a certain impetus now *within* the criminal justice system itself which is entirely expedient in its support for decentralisation. The argument is that the system has become too bureaucratic, too remote, too inhuman to deal with the current volume of crime and that greater efficiency could be achieved by breaking up parts of the system (Danzig, 1973). The 'community court', in particular, is seen as a way of reducing the social distance between judge and those who are judged, supposedly facilitating a sense of local involvement (Fisher, 1975).

The interests behind such proposals are unashamedly and naively correctional — crime will be reduced by increasing personal responsibility, justice, efficiency and a respect for authority — but the empirical models which are cited are worth examining. These include: informal work-group controls over such offences as pilfering;[16] more formal factory courts and arbitration procedures; dispute and conciliation mechanisms such as those used in non-Western societies (Conn and Hipler, 1974) and adaptations of procedures used in civil rather than criminal law. Most important for the argument about socialist legality, the models referred to include the various forms of community courts used in socialist countries: comrades' courts in the Soviet Union, peoples' courts in China, popular tribunals in Cuba and workers' courts in Poland. Despite the relative inaccessibility of the literature on these experiments, something at least is known about their philosophy (particularly the stress on the court's educational role) and operation to warrant serious examination by anyone advocating decentralised or community control.

A recent version of this argument — but one that is idealistic, in the sense that it explicitly does not claim that this mode of control will necessarily reduce recidivism — is to be found in Christie's call for conflict to be removed from the courts and the experts and given back to the community (Christie, 1976). Advancing this position from an Illich-inspired attack on professionals and specialists, Christie argues that models along neighbourhood court lines (such as the Tanzanian village court) give better opportunities for norm clarification and the staging of what are effectively political debates. Questions which relate judgements of blameworthiness to such factors as the size and power of the victims and the offender's status and background can be asked in direct, personal terms: '. . . decisions on relevance and on the weight of what is found relevant ought to be taken away from legal scholars, the chief ideologues of crime-control systems, and brought back for free decision in the court room' (Christie, 1976, p. 15). Thus guilt-neutralising statements such as 'They won't miss it' can be confronted in concrete moral and political terms. In conventional systems the loss of this personal confrontation through expert and professional controls means that the offender does not have the opportunity to be confronted with the type of blame which would be difficult to neutralise.

Besides the need to examine those experiments aimed specifically at creating new forms of social control, there is another valuable empirical reference point in the more ambitious attempts to create whole new micro-societies. Communes, *kibbutzim* and other Utopian communities have been founded with the explicit purpose of creating just and tolerant social orders. Some of the evaluative literature on these experiments (for example, Abrams and McCulloch, 1976) has concerned itself explicitly with questions of tolerance, diversity and rule enforcement. It is extraordinary that criminologists and sociologists of deviance have made so little reference to these experiments: they contain crucial sociological lessons about rules and boundary lines. Despite the obvious objection that such communities are but imperfect realisations of their original vision and that they are invariably parasites on the surrounding social order, these experiments are no less relevant than the macro-political attempts at creating new societies in this century. In both cases we might have as much to learn from the flaws as from the original vision.

But the debate on tolerance and diversity needs also to be extended in more theoretical and Utopian directions. Since Wilkins's early formulations about tolerance levels (Wilkins, 1964, ch. 4) few criminologists have even speculated about what the concept of 'tolerating' deviance actually means. It is by no means clear, for example, that tolerance would necessarily go along with greater decentralisation. And are trade-offs necessarily involved — more tolerance in one sphere of life resulting in more restrictions elsewhere? One matter is certain: the opposition between 'crime' on the one hand and 'socialist diversity' on the other is entirely unreal. Somewhere in the middle lies the much-abused concept of deviance (and derivative formulations about rule breaking, normalisation and so on). As Plummer implies (in his paper in this volume) the current attempt to switch back from a deviance frame to a crime frame means giving up many theoretical gains.

Finally, there is the need for more 'Utopian' theory construction. All the loose talk about legality, morality, justice and tolerance needs to be related to classic and current attempts (most notably those identified with Rawls, 1971) to specify the abstract properties of a just system. In addition, there is the vast anarchist and libertarian tradition of writing about the state: this addresses problems of tolerance more directly than Marxist literature. A work which brings together many of these separate strands is Nozick's compelling attempt to spell out what a minimalist state position would look like (Nozick, 1974). It is precisely such formulations which are needed to rescue the concept of tolerance from its purely subjectivist meaning.

STRATEGIES AND AGENDAS

Two lines of objection would suggest that much of my argument has been entirely unfair. In the first place, the demand for policy blueprints to be constructed or alternatives to be spelt out, clarified and made explicit can hardly be expected from *any* body of sociological theory, least of all the new deviancy theories which have had to establish themselves against an anti-theoretical, pragmatic tradition. And secondly, when one strand of this new theory adopts an avowedly revolutionary programme, it hardly seems appropriate to expect it to concern itself with the details of reformist policies. (Marxists would also presumably object to any separate examination of parts or derivatives of the theory without looking at the whole package — for example, the particular view about the nature of science or historical materialism.)

The first objection is justified, in the sense that the relationship between theory and practice in the social sciences is obviously not one which easily allows the precise spelling out of strategies and tactics for social policy. am asking less for such step-by-step strategies, though, than suggesting hat the new criminologies have manoeuvred themselves too tightly into heoretical positions whose immediate moral and political implications are not even put on the agenda. This is irresponsible, precisely because of the way these theories have evolved. At first — and understandably — the battle against mainstream criminology was fought not just against conservative correctional interests, but against any sort of policy interests at all. Particularly in the United States, rather than in Britain, the pretensions of he new deviancy school to be accepted into the sociological fold meant its shaking off of all identification with social work, or correctional or social policy traditions. In Britain this was never quite the case, and from the beginning of the National Deviancy Conference and its later more Marxist strands, it was patently obvious that the older policy interests were not to be replaced by pure naturalism (if that were possible) but by the construction of *new* policy interests. The struggle was to be on behalf of others — he deviants — and practical people like social workers were to be in the front line. If we were at all honest in this stance, then it seems to me disingenuous to imply that the consideration of policy and an active involvement in current policy debates is not our business.

As to the question of revolution and reform, it is tempting to do little more than recognise this as being the perennial question on the political agenda. In the specific context of radical criminology, Mathiesen's (1974) analysis has had a powerful effect in opening up this debate. The central argument against reformist politics remains: the danger not just of cooption but of pushing for reforms which would allow a society to present tself as more just and legitimate than it is. And similarly the dangers of Utopianism remain: in the meantime there are victims and sufferers, and heir plight is not relieved by suspending help till the revolution comes.

It should be possible — using, for example, the current struggle for ustice — to develop middle-range policy alternatives which do not compromise any overall design for fundamental social change. This does not mean simply employing this overall design to develop a theoretical critique of the justice programme, but actually being brave enough to speculate on ome policy alternatives, however unfinished and unworkable they might appear. Christie's vision of using the courtroom as a stage for acting out eal social conflict and for deciding the question of individual responsibility without the aid of experts is the type of example I have in mind.

The 'purer' theoretical tasks still remain on the agenda: to reconcile the wists of classical and positivist philosophies with a sociological conception of individual responsibility; to apply an abstract theory of ustice to the brute facts of the social order and the possibilities of a

different order; to understand what the notions of diversity and tolerance
would look like in the good society. But these tasks must be performed
with at least one eye open on the day-to-day world of crime and criminal
justice politics. When this world goes out of frame — as it has tended to in
the past — we lose the chance of influencing it. Conservative interests
have always kept this world in focus, for they are part of the frame. A
critical criminology has to combat not just knowledge, but the power of
knowledge.

NOTES

1. I am grateful to my fellow contributors and to Geoff Pearson and Jock Young for helpful comments on an earlier draft of this paper.
2. This was also true the further we ventured into the world of social work and these worries prompted me to write a paper (Cohen, 1975) which was interpreted as a polemic against *The New Criminology*. It was intended rather to reflect the inadequacy of both the interactionist and the Marxist versions of the new deviancy theories for translation into social work practice. The Marxist versions were treated more harshly because their claims and pretensions were, and are, more ambitious.
3. Only Pearson's (1975) account of this period deals with criminology's hidden moral agenda in the way I understand it in this paper.
4. In this context we might classify works such as Wilson (1975) as being on the Right with, say, Morris and Hawkins (1970) in the liberal centre. Schur (1975) might be more explicitly — though also far more problematically — on the liberal Left. There have only been a few isolated attempts — such as Greenwood and Young's (1976) intervention in the abortion debate — to stake out a coherent radical alternative.
5. I will comment later on some aspects of the Left's 'struggle for justice' debate. An archetypal public statement of the law-and-order repudiation of the treatment model of juvenile delinquency may be found in 'The Youth Crime Plague', *Time*, 11 July 1977, pp. 26-35. This conveys the flavour of the debate more clearly than any academic version.
6. Though Young's critique is very much to the point here, there is some confusion in the sort of argument which simultaneously attacks interactionist inspired theory for seeing the deviant as free *and* as the passive determined man on his back (see Plummer's and Rock's contributions to this volume for some discussion of this problem).
7. For a clear (crude?) example of this, see Quinney and Wildeman (1977).
8. One of the most revealing possible lessons from this period is to be derived from David Matza's story of receiving enthusiastic letters from police chiefs after his publication of *Delinquency and Drift,* his critique of positivism in the juvenile court. At last, they said, someone is coming out clearly in favour of punishment as against soft liberal treatment. Fatally, we have never understood the implications of such stories.
9. I am thinking particularly of the massive literature on the Nuremberg trials and such specific arguments as Hannah Arendt's on the Eichman trial (Arendt, 1965).
10. Her argument about this moral difference is, of course, not conclusive, though persuasive enough:

Though it would have changed nothing for the victims, most of us would prefer to think that those women and babies and old men had died in a raid rather than been singled out, one by one, for slaughter. Logic here is unpersuasive: the deliberate individual killing of unresisting people is more repugnant than the same result effected by mechanical means deployed at a distance and without clear perception of who or what is below. Even those who profess to see no distinction in Vietnam between the crime of war and single acts of homicide would be hard put to deny that distance does not seem to count in diminishing responsibility. Demonstrators shouting 'Hey, hey, LBJ, how many kids did you kill today?' were logically right in viewing Johnson as the final cause, insofar as that could be targetted in one person, but humanly they failed to convince, since he was not the proximate cause and could not even be said to have intended the slaughter of Vietnamese children in the sense that Hitler intended the annihilation of Jews in the gas ovens. (McCarthy, 1972, p. 42)

1. The obvious writings are those such as Hart's (e.g. 1968). For a useful secondary commentary, focusing on the issue of punishment, see Honderich (1976), especially ch. 5. A relevant recent addition to the debate is Ross's (1975) attack on moral nihilism, the view which denies the possibility of moral responsibility. Taking a pragmatic view of morality, Ross also attacks moral incompatibilism: the doctrine that moral responsibility is inconsistent with determinism. See also, Morris (1976).

2. The Report cites such analyses as Feinberg's (1970) for a statement of the just deserts position. For a more critical view, see Honderich (1976), ch. 2.

3. For demonstrations of this point in regard to recent penal policy, see Cohen (1977) and, especially, Scull (1977).

4. With reference to my earlier discussion about the unresolved question of individual responsibility, it is interesting to note that, in this context, Taylor and Young suggest an image which is less schizoid and more modest than earlier formulations: the individual is 'accountable' but in a 'context':

    Freedom and rationality in men is limited and repressed, not by an eclectic collection of 'extenuating circumstances' but by the systematic domination of the material and ideological unfreedoms in a class society ... The impediment to rational action in bourgeois society (and hence to the realisation of classicist ideals for the organisation of punishment and social control) is bourgeois society itself. At the same time as arguing against the notion of freedom in bourgeois society, however, we must avoid the trap of vulgar materialism, insisting on the accountability of actors within the context of the material and ideological circumstances surrounding them. (Taylor and Young, 1977, p. 43)

5. This slightly opportunistic element in the justice debate is paralleled in the shifting stances towards the welfare state. In the late 1960s the welfare state was attacked as the most repressive branch of the apparatus — most repressive because its control functions were disguised. Then, with the economic crisis, radicals jumped on to the other foot, forgot their previous critique of the welfare soft machine and started defending welfare against the cuts. The underdog sympathy remained, but now the underdogs had to be defended against new threats. Some of the older positions in deviancy theory and anti-psychiatry (for example, the analysis of stigma) became regarded as irrelevant or even reactionary. It remains to be seen — as in the justice debate — how these different types of attack can be reconciled.

6. Industrial sociologists are now building up an extremely interesting body of literature about informal control of 'deviance', such as pilferage (Ditton, 1977; Henry and Mars, forthcoming). The suggestion here is that these schemes of workers' control over hidden property offences should be extended actually to exclude the intervention of police and other formal control agents.

The Sociology of Crime, Symbolic Interactionism and Some Problematic Qualities of Radical Criminology [1]

Paul Rock

I assert that the Snark is the Absolute, dear to philosophers, and that the hunting of the Snark is the pursuit of the Absolute.
(F. C. S. Schiller, 'A Commentary on the Snark*', Mind, Christmas 1901)*

In place of a relativistic conception of reality we are developing a critical stance that permits us through our conscious being to get at the deeper meaning of reality.
(R. Quinney, 'Feature Review Symposium', The Sociological Quarterly, 14, Autumn 1973)

THE HISTORY OF SOCIOLOGICAL CRIMINOLOGY IN THE 1930s, 1940s and 1950s

The sociology of crime and delinquency has developed fitfully. Indeed, it may be misleading to describe it as an example of clear development at all. An impression of progress may only be the adventitious product of chronological succession. Intellectual events following one another in time are little more than random occurrences unless they are subjected to the imaginative work of synthesis, elaboration and comparison. That work has not distinguished the formulation of criminology, and there is no warrant to assume that each of criminology's stages represents an obvious and cumulative advance on what has gone before. It is difficult to demonstrate that functionalist criminology is more adequate than the writings of the Chicago School. Neither is strain theory manifestly more useful than functionalism. Rather, each is a separate and contained approach which opens up some perspectives and suppresses others. Each addresses some problems and neglects others. In this sense, every phase of criminology may be depicted as an intellectually discrete episode which borrows little from its predecessors and bequeaths little to its heirs.

Those who bear the criminological tradition have occasionally felt obliged to impose a superficial order on its evolution. They tend to discuss its practices as if they followed the canons, methods, style and transformations of a normal sociological discipline. They implicitly portray criminological thought as reflexive, suggesting the existence of an imagination which refers back to the past and anticipates the future. After all, some communicable logic of growth and direction must be established before criminology can be reproduced. If there were no such logic, there could be no seminars, lectures, reviews and books. That animating logic may well be abstracted from areas of sociology which do display an intelligible pattern of evolution. Science is so rarely represented as a haphazard or muddled enterprise that any discipline claiming a scientific mandate is assumed to be coherently organised. Criminology itself has been called a science, and its accumulated writings have been correspondingly interpreted as an ordered and purposefully designed whole. In this fashion criminologists have adhered to the ordinary conventions of teaching and research, and those conventions have automatically lent structure to their materials. They have subscribed to a rudimentary history of ideas, and the history of ideas defies presentation as flux. Further, many criminologists are committed to a scheme whose claims are in competition with those of such orthodox undertakings as the sociology of religion and the sociology of development. They would be disadvantaged if they defined it as an unusually confused and static branch of learning. But criminology *does* lack the incremental character of much science. It has lurched from one stage to another in a manner that only the benevolent could actually describe as a series of intellectual advances.

This erratic development flows from what has become a distinct division of academic labour. The precarious continuity of criminology has been preserved by specialists housed in research institutions and departments of law, sociology, social administration, social work, psychology and criminology itself. The specialists have reproduced, sustained and modified what passes for criminological knowledge. They have undertaken research and championed the legitimacy of their calling. Yet only rarely can those professional custodians be identified as innovators.[2] In the main, they have been dependent on ideas which have been deposited by others who owe no allegiance to the criminological profession. They have diligently explored and embellished materials provided by others. The outsiders have not necessarily asked criminological questions or furthered criminological objectives. Durkheim, for example, was chiefly concerned with pathological states of social integration when he offered the thesis of anomie. Similarly the work of the Chicago School was not expressly focused on the deviant and the criminal. It was devoted to an ethnographic charting of the city. Deviant worlds formed part of the city, and they were mapped in their turn. Some members of the Sociology Department at the University did have an overt interest in criminal phenomena; but Little Sicily, Polonia, newspapers, crowds, restaurants, hotels and rooming-house districts were held to be equally engaging analytic subjects. Deviance contained nothing which was substantively distinctive or compelling. It was one form amongst others, and it did not command a peculiar vocabulary of explanation.

The functionalists, too, have explored deviance as if it were a matter of secondary analytic importance. Parsons himself barely touched on rule breaking, dismissing it as a consequence of disjointed interaction or strain in the social system. Malinowski examined crime, but only to illuminate concealed properties of social structure. Others have turned to deviance in order to document facets of the larger functionalist vision. Seeming pathology has become latent functionality, anomaly has been revealed as hidden consistency, and the competence of the sociologist has been confirmed. Merton, Bell, Coser and Davis cannot be recognised as properly ratified criminologists. At best, they made analytic excursions into deviance for criminologically eccentric purposes. Their work serves interests which lie outside the boundaries of criminology. It is in this sense that the history of the Chicago School and functionalism could be written without much allusion to the study of crime, but the American (if not the British) history of criminology would be void without the achievements of the functionalists and early interactionists.

Such innovators have usually swept in and out of criminology, leaving confusion in their train. They have not always been steeped in criminology. Neither have they believed themselves its guardians. They have not always phrased their analysis in a style that can be grafted on to the tradition, that draws upon its arguments, that reinforces its theses or that ensures its tenability. Instead their interests have generally been instrumental and evanescent. Coser entered deviance briefly so that he could inject a Simmelian dialectic of conflict into functionalism. Davis investigated prostitution and illegitimacy to adorn his demography. Cicourel examined the construction of crime statistics and juvenile delinquency, but his preoccupation was with the constitution of *any* social practices. Behaviour at a circus or in a lecture theatre would have served just as well. In all this work deviance simply presented an array of research opportunities. It was not a problematic or fascinating object in its own right. Indeed, few rigorous sociologies have ever become firmly attached to just one substantive area. Their concern is with the forms of life, not with some specific content.

Many of the principal authors of criminology have thus been uninterested in nursing the tradition which has claimed them. They have typically exploited its materials for idiosyncratic reasons. Their problems have flowed from questions which have little immediate bearing on the central themes of criminology itself. Once resolved, those questions have largely been abandoned. Although they posed criminological dilemmas which have remained unanswered, the innovators have not returned to settle them.

The production of criminological knowledge has been framed by extra-ordinary conditions. The intellectually curious have promoted their special analytic concerns. Their ideas have not welled out of a peculiarly criminological environment. They do not rest on a common foundation of perspectives and problems. On the contrary, they refer laterally to a series of parent sociologies: symbolic interactionism, functionalism, phenomenology, positivism, Marxism and ethnomethodology. Because they are so focused, there has been little resort to the body of explicitly criminological writings. It is as if that body did not exist at all. Merrill, Taft, Tappan, Reckless, Ohlin, Wolfgang, Mannheim, Teeters, Clinard, Toby, Savitz and Johnston may have provided a context for their fellow criminologists, but they are unacknowledged by the sociologists of crime. They have furnished commentaries which are unread, arguments which are unanswered and analysis which is unused. Criminology may accordingly be described as a drama whose chief actors recognise no master script or supporting cast. Indeed, they sometimes appear not to understand that they are participants in a play at all.

Every criminological paradigm consequently tends to consist of a welter of unrelated conjectures, unfinished work and oblique solutions. It is a repository of ideas which have centred on crime, an almost antiquarian accumulation of observations, hypotheses and problems. Its boundaries are drawn by reference to the substance of crime, not to the forms of theory, and they reflect no coherent intellectual organisation. The custodians may accomplish a certain amount of exegesis, synthesis and explanation, but their materials have been assembled in a disorderly fashion. No amount of rearranging can transform the older criminology into an integrated corpus of thought.

Textbooks do, however, retrospectively cast each sustained intellectual foray as a cycle or movement in the emerging history of criminology. Sociologists are identified as criminology's own, although they may disown affiliation. A kind of specious collaboration has been plotted out, suggesting connections and commitments which are less substantial than many criminologists would suppose. The sociology of crime has been correspondingly deformed. Its course has been twisted and manipulated to address a litter of unrelated problems. Comprehensive answers to those problems cannot be discovered in criminological tracts themselves but in the larger sociological schemes which first prompted enquiry. Anomie is incompletely understood unless Durkheim's examination of social solidarity and the division of labour is first mastered. *The Hobo* and *The Taxi-Dance Hall* can be properly interpreted only in the context of pragmatism, formalism and ecological sociology. A close investigation of those intellectual matrices will turn the sociologist away from the uniquely criminological and direct him at questions which are tangential to crime. It follows that criminology itself cannot proffer an interpretative framework for its own component writings. The arguments assembled in a single phase do not compose a coherent environment of explanation for one another: they must be locked into a wider scheme outside criminology. The arguments of different phases are even more discontinuous. The works of the Chicago School do not elucidate functionalist contentions, and functionalism does not usefully amplify symbolic interactionism. In short, much criminology is no more than a conglomeration of partial questions, elliptical answers and fractured perspectives. It is a congregation of fragments without overall design or organisation. It feeds upon a sociology which becomes partial, disordered, deracinated and non incremental in use. If that sociology ever did have strengths, it was likely to become emasculated when it was absorbed by criminology. The analytic edifices which supported its contentions, the larger system which awarded them significance and the reservations and qualifications which supervised their application were all surrendered. In their place, much vulgarisation and simplification have been introduced.

The insubstantial and fissured character of the criminological tradition has been amplified by another critical quality. Until recently criminology has tended to be taught and practised as an applied discipline. Such a subordination to practical concerns cannot be described as necessarily discreditable. After all, much sociology cannot even claim to be justified by social utility. Few writings are either useful *or* analytically potent. Yet the grounded, focused and immediate aspects of criminology have inflicted analytic wounds on the tradition. Those aspects have become pervasive. The bulk of criminology is composed of pieces which have suffered from being closely tethered to the time, place and concerns of their originating context. They have offered descriptions which rapidly lose all theoretical and practical significance. In this sense the discipline is a graveyard of excessively concrete thought: study upon study is piled up in the mausoleum of textbooks and journals, each limited in scope and depth. Even those arguments which are presented in academically remote settings tend to be infected by a style which is rooted in the concrete.

The problem is compounded because there is little recognition of the mortality of criminological research. Ideas are displayed without an awareness of how hazardous speculation can be. Tacitly, at least, that research is held to explore what is tantamount to a collection of criminological essences. The beings and groupings that inhabit crime's bestiary are apparently thought to be simple, unchanging, discrete and analytically transparent. Work on juvenile delinquency, for instance, has been managed as if it were a single, prolonged assault on one essential problem. An article written on New York gangs in the 1950s can be celebrated as a refutation of assertions made about the Chicago of the 1920s. Observations on Californian delinquents in the 1960s can, in turn, upset conjectures about East Coast society. British examples are flourished to counter American theories. Such a conception of science can exist only when delinquency is translated into a Platonic form which reveals itself in different places and at different times to different people. Matza's drifting boy, Thrasher's mild hedonist, Yablonsky's sociopath, Cohen's frustrated aspirant and Goodman's anarchist become no more than glimpses of the Absolute Delinquent. They are glimpses which may be contrasted, ranked and filtered. This attribution of a noumenal core to deviant phenomena has encouraged the development of a number of arguments in which unlike is pitched against unlike. It has been revived by radical criminologists who assume that all criminology has been directed at the explanation of identical processes and events. Crime is so defined by radical criminology that it becomes an absolute which permits only one master scheme of interpretation. I shall discuss the ramifications of the new absolutism below, when I compare the phenomenalism of the symbolic interactionists with the essentialism of the new criminologists.

In the older criminologies of the 1930s, 1940s and 1950s practicality brought about the wholesale abandonment of reflexivity. Imported into criminology, sociological theorems were stripped of all their epistemological and ontological subtlety. The covert division of labour between custodians and producers also embraced a divide between those who were incurious about metaphysics and those who were curious. Few professional criminologists were taxed by problems of meaning, descriptive authenticity and epistemological adequacy. The larger conceptual baggage of sociology was almost invariably discarded at the frontiers of their discipline. As a result criminology has tended to resist generalisation, comparison or analytic elaboration. Its ideas have not been extended to describe alien realms. Indeed, they are not entirely amenable to extrapolation over time or across different situations. Criminologists may have depended on other disciplines for ideas, but they have offered little in return. Few sociologists of politics or religion lean on the writings of Tappan, Walter Miller or Albert Cohen. In this manner criminology has been the mute of the social sciences: its voice has not been heard by sociologists at large. Stanley Cohen and Laurie Taylor, have for instance, alluded to the pariah status of the criminologist in the sociology department of the 1960s, claiming that no professional shame was revealed by those colleagues who knew nothing of criminological thinking (cf. Cohen and Taylor, 1975).

I have observed that self-scrutiny was largely absent in the early criminological tradition. Some limited reflexivity has lately appeared, but it has tended only to magnify the inchoate features of criminology. The criminological mind has newly folded back on itself in *The New Criminology* (Taylor et al, 1973a), *Critical Criminology* (Taylor et al, 1975a) and *The Deviant Imagination* (Pearson, 1975). A version of the sociology of sociology has been constructed to inspect the development and contents of the analysis of crime. Following Gouldner, a few criminologists have examined their own tradition and contributed to its incoherence. Managing criminology as an insulated and independent enterprise, they have compounded the fractures and discontinuities which plague the discipline. Radical criminologists have criticised the work of their predecessors and colleagues as if it consisted merely of the theoretical outcrops which have obtruded into criminology. They have failed to recognise the importance of the division of labour between innovators and custodians, acknowledging only those materials which have been explicitly identified as criminological. The truncated, distorted and inarticulate remnants of sociological perspectives are consequently discussed as if they were whole. The intentions, epistemology and strategies of innovators are inferred from the arguments which the custodians choose to preserve. To add additional confusion, the innovators are represented as men who confronted the one Absolute of the radical criminologists. As I shall argue, radical criminologists make no provision for the possibility that there is no Absolute or that men may not entirely share their yearning for the Absolute. Not all criminologists are enamoured of metaphysical pathos.

The reflexivity of the new criminology, accordingly, retains the emasculated conceptions of the old. There can be very little reference to ideas which did not expressly bear on crime, although much of the older innovative work was framed by conceptions that were criminologically extraneous. It has thus come about that *The New Criminology* can discuss symbolic interactionism without invoking the neo-Kantianism of Simmel and the pragmatist reconciliation of philosophical dualism. It can proceed without citing Dewey, Blumer, Hughes and Strauss. It can exclude even the relatively minor strains of interactionist sociology. The self is not lodged in its dialectical background. Phenomenalism is ignored. The rejection of Aristotelian reasoning is unmentioned. An interactionism without those authors and themes is a sociological corpse which lacks any robustness or life. It can be dismissed with ease. Phenomenology, too, has been examined as if Husserl, Renouvier, Bergson, Kant, Heidegger, Jaspers and Merleau-Ponty had never written. The interests, perspectives and intellectual landscapes of criminological innovators are thereby extinguished. Everything that lent substance and order to their works has been critically obliterated. Instead a gross sociology of knowledge has been expounded to demonstrate how such rootless and partial theses could have been produced. The radical criminologists have generally taken to working a complete reconstitution of the ideas of others before criticism can proceed. They displace the world of rival authors and insert class interest, cerebral infirmity or servility in its stead. In the main that new context is utterly simple. It is compounded of the ideology which the radical criminologists advance. Other sociologists are accused of not deferring to such an ideology, although they may well have substantial if unstated reasons for not doing so. Radical ideology has fabricated a new environment for old criminology. Anachronistic connections are established and motives are imputed. Thus Gouldner has accused Becker of being swayed by financial agencies which he never approached (cf. Gouldner, 1968). Pearson has asserted that symbolic interactionism refracted the concerns of the Frankfurt School, although interactionism was fully formed before the Frankfurt School emerged and no interactionists refer to its arguments (cf. Pearson, 1975). A superficial affinity

exists which justifies no statement about intellectual ancestry or
influence. The absolutism of the new criminology allows bizarre empirical
links to be established by a school which disdains empiricism. This, too, I
shall amplify below.

   Radical criminologists are themselves exempt from the criminological
filter. They do not expunge their own past when they develop an onslaught
on their fellows. They make use of the entire armoury of Marxist and allied
arguments when they attack the mutant husks of interactionism and
phenomenology. Their project is ensured success because it has been
provided with an invincible design.

THE INTERACTIONIST PHASE

The criminology of the 1950s was a loose congregation of ideas distilled
from theories of differential association, functionalism and anomie.
Anomie was an especially incisive conception, which was to become the
theme of a reasonably extended period of analysis and research. Merton's
reformulation of Durkheim's work was to be followed by Cloward and
Ohlin's *Delinquency and Opportunity,* Cohen's *Delinquent Boys,*
Spergel's *Racketville, Slumtown, Haulburg,* Downes's *The Delinquent
Solution,* and a great spate of articles. Yet, like its predecessors, anomie is
a most delicate and intricate idea which was rather crudely amputated
from sociology proper. It conjures up complex questions about the nature
of symbolic universes, processes of moral disarray, and the dialectical play
between man and the collective representations. Ushered into criminology, it was transmuted into a description of contradictions between
societal goals and means. Culture became a monochromatic and flat
collection of simple imperatives. Men became the isolated, rational judges
of life-chances which were strewn over long expanses of time. Deviance
was cast as a virtually indelible status into which men leapt from a position
of unalloyed virtue. In sum, anomie theory was characteristically bowd-
lerised during its phase as an object of criminological interest. Moreover,
its advocates did not pursue its analysis for very long. Some had appeared
from the world of social work and correction. Others turned to it. Anomie
theory was the particular province of those who devoted only a limited
time to academic reflection. Cohen, Spergel, Cloward and Ohlin were
immersed in problems of practical intervention, preferring not to undertake an exhaustive examination of what they had brought into being.

   Even in the late 1950s, then, criminology was vulnerable to almost any coherent analytic attack. The discipline was so poorly articulated that every whole sociology became formidable in contrast. Ironically, the sociology which *did* migrate into deviant terrain was itself loosely constructed and ill-defined. Symbolic interactionism is a most unusual sociology, which has only occasionally colonised areas of substantive knowledge. Its constitution discourages the adoption of an imperialistic or proselytising stance, and that constitution must first be described before it is possible to explain the sociology's drift into criminology, its reshaping of that discipline and its eventual displacement by radical criminology in Britain and parts of America.

I shall dwell on interactionism for two principal reasons. One is that it is a sociology which did lead to a definite break in the criminological tradition. The interactionists produced a sustained and co-operative exploration of the problems attending deviant phenomena. Their accomplishments were substantial, constituting an important alternative to the radical phrasing of criminology. As important, those accomplishments have been somewhat misrepresented by their radical critics. The attacks on interactionism have distorted and simplified their object, but they have not been seriously challenged. In turn they have come to stand as definitive judgements for a number of criminologists. My intention is to put something of the interactionist case, attempting to restore proportion to the arguments which surround the competing sociologies.

The epistemology of symbolic interactionism flows from a fusion of formalism and pragmatism. It endows knowledge with a special province and a special significance. Valid knowledge is held to reside neither in the subject nor in the object but in the transactions that unfold between them. It is not the creature of analytic *a priori* reasoning, science or spirit, because its objects are independent of mind and cannot be understood by logic or the imagination alone. It does not inhere in the very nature of phenomena themselves, because those phenomena must be actively grasped by the intellect. It represents the emerging product of active encounters between consciousness and the materials which consciousness surveys. Interactionism thus tends towards a conception of science which is based on the phenomenology of the act but, unlike phenomenology, it does not award privileged understanding to reflexivity. The self and its ideas are not transparent to the mind which creates them. Culture, identity and thought are as opaque as any other facet of the world. Folding back on itself, consciousness becomes its own problematic object. As its own uncertain and seemingly alien object, it must be interpreted tentatively and without the assurance of the phenomenological reduction.

Grounding knowledge in the reflexive act, symbolic interactionism does not entertain a vision of truth as an unchanging, monolithic unity. Rather, it embraces a pluralistic realism in which perspectives can be complementary, independent or conflicting but never total. There can be many truths and many realities: each rooted in a knowing-known transaction; each secure in its time and place; each contingent on purposes, context and experience; and each hostile to precise ranking and comparison with other expressions of existence.

For the pragmatist who has achieved a special synthesis of the thought of Hegel and Darwin, those realities are an integral part of nature itself. They are the interplay between different facets of the natural world. The human reflex is not ontologically distinct from the rest of its environment, and it cannot be considered alien or strange. Prepredicative knowledge is not an estranged or unnatural state, and its authenticity is as substantial as any physical or organic process. It is not superadded or apart from the world: it is *in* the world, changing and being changed as other parts change. The understanding of a man prepares particular horizons of possibilities. It arranges the world with the formation of projects. Each organisation is valid in itself. It is not solely a mental conception but a synthesis of what is within and without. Indeed, the pragmatists refuse to demarcate frontiers between mind and its objects. They seek to transcend the Kantian disjunction between observer and observed, fusing the two in an active process of knowing.

For the formalist, the prepredicative knowledge of the pragmatists is intellectually unmanageable. It is the incommunicable content of social life, becoming analytically available only when it is mediated by the collective forms of consciousness. Contents are indescribable without the structures of social life. Those structures give shape to experience, creating public and private realities. They are social accomplishments which cannot be matched with one another. Society, social organisation, the individual and a piece of art are all assemblies of forms. None is ontologically superior to the others. Each is a social fabrication, and it is absurd and profitless to enquire which fabrication is the most real.

The interactionists amalgamated pragmatism and formalism in an attempt to produce a viable sociology. Pragmatism had offered a vision of lived experience which no sociology could assimilate. Betrayed by any analysis, that experience could not be interpretatively exploited or reproduced. It had simply to be *lived*. When it was transmuted by the social forms, however, experience could be treated as a social reality which was adequate for all sociological purposes.

Humanity was still at one with nature, but its consciousness was ordered by structures which gave a particular organisation to experience. It was an embedded consciousness, joined with the environments which became its objects. It could not be regarded as transcendental, and it did not deliver metaphysical truths. It furnished local realities which are valid despite their parochialism. Interactionism, then, holds that truth is not the peculiar possession of any one group, individual, theory or situation. Neither is it inevitably orderly, harmonious and whole. It requires the most momentous act of faith to assert that the truth is one: discontinuity and confusion may be as much its characteristics as logic, consistency and neat definition. There are no binding reasons why knowledge should be subordinated to a single master scheme which explains all the separate appearances of reality. Indeed, the production of such a scheme would only remove men from practical activity and intellectual exploration. It would alienate them from the experiences which underpin useful understanding.

Interactionist epistemology brought about a sociology which avoids both monism and dualism, idealism and crass positivism. I shall relay the arguments which impelled the interactionists to produce a new conception of knowledge and man. In so doing, I shall resurrect some of the criticisms which interactionists once directed at rival phrasings of science. The special vision of interactionism might then become clear, preparing the way for a review of the radical criminology which is beginning to replace it.

Analytic *a priori* thought makes mind global in a world of objects which are distinct from consciousness. It implies that the resources of thought are sufficient to comprehend things which do not belong to thought at all. In turn, it forces a correspondence between the structure of description and the structure of what is described. It declares that philosophy and its objects are one. Explanation proceeds by means of a sympathetic magic: as descriptions change, so must their objects. Such idealism must necessarily lodge knowledge in some disembodied realm of pure reason. It demands the existence of an Olympian plane which reveals the Absolute. It reifies thought and divorces it from the practices of the thinking mind which produces it. It can proceed only by creating an alienated process called theorising which houses the sure understanding that is foreign to ordinary men. In that manufacturing of an estranged universe, idealism removes consciousness from conscious men. It separates ideas from the things which ideas portray. It mystifies the workings of the reflexive act. Thoughts are transferred to an autonomous sphere which is sited neither in mind nor in mind's physical and social environment.

Interactionists largely discard such axiomatic reasoning. Of course, even interactionist analysis must be supported by conjecture and *a priori* speculation. But it adamantly defines objects as external to the thought which tries to interpret them. In turn, the interactionists would state that understanding can be adequate only when it is open to transformation by phenomena outside itself. That transformation cannot occur unless men experience the world as objectively real and obdurate. The distance created by analytic *a priori* schemes need not confer an experience of constraint. It reduces all to subjectivity. It is quite evident that an apprehension that nature restrains is still an *apprehension.* It does not emancipate men from subjectivity because the external world must be considered and assessed. But it does represent the only practical escape from rampant idealism. It obliges sociology to refer to the interplay between reflexive acts and the settings which anchor them. It suggests that any other focus must entail an examination of ideas which are independent of minds, subjects without independent objects and men who have no recalcitrant environment.

The symbolic interactionists reject subjective idealism because they acknowledge the stubborn facticity of the world. Yet they also resist the gross empiricism which depicts objects and relations as laden with innate meaning. They claim that the world cannot be known until it has been transmuted by the structures of thought and observation. There can be no understanding without the synthetic *a priori* forms which shape all content. Those forms are the socially mediated and socially accomplished architecture of experience. They lend order to existence and are existentially ordered in their turn. It is in this sense that the world defies direct, unmediated inspection. It does not passively await an observing mind which will work no changes on it. It is changed when it is viewed and, being changed, it becomes doubly social: as a collection of objects which are patterned by collective representation and as objects which are transformed by collective action. When men touch, smell, move and work on phenomena, they impart significance and organisation which stem from the social order itself. Knowledge is therefore a transaction which cannot be dissolved into its component parts. It is not a state of contemplation or a vehicle of immutable truths. On the contrary, it is a *process* and the truth changes as every transaction evolves. The very word 'knowledge' is mischievous because it suggests a finality or consummation. It should not be a noun but a verb. So defined, knowledge becomes knowing, a dialectical exchange. It constitutes and is constituted by its objects as it unfolds.

Meaning must, then, be creatively discovered: it is neither invented nor self-evident. In turn, there can be no route to the real and fundamental meanings of society and nature. Those meanings have no existence or substance outside the play of practical consciousness. All useful knowledge must be fluid, local and incomplete. It cannot but be a partial organisation of the world, an organisation which is circumscribed temporally, spatially and imaginatively. It can retain its focus only by blurring and ignoring large tracts of matter. It may always be upset by new discoveries and new syntheses. In short, it can never be general or absolute. It does not offer access to a clearly structured domain of essences. Knowledge produces specific configurations which are parochial rather than universal, emergent rather than static, and dependent on the consciousness which engenders them. There is no one objective or transcendental order which can be properly studied by the sociologist. All sociologies which do pretend to sure knowledge of social totalities are consequently defined as meretricious. They contemplate metaphysical Utopias of their own making.

Just as the essence of society is unascertainable, so it is impossible to establish a systematic theory of society. All perspectives are tied to one or more minor social locations. There is no vantage point which offers the sociologist a view of society at large. Society can be grasped only in the imagination: it is the creature of reified metaphor, *a priori* intuition or impermissible induction. As an imaginary entity, its alleged attributes must always be regarded with the greatest suspicion. Some modest generalisation of the social forms may be possible, but detailed descriptions of society merely present a scientific chimera. Indeed, there would appear to be no convincing reasons why 'society' should be analysed as one intelligible unity at all. It is permanently beyond the reach of any defensible research strategy. However urgent questions about society might be, interactionists would argue that valid knowledge is irreparably circumscribed and partial. They would maintain that sociology should not dwell on unanswerable problems. Rather, it should slowly navigate those areas which might fall before a reasonably sound methodology.

It is this abandonment of the Absolute which distinguishes interactionism from many other sociologies. Interactionism denies that society can be an object of pure thought. It argues, instead, that sociology and common sense must both defer to the phenomenal reality of the social world. Any imputation of essential, noumenal, deep or hidden structures flows only from the exercise of a speculative reason which is entitled to no interpretative authority. Aristotelian logic is inappropriate to sociology because valid observations can emerge only out of the rooted practices of acting selves. It is those practices which create the specific forms of the social world, and there would be nothing knowable without them. In turn, phenomena are defined as irreducible and real. They are the 'truth' of embedded consciousness, the sole truth which men can know with confidence. They cannot be dismissed as mere indices of an invisible, untouchable and inaudible Absolute. What is real for men is real for all practical purposes. It is not epiphenomenal, superstructural or the manifestation of false consciousness. Indeed, the only false consciousness recognised by the interactionists is the contemplation of an alienated mind which retires to a place of distant analytic reflection.

The sociologist must then launch his own self into the social world when he seeks understanding. His consciousness does not afford privileged insight into itself or society. Introspection, intuition and rational surmise can guide neither self-understanding nor an understanding of the wider environments of the self. Instead, analysis must be conducted in the social settings which it seeks to explore. It must be an integral feature of its own problems.

In this fashion, interactionists have upset the conventional hierarchy of sociological priorities. Instead of subordinating inquiry to pressing problems, they have set themselves manageable but unremarkable projects. Orthodox sociologists have accused them of being preoccupied with the petty and ephemeral. In reply, they would define much sociology as a latterday hunt for the questing beast. They have not given themselves impossible tasks which offer the illusion of profound solutions: they are not Snark hunters. On the contrary, they have sought to build a 'scientific mosaic', an assembly of interlocking minor studies. They have turned to ethnography, rejecting the architectonic schemes of high sociology. That course is uncongenial to most sociologists. The construction of a mosaic is neither an ambitious nor a massively satisfying enterprise. Interactionism provides little reassurance that every significant problem can be subdued, that sociology represents an especially powerful or privileged medium of thought, or that the sociologist can hope to accomplish much. Sociology is translated into a relatively humble undertaking which is pursued without any prospect of palpable success. It can progress only when the sociologist acknowledges uncertainty.[3] It is devoted to a meticulous observation of the social forms, not to an embellishing of axiomatic schemes.

No volume of work can transform those schemes into their objects. In only one sense can they be understood as identical with what they portray. When Marxists, functionalists or structuralists act as if their sociologies were true, they become the authors of a phenomenal realm which is real enough in its consequences. Their sociologies may fold back on them as an alien reality which does constrain and move action. But they do so in a novel, synthetic *a priori* form, not as an analytically adequate account which others must accept as a proper explanation of society. They have an experiential validity in their own small situations, but no metaphysical and universal truth which all must recognise.

SYMBOLIC INTERACTIONISM AND DEVIANCE

Interactionism was proposed as a sociology which could avoid some of the hazards of philosophical dualism and subjective idealism. Its originators advocated a return to the social world. Ethnography became the praxis which might underwrite knowledge. It transformed lived experience into the supreme centre of the sociologist's attention, a centre which produced authentic understanding. Transcribed into the social forms, that experience became publicly analysable and publicly communicable. It became a fitting material for sociological work.

The epistemological foundations of interactionism were to have curious consequences. They were to lead to a kind of intellectual suicide or disinheritance. Organised around a philosophy which disowned philosophy, interactionism denied its own past. A reasoned rejection of propositional logic brought about a sociology which recognised no comprehensive philosophical legitimation or direction. The interactionists tend not to refer back to their roots in pragmatism and formalism. Instead, they have produced a creation myth in which their sociology was given a virgin birth in the Chicago of the 1920s.

Symbolic interactionism has become a sociology without an overt system of axioms. It is not propelled inexorably towards certain goals and certain objects. Neither does it mobilise a closed and schematic theory when it advances on particular problems. Clearly, it does display something more than mere intellectual drift. But, unlike more orthodox sociologies, it is not barred from analysing specific forms of life. There are no taboo or illegitimate phenomena. Society is not so firmly prestructured by the minds of sociologists that its parts may be treated as known in advance of enquiry. In this sense, there was no reason why deviance should *not* have been studied at some stage in the history of interactionism. Deviance is one sector of the phenomenal realm; it is as real and beguiling as any other, and it is as worthy of mapping. As the ethnographic work of the interactionists advanced, so deviance was itself mapped. It was not removed from scientific inspection by theoretical *fiat*.

The exploration of deviant phenomena then arose because there were no barriers to its pursuit. It was not awarded greater importance than research on education, the mass media, occupational careers, medicine or communal life. Indeed, it was not held to demand a substantially different methodology. Deviance is the emergent outcome of social forms, and forms may be prised away from their contents. *A priori,* the forms which generate, sustain and modify deviance need not be dissimilar to those which organise other social phenomena. Formalism discouraged the assumption that deviance was unique. Pragmatism discouraged the assumption that it could be charted by inferential thinking alone. There were resources within interactionism to examine deviance, but none to pronounce its nature until ethnography had taken place.

Interactionist methodology itself is controlled by two contradictory imperatives. Participant observation requires the sociologist to be both inside and outside the social scenes which he explores. As an insider, he is supposed to become familiar enough with a world's forms to reproduce them himself. He may then understand, and hence relay, the procedures which are employed to construct that world's phenomena. Yet such mastery may induce him to take those selfsame forms for granted. Whether he is in real or spurious command, the forms may recede into an unproblematic background where they are no longer open to analytic scrutiny. As an outsider, the sociologist is a monitor who defines the routine as bizarre, the seemingly natural as arbitrary and the unremarked as remarkable. He exercises an appraising rationality in situations where none may have been employed before. He records and organises what would otherwise have been evanescent and unexamined. He maintains a distance where others would not do so. In sum, the fieldworker is one who estranges himself from everyday life in a manner that might be read as subversive, calculating and abnormal. He uses his own self as a research instrument, tailoring it to extract materials. He thereby risks alienating himself from the very meanings which he wishes to understand. In all this, there is an irreconcilable disparity between interpretation and analysis. Hughes identified that disparity as the necessary dialectical tension which animates the research process.

The tension can never be wholly dispelled. The two opposing stances may be alternated in a sequence of internal and external positions. By undergoing withdrawal and return, the sociologist may segregate the antagonistic facets of his work. A second strategy is to proceed as if the tension did not exist at all. The sociologist may rely on a prepredicative resolution of his seeming conflict. He may assert that the tension flows from a logical contradiction which tends to disappear in practice. The actual experience of fieldwork makes perfectly manageable what appears to be methodologically impossible. The contrary states of participation and observation are intolerable only when they are brought to consciousness. They need present no practical impediment to the business of research.

Other interactionist ethnographers have attempted to exploit the tension by moving to those situations where it may be usefully harnessed. There are certain areas which enclose the unfamiliar within a larger landscape of the familiar. Deviant settings, in particular, are made up of apparently strange phenomena surrounded by the less strange. They may be assumed to refract and rearrange known forms in a manner that is peculiarly congenial to ethnography. The conventional which is dressed in an unconventional guise may excite just that tension which is vital to useful analysis. Instead of hampering understanding, it may lead to what Goffman has called a 'stumbling into awareness'. The sociologist can then traverse the boundaries between orthodox and unorthodox scenes, being both native and stranger. The American fieldworker who explores American deviance and the English fieldworkerk who investigates English deviance can appreciate recognisable figures in a jarring form. In this sense, deviance presents an array of methodologically propitious phenomena which attracted interactionist interest.

But there is one other reason for the emergence of an interactionist sociology of deviance. Many symbolic interactionists were themselves marginal figures.[4] They existed on the interface between convention and disreputability, already occupying those positions which enlighten through contradiction. Becker was a jazz musician, Polsky was a pool player, Irwin had been an inmate. Others had been in asylums, or had taken marijuana at a time when use was not widespread, or had straddled sexual roles. The very recruitment of some major interactionists encouraged a focus upon deviance. Marginality became a resource, its strains being cultivated. It eased passage between the university and certain eccentric worlds. It did not present insuperable problems because the cosmology of symbolic interactionism is not markedly discontinuous with that of the larger world. It does not impose arcane beliefs upon its adherents. Neither does it dismiss the phenomena of social experience as a series of deceits. Rather, it may be exported into mundane settings without any of the violence which is associated with the high sociologies.

It is not really necessary to provide an exhaustive inventory of inter-actionist accomplishments in the sociology of deviance. They flow from the hidden epistemology which I have sketched. Extending their synthesis to the domain of rule breaking, interactionists have concentrated on the symbolic construction of deviance. They have taken deviance to be an unfolding form which is reproduced and altered in conversations between and within selves. It is to be discovered neither in the deviant alone, nor in those about him, but in the discourse of significant gestures. It is inevitably unstable, emergent and incomplete, permitting further modification without end. Found only in the dialogue of forms, it does not enjoy an absolute or autonomous existence. It is not the property of some mysterious and invisible entity called Society. Its sole site is in the activities of observable selves, and the voyagings and transformations of those selves must become the prime objects of interactionist analysis. In particular, they must be explained by the synthetic *a priori* forms of social life. The career, primary and secondary deviation, commitment, conflict, collusion, symbiosis and co-operation are members of that vocabulary of forms. They lend order to what might otherwise be an incoherent agglomerate of unique and indescribable events. They draw deviance into the realm of the normal, suggesting that abnormal contents are organised by wholly conventional processes. They contribute to a set of minor theorems about the geometry of social life.

Those theorems do not lay themselves out as a system which may be treated as an exact mirror of life. They cannot be manipulated to compose an axiomatic scheme which is entire in itself. Instead they must be used as a collection of interpretative guides which cannot be extrapolated and generalised without research. The interactionist possesses no mandate to proclaim all the shapes and qualities of deviance. He offers no more than a vision of possibilities.

THE 'RADICAL' PHASE OF CRIMINOLOGY

I have argued that orthodox sociological theory either tended to ignore crime or else used it for very particular purposes. In the main it defined rule breaking as an insignificant area which could be appraised by inference alone. Inference taught that crime was peripheral, that it could be mastered by general explanatory principles and that there was little profit in exploring it. By contrast, the symbolic interactionists suggested that such *a priori* reasoning might have failed sociology. They so transformed criminology that it came to present novel problems and opportunities. They were the colonisers of the discipline, preparing it for later invasion by the advocates of conventional theory.

The interactionists had abandoned propositional analysis, turning instead to phenomenalism and modest ethnographic research. It was that strain in their approach which translated crime into a legitimate intellectual object. But it was that strain which also encouraged some ordinary sociologists to seize the object and make it their own. Although interactionism had made crime analytically attractive, interactionism was itself thrust aside. The sociology had reduced the scope and depth of possible theorising; it had refused to establish extensive structural connections; and it emphasised fluidity and uncertainty. The conventional theorist is unprepared to accept such analytic restraints. His sociology is less circumscribed. Buttressed by a coherent metaphysics of the social world, he can launch an attack which no phenomenalism can withstand. The comprehensive and logically rigorous theory lends crime a much greater significance than any envisaged by the interactionist. Further, it yields criticisms on a plane which no interactionist can reach. If the symbolic interactionist answers metaphysics with metaphysics, he has betrayed his own epistemology and lost his case. Hence it has come about that the assault made by radical criminologists in the early 1970s was superficially successful. It seemed to offer the prospect of a richer and profounder sociology, and the interactionist offered no defence. What was abandoned was discipline and a modesty of aim. The new criminology is not seated in a commerce with the phenomenal world. It strains towards the Absolute and a rampant idealism.

Radical criminology reasserted *a priori* theorising, restored absolutism and denied the sovereignty of the phenomenal world. As Taylor, Walton and Young have themselves observed, the new criminology is not new at all. It is a resuscitation of high sociology. The new criminologists have displaced the interactionists, lamenting 'the failure of social reaction theorists . . . to build a bridge with . . . the tradition of grand sociology from which [the] area of study has grown'. They state that that failure is an 'outstanding omission' (Taylor et al, 1973a, p. 168). The nature of that omission, the competing claims of phenomenalism and absolutism will form the basis of all that follows. Radical criminologists have generally depicted symbolic interactionism as a sociology which is deficient in reason or vision. The world which they celebrate is taken to be overwhelmingly real. Those who deny its facticity are held to be its inhabitants despite themselves. It is only grand theory that can comprehend that world, and a refusal to employ it is construed as a sign of myopia or timidity. That is the absolutist conception. But there is another conception, and it is one which I wish to champion. That latter interpretation

maintains that the bridge with the traditions of grand sociology is no more
than a Jacob's Ladder leading to an uncertain heaven of speculative
metaphysics. The worldliness of the radical criminologists is more
properly defined as otherworldliness, a retreat from what may be known to
what can never be known.

Arthur Lovejoy has described otherworldliness as:

> . . . the belief that both the genuinely 'real' and the truly good are
> radically antithetic in their essential characteristics to anything to be
> found in man's natural life, in the ordinary course of human experience,
> however normal, however intelligent, and however fortunate. The
> world we now and here know — various, mutable, a perpetual flux of
> states and relations of things, or an ever-shifting phantasmagoria of
> thoughts and sensations, each of them lapsing into nonentity in the very
> moment of its birth — seems to the otherworldly mind to have no
> substance in it; the objects of sense, and even of empirical scientific
> knowledge are unstable, contingent, forever breaking down . . . [The
> real is] to be found only in a 'higher' realm of being differing in its
> essential nature, and not merely in degree and detail, from the lower.
> (Lovejoy, 1960, pp. 25, 26)

Radical criminologists would have it that their sociology is simply more
comprehensive, embracing self-evident political realities which interactionists are loath to acknowledge. In turn, interactionist epistemology is
cast as a mere outgrowth of liberal ideology, a subservience to capitalism
and all its works. When the conflict between the two sociologies is
rephrased, however, it becomes apparent that it is more fundamental and
more antique than the new criminologists suppose. Interactionists are the
heirs of Heraclitus. Radical criminologists affirm a Platonic philosophy.
The dispute between the phenomenalists and the absolutists is not
resolved. Indeed, it probably defies final resolution. It certainly cannot be
settled by treating it as a battle between those who are politically adven-
turous and those who are not, between those who recognise reality and
those who do not. Rather, it revolves around worldliness and otherworldliness, the question of the scope and nature of reason.

RADICAL CRIMINOLOGY DESCRIBED

Just as I have been forced to construct a personal ideal-type of symbolic
interactionism, so it is necessary to create an artificially coherent model of
radical criminology. The new criminologists are an assembly of English
and American sociologists whose ideas stem from Marxism, populism and

conflict theory. They are not bound together in a massive unanimity of thought. But it is possible to discern a collection of central themes in their writing, and those themes are markedly opposed to the interactionist formulation of criminology. They emphasise the authority of the original great charter of sociology. With Marx, Tönnies, Durkheim and Comte, they conceive sociology to be a science which examines the major pathologies of society. Alienation, oppression, the collapse of community and the fate of mankind are the central, fitting topics of a discipline which was designed to redeem the world. Any lesser objectives would not justify the pursuit of sociological knowledge. That knowledge is believed to be capable of rendering the truth transparent. There can be but one truth, and its rivals are decoys and snares. It strips the world down to its inner core, its essence, and discards all else as irrelevant and superficial. By extension, the thinker who wields sociology is himself translated into a vehicle of truth. He is one whose understanding transcends the consciousness of Everyman. Everyday life is redefined as a panorama of petty and ephemeral matters. Those who defer to its reality are deluded by epiphenomena. They are mystified.

Instead of undertaking the focused studies of interactionism, a radical criminologist charts an entity which has been named 'social totality'. That totality is the noumenal truth of society, the otherworldly reality which comprehends all that is important and fundamental. It is an analytic distillation, one must assume, of *everything* that is socially significant. The new criminology, accordingly, invokes the 'real world' (Taylor et al, 1973a, p. 164), a world which others have neglected. That world embraces the essential character of society. Those who study it must commit themselves to 'doing theoretical work in the total society' (Taylor et al, 1975b, p. 19), to placing models in a 'total analysis of social processes rather than merely in one aspect of them' (Taylor et al, 1973a, p. 157). Social totality then demands total analysis. It may be mastered only by resort to the 'traditions of grand social theory' (Taylor et al, 1973a, p. 273).

Social totality looms large in radical criminology. It is the *Leitmotiv* which justifies the claim to a 'fully social theory' (Taylor et al, 1975b, p. 18). Advancing that claim, the new criminologists believe that they have superseded all other modes of interpretation. But it is evident that radical criminologists mean something rather special by the word 'total'. The meaning is less than certain. At one level, it appears to refer promiscuously to all the infinite detail of social life, and especially that detail which touches on supposed political economy. It is not a mere analytic incision, a partial perspective, because it comprehends the whole. Explanations which do not allude to that whole are criticised for their incompleteness: they illuminate only 'one aspect' of total analysis. Indeed, partiality is so utterly rejected at points that every rival model of process is dismissed as selective. None but the radical criminologist can know the whole, and he appears to stand outside the confines and organisation of thought itself. If thought imposes order on the world, obscuring some details and obliterating others, all theorising must be parochial and less than total. The radical criminologist who experiences totality must then emancipate himself from the shackles of theory. Thus Quinney can discard ethnomethodology because it 'questions the existence of an objective reality apart from the individual's imagination. . . . The epistemological assumption of social constructionist thought is that observations are based on our mental *constructions,* rather than on the raw apprehension of the physical world' (Quinney, 1975, p. 184). Similarly, Taylor, Walton and Young argue 'our final assessment of ethnomethodology's contribution to the study of deviance is that in "bracketing" away the question of social reality, it does not allow of any description of the social totality we assert to be productive of deviance' (Taylor et al, 1973a, p. 208). It would then seem to follow that radical criminologists are able to grasp reality without the mediating and distorting effects of consciousness. They can think without thought, know without knowledge, theorise without theory. They somehow divine the social totality, and their models have an oracular quality. Their grasp of totality empowers them to examine the correspondence between other theories and truth. Standing apart, they adjudicate between those ideas and the world *as it is,* unmarred by ideas. It was for this reason that Quinney must have felt himself entitled to observe 'the concern of the social constructionist is not primarily with the correspondence betwen "objective reality" and observation . . .' (Quinney, 1975, p. 184). That is, the ethnomethodologist and phenomenologist are lambasted for not comparing an unobserved world with the observations that are made about it.

At another level, it becomes apparent that radical criminology is not intended to study every face of every moment of every social scene. Even a sociology as ambitious as the new criminology is unable to compress all that passes for social into one description. Rather, tacit principles of selection are advocated. Those principles cannot bring about the production of mere abstractions or limited perspectives. After all, they are designed to accomplish a description of totality, and totality would be betrayed by an approach which treated wholes as divisible. The truth does not lend itself to diverse expression. Thus 'liberal' theory is not recognised as an authentic complement to radical criminology (Taylor et al, 1975a, p. 22). There is only one truth, and every rival to the new criminology deforms it. The new criminologists castigate the journal *Social Problems* for publishing articles that 'undermine all that is progressive in modern deviancy theory' (Taylor et al, 1973a, p. 133). Eschewing 'a relativistic conception of reality' (Quinney, 1973, p. 592), the radical criminologist cannot argue that his selection is simply another refraction of a complex and recalcitrant whole. It is not even a choice between alternative vantage points. Rather, it is a mining or tapping of the social noumenon. It condenses reality into its purest form. All that is marginal is then shed, leaving the essence of society in its unadulterated state. The total analysis of social totality is thereby transformed into a massive interpretational act, a piece of major intellectual surgery. As Taylor, Walton and Young contend, 'a precondition for a radical criminology is the separation of the essential from the inessential . . .' (Taylor et al, 1975a, p. 46).

The essential is that otherworldly realm of real processes which must not to be confused with mundane appearance, everyday belief and social phenomena. It cannot be understood by entering the lifeworld of those who actually experience those processes. The consciousness of essential truth is distinct from the false consciousness of ordinary people. Everyday life is riddled by ideologies and untruths. Even theories espoused by colleagues are 'little more than rationalisations for an individualism that serves a capitalist system' (Quinney, 1973, p. 590). It is necessary to disentangle reality from unreality, prising apart false beliefs from those which are correct. As Taylor, Walton and Young remark, the Fascist may resort to explanations which are 'the products of false beliefs about the underlying social structure' (Taylor et al, 1973a, p. 174). It is the radical sociologist, not the Fascist, who can divine the truth of the Fascist's life. Underlying social structure is ontologically different from the environment of those who dwell on the surface. The surface-dweller can only see phenomena, the new criminologist *knows* noumena. For some, a protracted involvement with phenomena must lead to mystification and enchantment. Phenomenalism must be replaced by a new consciousness of deep truths: 'We do not adequately understand our present existence. Our comprehension of the present, as well as the past, is mystified by a consciousness that only serves to maintain the existing order . . . Only with a new consciousness — a critical philosophy — can we begin to realise the world of which we are capable' (Quinney, 1975, p. 181).

Those who explore phenomenal landscapes are transformed into the celebrants and navigators of false consciousness. They dissolve totalities into meaningless parts; they mistake knowledge of the commonplace for true understanding; and they are responsible for animating the ideologies which support deceptive appearances. Radical criminology has therefore adopted something of the intellectual stance of a Durkheim or a Lukács. It rejects a dependence on empiricism and *Verstehen*. Instead, it turns to the enlightenment which flows from the workings of an analytic mind. After all, empiricism merely investigates the sensory world, a world which is not metaphysically authentic. *Verstehen*, too, simply reproduces false consciousness and is incapable of explaining what is real. Thus, the British 'empiricist culture' (Taylor et al, 1975b, p. 9) is disowned, and the 'use of ethnographic research procedures . . . [is thought] to prove inadequate for the task of constructing a fully social theory of deviance . . .' (Taylor et al, 1975b, p. 18). Science has also been overthrown by some because: 'Only now are we beginning to recognise the unseen that has been excluded by our impersonal rationality. The scientific model has systematically excluded anything that could not be known through sense experience. We have naively suspended other means of knowing from our methodology' (Quinney, 1972b, p. 325).

Rationality has been denied by a number of radical criminologists. Even contradictory facts are dismissed. They cannot fetter the processes of the new imagination. Facts are also taken to be matters of the surface, creatures of false consciousness, political accomplishments. It is in this fashion that Quinney asserts 'without critical thought we are bound to the only form of social life we know — that which currently exists' (1975, p. 189). Such existence is, of course, specious and transitory. It should not impose a check on the development of thought. Similarly, and more pointedly, Taylor, Walton and Young claim ' "facts" are a product of the work of those with the power to define what is taken to be "factual" and of the willingness of those without such power to accept the given definitions' (Taylor et al, 1973a, p. 26). Without a principled adherence to empiricism, ethnography, science, rationality and facts, there is no obdurate world which defies thought. All that remains is the projection of a fertile imagination, the other world, which is the sport of analytic *a priori* reasoning. The new consciousness probes reality. Unrestrained, it may proceed to intuit the shape of the whole. New criminology is truly liberated.

Discussion has consequently shifted to a detailed examination of the internal organisation of radical criminology. It is there that reality grows. Postulates are scanned and rejected, axioms are arranged and rearranged, logic is formed and reformed, orthodoxies are advanced and countered. As Quinney remarks, 'the "findings" of science have always been the constructs of the observer. All phenomena that we perceive are the results of the operations of our mind and soul. Our explanations are the consequence of the manipulation of our own constructions' (Quinney, 1972b, p. 319). Speculation has thereby replaced mundane exploration: 'In the immediate future, empirical radical research is likely to be minimal. The debate amongst radical criminologists is about the appropriate and correct departure points for research . . .' (Taylor et al, 1975b, p. 28-9). Indeed, that radical empirical research is unnecessary, because there is little that it can achieve which cannot be more elegantly engendered by contemplation. It is contemplation which plots totalities, and argument has begun to revolve around contemplative doctrines alone. The new criminologists have invaded territories which are ruled by rival metaphysicians. Their disputes are no longer about phenomena, but about competing rights to define noumena. They are required to answer the charges of such Marxists as Paul Hirst who refuse to recognise even the noumenal existence of crime: 'There is no "Marxist theory of deviance", either in existence, or which can be developed within orthodox Marxism. Crime and deviance vanish into the general theoretical concerns and the specific scientific object of Marxism': (Hirst, 1975, p. 204). Criminology has become a form of secular theology, a squabble about the population of a theoretical heaven. It is of little moment that people are daily frightened and hurt, that the phenomena of crime are created daily and that policies are formulated and pursued.

The total analysis of social totality has then become a mapping of fantasy. Social totality is an alternative or parallel universe, whose structure is magisterially dictated by the radical criminologist. It is the child of will. Appropriately, the new criminologists recognise none of the entities which fill the world of common sense. Everything becomes changed in a system which acknowledges no authority but the new consciousness. Most significantly, crimes are themselves transformed. They are no longer what criminals, victims, policemen, probation officers, judges, social workers, psychiatrists and Everyman believe. All the activity which manufactures the phenomenal reality of crime is deceptive. The consciousness of these people is spurious, uninformed by critical philosophy and an otherworldly mind. In an essentialising sociology, lay definitions are immaterial. Behaviour becomes intrinsically meaningful because it partakes of the social essence (cf. Walton, 1973). Its significance is not ascribed. Neither are its boundaries to be defined by practical knowledge. Rather, crime becomes what radical criminologists proclaim it to be (Schwendinger and Schwendinger, 1975):

> In accepting the State and legal definition of crime, the scope of [conventional] analysis has been constrained to exclude behaviour which is not legally defined as 'crime' (for example, imperialism, exploitation, racism and sexism) as well as behaviour which is not typically prosecuted (for example, tax evasion, price fixing, consumer fraud, government corruption, police homicides, etc.). (Platt, 1975, p. 96)

In this sense, a noumenal society is awarded its own noumenal crimes. It is to be analysed by a noumenal philosophy and replaced by a noumenal politics, 'real socialism' (Taylor et al, 1973b, p.402), which may be contrasted with all the false socialisms which actually structure the world. That society is populated by noumenal men, the 'fully human', who may be recognised by a 'natural image of man that is self-evident. Radical is God-given . . ., (Quinney, p. 1972b, p. 324). This process of recreating the world is somewhat perversely identified as 'demystification'. There are two ontological realms, one real and the other imaginary. The real is known to the critical thinker, the imaginary is known to everybody else (Pearce, 1973). It would seem that demystification will occur when everybody's realm is usurped by that of the radical criminologist. Society would then be robbed of all the events and processes which make it familiar to its inhabitants. All phenomena would be excised, leaving an invisible order which is either essentially true or *in utero*. The essence of that order is discovered by a vehicle of the imagination, a critical consciousness, which is its own guide and legitimation. It must not be shackled by anything that stems from the unreal domain of common sense. It must not be captive to the actual appearances of things. Instead, it must liberate itself from every possible source of contradiction:

> A critical philosophy is one that is *radically* critical. It is a philosophy that goes to the roots of our lives [sic], to the foundations and the fundamentals, to the essentials of consciousness. In the rooting out of presuppositions we are able to assess every actual and possible experience. The operation is one of demystification, the removal of the myths — the false consciousness created by the official reality. Conventional experience is revealed for what it is — a reification of an oppressive social order . . . The liberating force of radical criticism is the movement from revelation to the development of a new consciousness and an active life in which we transcend the established existence. (Quinney 1975, p. 188)

Conventional experience having been exposed and established existence transcended, what remains to direct the new consciousness? Clearly, there nothing in the visible, audible, tangible or sensed world which can ovide that assistance. The search for objective reality is obliged to turn that most subjective of all mentors, ideology: 'Better are the ideas that me from those who are involved in the struggle of human liberation' uinney, 1972b, p. 321). It is the correct political vision which offers velation of the truth:

The fight for a liberated criminology should not be waged on the basis of making the discipline intellectually respectable, nor to rescue and integrate redeemable strands of liberal theory, nor to earn the respect of our antagonists. Rather, we must develop radical theories of human potentiality which help to explain the dynamics of exploitation and serve to advance the struggles of oppressed classes. (Platt, 1973, p. 599)

This, then, is the most curious paradox of radical criminology. Critical ought offers pontifical definitions of objective reality; it berates its rivals r the subjective and ideological strands of their thought; asserts that ch thought is a subjective deformation of truth; and then justifies its vn definitions of truth by celebrating its own subjective ideological ctitude. Facts are the puppets of power, and the new criminologist tempts to be a master puppeteer. In a mental universe which is regulated by any canon but that furnished by the new consciousness, cology gives objective reality and objective reality gives ideology. The dical criminologists have erected a closed scheme which is organised ound a massive and simplistic tautology.

Further, they have employed that scheme to belabour their competitors. sitivism, symbolic interactionism, the older conflict theory, phenomenology, functionalism and the like are not diligently examined for what they ay offer methodologically, sociologically, ontologically and epistemogically. They are not regarded as possibly competent alternatives to tical criminology. Their pretensions are not seriously discussed. ather, every intellectual contender is neutered and suppressed by placing n a context of ideological significance. Ideas are no longer essentialist or enomenalist, pragmatist or formalist, functionalist or idealist alone. ley are reduced to being 'liberal', 'conservative' or 'radical'. Consider att's remark: 'the dominance of liberalism in criminology is not an cident or fashion but rather reflects fundamental relationships between e state, social institutions and the intellectual community' (Platt, 1975, 99). 'Liberalism' is not taken to be intellectually persuasive. It is merely rt of the currency of power. Consider Quinney's remark: 'The political lure of positivist thought . . . is its acceptance of the *status quo*' uinney, 1975, p. 183). Consider yet another remark by Quinney: 'A critical criminology has an important role in the struggle. Ideas are to put at the service of the community, not to the service of the capita state' (Quinney, 19   , p. 594). It is not those ideas' merit but th political employment which determines their truthfulness. Again, c sider remarks offered by Taylor, Walton and Young:

> Conservative social scientists are engaged, by and large, in the furth and more detailed characterisation of existing social arrangements [Liberal social science] is engaged in . . . at the behest of the powerful alternatively is intended for their consumption after production, i work which also serves either purposively or latently to legitim existing social arrangements . . . (Taylor et al, 1975b, pp 21, 22).

The reiterated theme is that there is an objective reality known radical criminology but unappreciated by others, and the significance others' thought is to be discovered only within the framework of t' reality. As I have argued, this framework is yielded by ideology and analytic *a priori*. There are no persuasive reasons why any criminolog but radical thinkers should accept its authority. Proclamation alone is sufficient. In turn, there is a failure to question how and why that *a pr* framework should be regarded as compelling. It represents the base fr which all argument proceeds. Reality is disputed, but it is held to indisputable. Social totality is not universally accepted, but it is asserted the only proper province for sociology. As a result, the radical crim ologist can understand rivals only when he resorts to a crude sociology knowledge. He does not argue with them. He *discredits* them. He alle that their motives are dishonourable, their vision myopic and their int pretation flimsy. When there is only one true consciousness, any oth sociology becomes false consciousness.

The criticism which rests on impugning integrity can work mu mischief. Platt, for instance, accuses *The New Criminology* of courte He believes that his most important criticism is couched in the followi question:

> What was and is the political practice of theorists like Sutherla Cressey, Lemert, Turk and others in terms of their support of strugg against oppression? This is not simply [a] rhetorical or 'practi [question']. Rather [it goes] to the root of explaining how ruling-cl ideologies are formed and sustained and why it is important undermine the hegemony of liberal theory. (Platt, 1973, p. 598)

The implication is clear: a valid sociology with uncongenial politi ramifications must surrender to an invalid sociology whose ramificatic are pleasing. That is, political consequence and not sociological adequa

...s become sovereign. It would, of course, be useful if the intellectually equate and the politically progressive were one. *A priori*, there is no cessity for them to be so. The unpalatable consequences of ideas must be ken seriously; they should not become the source of automatic rejection. he drift into otherworldliness has been virtually completed by the ceptance of political rather than sociological criteria, and by the refusal enter into considered exchanges with rivals. There is now little left to nd radical criminology to the everyday world of ordinary people and the tellectual world of other sociologists.

Truth so recognised lays a road to totalitarianism. It encourages the rcible rescue of 'fully human' man from the trappings and deceits of the npirical world. It speaks in the name of a noumenal humanity, whatever e actual protestations of people may be. It leads to a stance which urges e forcing of men to be free. None but the sociological élite can know the al condition of man and the real nature of liberation. Such a sociology d a politics are obedient only to the intuition of a group which resists most every intellectual discipline. They can ward off all criticism cause they have become detached from rationality and sublunary alities. But they are also dangerously akin to the Boojum, threatening to vallow their adherents in a whirlpool of uncontrolled idealism. One may nclude with Schiller that 'the verdict of Philosophy must be: "So perish who brave the Snark . . ." ' Perhaps that fate will menace the critical iminologist, and him alone. Others, and the symbolic interactionists in rticular, are wary of Boojums and Snarks. They prefer to undertake ests for more tractable and less perilous beasts.

CONCLUSION

or certain descriptive purposes, the course of criminology may be nderstood to have passed through three stages: the antiquarian, the teractionist and the radical. There is a great gulf between the latter two nases. Radical criminology searches for the roots and essences of social e: it is directed at the discovery of an absolute society which subtends all e mundane appearances of experience. Distrusting all that may be nsed, it eschews every exploratory use of the senses. It places reality in a alm which can only be intuited by a consciousness which is ideologically tuned. By contrast, symbolic interactionism affirms that phenomena are al enough in their practical consequences. They shape the contours and

materials of the social world and nothing else may be as surely mapped.
phenomena are denied, the intellect can run amok, conjuring up a
phantom or Erewhon which it chooses to devise. There is no science
discipline in such a berserk mind. At most, its productions may be judg
artistically as ideas which please or displease the aesthetic sensibilities. N
other canon may be employed. It is as art that radical criminology must
appreciated. It may have political consequences, but it is not adequate
politics or sociology.

Critical criminology has affected the thinking of many students
Britain and Europe. Its attractions are quite apparent. Instead of t
seeming incoherence, disorganisation and modesty of the interaction
sociology of deviance, radical criminology offers a succint, programma
and allegedly exhaustive master scheme. Confusion has been replaced
order, a limited strength by power, and an exhortation to observe by
metaphysics which explains all. In particular, interactionism is chie
promoted by exposure to organised research. It does not lend itself to
entirely satisfactory reproduction in the class room or textbook. I
appreciation stems from a set of grounded ethnographic experience
experiences which are inevitably foreign to most students. But critic
criminology will probably not survive for any great length of time. Bu
around a number of unruly ideas, it cannot maintain either its integrity
its continuity. One major source of difficulty is that which stems from th
conception of a new consciousness. It is a paralysing conception whic
turns the mind inwards towards contemplation and away from research.
is similar to the teachings of the Hegelians at the beginning of th
nineteenth century. Conveying a sense of power, it nevertheless brin
about a withdrawal from the world. The politics of that consciousness ar
by extension, akin to those which Marx mocked in *The German Ideolog*
The activity promised by critical criminology will become a form
quiescence for some. It is clear that the disdain for research is n
universally accepted by all radical thinkers. Jock Young, for instanc
would seem to have embarked on a return to a version of empiricism. In h
recent work and in 'Working-class Criminology' (1975) in particular,
novel scepticism has appeared. The formulaic logic of *The Ne
Criminology* has been replaced by a respect for the imponderable qualiti
of the phenomenal world. A few radical criminologists may then aband
the grander claims of critical philosophy.

Another difficulty flows from the focus on essences and totalitie
When phenomena are discredited as unreal, the organising centre of
discipline will itself become weakened. Attempts have been made

state a class of ideal forms, noumenal crimes, but criminology is defined by its exploration of a substantive field. It cannot remain coherent unless it adheres to that definition. The invocation of a real order makes that adherence precarious. Crime itself threatens to become part of the epiphenomenal realm, a ghost of the surface rather than a creature of the essence. As the political economy of the underlying structure continues to be advanced, so crime is likely to become more and more marginal as an intellectual object. Its significance will pall besides the massive transformations of a class society. Platt and the Schwendingers have tried to make crime an integral feature of those transformations, but total analysis of social totality will lead to more salient problems. Paul Walton, for example, has increasingly moved towards a discussion of the pivotal questions of Marxist theory. Crime itself has been left behind, emperilling the future of a radical criminology.

In addition, there are substantial problems accompanying the realisation of a radical criminological argument. The claims for totality are urgent at the level of criticism or manifesto, but they become obstructive when there is any attempt to undertake focused or substantive analysis. It is evident that no argument can sustain the global commitment to totality unless it remains part of a general abstract thesis. There has been an accompanying tendency practically to disregard the radical programme whenever work descends to earth. Walton's diligent exploration of the social production of news, Ian Taylor's intriguing work on the intellectual foundations of the welfare state, and Young's history of abortion law all chronicle the tension between the claims and performance of radical criminology. On one plane, the analysis is largely competent and interesting. On another, it is subversive to radical conceptions of an all-encompassing vision. It is probable that that vision will recede, principally because of its sheer unattainability.

More minutely, there are stresses and instabilities in the social organisation of radical criminology as an enterprise. The coalition of Marxists, anarchists, populists, conflict theorists and libertarians is prone to some internal dissention. The emergence of that coalition was made possible by a common group of adversaries, the liberal criminologists. Its future hinges on the resolution of internal contradictions. Anarchism and Marxism are not entirely complementary. Neither are libertarianism and structuralism. It is conceivable that radical criminology will shatter into a host of subordinate criminologies, each veering towards a parent world view. But the new criminology does not only associate itself with writers and thinkers. It depends upon an advocacy of praxis, joining with groups

who represent, or claim to represent, prisoners, mental patients, welfar
claimants and the like (Taylor, 1973b). Organisations which champio
the dispossessed and the incarcerated are somewhat volatile. Their fate i
often determined by the work of a few men, and those men tend to b
changeable. Lacking a firm bureaucratic base, substantial finance and
powerful membership, these groups are also threatened by the politics c
disrepute. There are taxing problems of legitimacy and political conse
quentiality (cf. Mathieson, 1974). Confronting established and powerfu
agencies, they are strategically and tactically weak. In the main, th
principal parties of the Left are unreceptive to their vision. As a result, th
politics of the marginal are marginal politics, drifting into inaction c
expressive displays.

Radical criminology may leave a legacy which will be useful. It ha
restored a concern with the traditional problems of orthodox society
completing the courtship which was initiated by the symbolic inter
actionists. Those who address police work may then begin to lean on
Weberian analysis of bureaucracy or a Simmelian description of the dya
and the triad. The politics of deviance may be renewed by Marxist ideas o
ideas flowing from Mosca and Michels. The gulf between criminology a
an antiquarian repository and sociology as an innovative stimulus woul
accordingly be bridged. But the bridge would not be a Jacob's Ladder. I
would unite disciplines which have little commerce with essences, dee
truths and total analysis.

NOTES

1. I am indebted to Stan Cohen for helpful comments on an earlier draft of this paper.
2. Edwin Sutherland and his colleagues at the University of Indiana *were* exception
    But there have not been many such exceptions.
3. Of course, high sociologists tend to be beset by uncertainty as well, but it is a
    uncertainty typically born of despair. There is a peculiar pathos which attends th
    rise and fall of grand sociological systems; cf. Hawthorne (1976).
4. The very marginality of interactionists opened up significant intellectual an
    methodological opportunities. But it has also been exploited by critics to emphasis
    the discreditable qualities of their work. A false syllogism has been propounded b
    such men as Alvin Gouldner: it argues that the socially marginal must be someho
    intellectually marginal, as a kind of hippy excrescence. Such criticism is not only *a
    hominem,* it also belittles the analytic consequence of work by alluding to th
    'inconsequentiality' of its object. As many sociologists have demonstrated, there i
    no necessary affinity between social importance and intellectual importance
    Neither is there always an affinity between the grandeur of a problem and th
    gravity of its explanation.

Misunderstanding
Labelling Perspectives

Ken Plummer

The past decade has seen striking changes in the prominence given to sociological theories of deviance. Most notable is the changing status that has been accorded to labelling theory. Whilst far from new, in the early sixties it was seen as a 'radical, underground' theory, attracting the 'young Turks' of sociology who used it as a basis for developing critiques of the dominant paradigms in deviancy analysis. By the late sixties (in America at any rate),[2] the theory had been co-opted into the mainstream of sociological work — enshrined in formal statements, texts, readers and Ph.D. theses, taught widely on undergraduate sociology and criminology programmes, and absorbed into much 'positivistic' social research (cf. Cole, 1975; Spector, 1976). This acceptance of the theory has been followed most recently by the growth of criticism of it from a number of contrasting perspectives, most notably ideologues who are critical of its biases, limitations and liberal assumptions (e.g. Manders, 1975), and 'positivistic' researchers who find it empirically falsified (e.g. Gove, 1975). In just ten years, labelling theory has moved from being the radical critic of established orthodoxies to being the harbinger of new orthodoxies to be criticised. Yet as one recent defender so forcefully put it:

> The sheer volume of the critics could easily lead one to presume that labelling theory is dead and already buried. But when the criticisms are considered one at a time labelling theory emerges as a still lively and viable theory. Indeed, to the extent that the criticisms call for clarification and specification of the theory it may be fairly claimed that labelling theory is strengthened by going through the process of challenge and response. The volume of criticisms may be seen as a tribute to the power of the theory. (Conover, 1976, p. 229)

In this article, I wish to consider some of these criticisms that have engulfed labelling theory in recent years and to show that they have far

85

from succeeded in dealing the death blow to it. I will begin by considering precisely what labelling theory is, and will argue that it is most usefully conceived as a perspective *whose core problems are the nature, emergence, application and consequences of labels.* I will suggest that there can be many differing theoretical approaches within this perspective, and will go on to argue that the failure to be precise about the kind of theory one is using has led to many confusions. Symbolic interactionism is only one such theory, and hence criticisms of such a theory should not be seen as synonomous with criticisms of labelling theory. My own preference, however, is for an interactionist theory of labelling; my subsequent comments will therefore be erecting a dual defence.

The main body of the discussion will then centre on three clusters of criticism: the charge of *confusion* especially over definitional and value problems); the charge of *bias and limitations*; and the charge that the theory has been shown to be *empirically falsified.* My goal throughout is to clarify the foundations of the labelling perspective so that it may continue to grow as a most fruitful approach to the study of deviance.

WHAT IS 'LABELLING' — A PERSPECTIVE, A THEORY OR A PROPOSITION?

Because the labelling perspective is seen alternately and simultaneously as a perspective, a theory and a proposition, it becomes an easy target for attack and a ready refuge for defence: it is all things to all men. In looking at this muddle, I will identify those sociologists most commonly viewed as labelling theorists, locate their views on the nature of the theory, consider why confusions arise and propose some standardisation of terms.

First, who are the labelling theorists?[3] In a review of twenty standard books and articles at hand, I found four groups of theorists referred to as labelling theorists:

   (a) Becker and Lemert — mentioned by nearly everyone;
   (b) Tannenbaum, Kitsuse and Erickson — mentioned by well over half;
   (c) Goffman, Schur, Garfinkel and Scheff — given between six and eight references each;
   (d) a diverse sprinkling of names referred to only once or twice — Matza, Waller, Platt, Lofland, Lorber, Simmons, Sudnow, Piliavin and Briar, Cicourel and Quinney.

Now if one takes this list as representative, it is clear that 'labelling' can only be a perspective; there is no unanimous proposition that these writers are testing (cf. Erickson (1966) on issues of boundary maintenance; Becker (1963) on moral enterprise and deviant careers; Schur (1963) on victimless crimes; Platt (1969) on the historical origins of delinquency categories; Wilkins (1964) on deviancy amplification; Matza (1969) on techniques of neutralisation and signification; Piliavin and Briar (1964) on the screening process), and there is considerable theoretical diversity — functionalism (Erickson), dramaturgy (Goffman), phenomenology and the sociology of law (Quinney), systems theory (Wilkins and Scheff), naturalism (Matza), interactionism (Becker) and ethnomethodology (Kituse and Garfinkel).[4] The same conclusion is reached by looking at both the main exponents of labelling theory, Lemert and Becker. Neither restricts his analysis to a major proposition, and while one is a symbolic interactionist, the other is only reservedly so (Lemert, 1967, p. v; 1974). On this score, then, 'labelling' is a perspective, which raises a series of problems and suggests a few themes.

Further, none of the theorists above actually began by identifying himself as a labelling theorist: rather ironically, they had that label thrust upon them by others and only later came to incorporate it into their own sociological identities (cf. Kitsuse, 1972; Goode, 1975). Thus neither Becker nor Lemert seems at all happy with being identified as a labelling theorist; neither used this tag in his earlier work. Indeed, by the early 1970s Becker was publicly stating his preference for being known as an interactionist rather than a labelling theorist (Becker, 1974, p. 44), while Lemert was disassociating himself from the 'conceptual extrusions' and 'crudities' of labelling theory (Lemert, 1972, p. 6). Goode's review of the field also concludes that Becker and Lemert (as well as Erickson and Kitsuse) 'cannot be called labelling theorists' (Goode, 1975, p. 571). It is important to stress both this lack of self-recognition by labelling theorists and their diverse theoretical concerns: *for the labelling perspective has only emerged from the retrospective selection of a few select themes largely from diverse theoretical projects.* They are united by some common substantive problems but not common theories. There are often much wider discrepancies than overlaps. Erickson's brand of functionalism can hardly be equated with Cicourel's ethnomethodology, while Lemert's focus on putative deviation (which implies a non-putative or objective deviance) jars markedly with Kitsuse's relativistic 'imputed deviance' (which denies an objective reality of deviance) (cf. Rains, 1976).

What are these common substantive problems? Becker suggests the following: 'We [should] direct our attention in research and theory building to the questions: who applied the label of deviant to whom? What consequences does the application of a label have for the person so labelled? Under what circumstances is the label of a deviant successfully applied?' (Becker, 1964, p. 3).

While these questions have certainly received much attention from labelling theorists in recent years, they are unnecessarily narrow (and in practice Becker dealt with a wider range of problems). Since the theme of the tradition is 'labels' we should seek to discover all that we can about this phenomenon and not just a limited portion. Basically, therefore, labelling theory should centre on asking:

1. What are the *characteristics* of labels, their variations and forms?
2. What are the *sources* of labels, both societally and personally.
3. How, and under what *conditions,* do labels get applied?
4. What are the *consequences* of labelling.

All would seem clear: the labelling perspective constitutes neither theory nor proposition, but is a useful series of problems designed to reorientate the former mainstream study to the consideration of the *nature, emergence, application,* and *consequences* of deviancy labels. Yet it remains unclear because of (i) the confusions of labelling proponents themselves, and (ii) the narrow orientation fo their critics.

Labelling proponents have added to the confusion by either rejecting the tag of labelling theorist or by seeking to co-opt it into one narrow kind of theoretical stance. Since their first allegiance was never to a reified, academic 'labellilng theory', but to 'social control processes', 'interactionism', etc., they have not seen fit to defend it. Thus Lemert equates labelling theory with interactionism, and sees his own intellectual task as altogether more eclectic (Lemert, 1972, p. 6; Lemert, 1974); while Becker equates the general orientation with interactionism, and then opts to call it 'an interactionist theory of deviance' (Becker, 1974, p. 44). So for these writers labelling theory is not an orientation; rather, it is synonymous with interactionism. But if this is so, we cannot include Lemert, Erickson, Garfinkel, Scheff, Matza or Cicourel so clearly under that banner anymore. Schur, who also views it as an orientation embracing different theories (phenomenology, conflict, functionalism, and prediction theory), seems to assume an interactionist base.[5] But if it is an orientating series of problems, it does not have to entail a commitment to one theory. The problems of labelling may be dealt with by Marxists, ethnomethodologists, functionalists or positivists, there is no endemic link to interactionism, and it is interactionist imperialism to suggest otherwise.

More muddling than labelling theorists themselves are critics of the theory. While most vaguely acknowledge labelling to be a conception, the attacks are actually levied either at its interactionist base (e.g., Taylor, Walton and Young, 1973a; Gouldner, 1968; Warren and Johnson, 1972) or at a narrow proposition attributed to it (e.g., Mankoff, 1971; Davis, 1972). Of the four problems I have mentioned above, critics usually focus primarily upon only *one* possible answer to the third and fourth questions — the independent and dependent variable issue (cf. Gove, 1975). They suggest that labelling theory may be characterised by the following proposition 'that societal reaction in the form of labelling or official typing, and consequent stigmatisation, leads to an altered identity in the actor, necessitating a reconstitution of the self' (Davis, 1972, p. 460); Or: 'Rule breakers become entrenched in deviant roles because they are labelled deviant by others and are consequently excluded from resuming normal roles in the community' (Mankoff, 1971. p. 204); or, most crudely: 'People go about minding their own business, and then 'wham', bad society comes along and slaps them with a stigmatising label. Forced into the role of deviant, the individual has little choice but to *be* deviant' (Akers, 1973, p. 24).

Through these propositions, labelling theory is vulgarised into a narrow theory which can be readily refuted. It can be easily shown that many people become 'deviants' without being directly labelled by others (cf. Mankoff, 1971; Becker, 1963, ch. 3), or are labelled because of their behaviour and not merely because of the contingencies that surround them (cf. Williams and Weinberg, 1971). Yet any criticism based upon this limited view is grossly unfair, because it tends to suggest that labelling theory is concerned with labelling that is overt, public, direct and unrelated to the act: and this is simply not the case. It is true that a few studies have *implied* this kind of limited argument (e.g., Scheff, 1966), and that some illustrations have been unfortunate (e.g., Malinowski,1926) in Becker, 1963, but in general labelling theorists do recognise a multiplicity of answers to the problems of the conditions and consequences of labelling. Thus, for example, even the classic writings are not guilty of all that has been attributed to them. Becker's own statement of 'marijuana use and social control' does not deal with matters of formal control, as labelling critics would have us believe. As Paul Rock astutely notes:[6]

> Becker's becoming a marijuana user dealt entirely with its significance to the self. It had no reference to official control, but concentrated instead on the way in which significance was built up introspectively. I have always found that critics have neglected this basic article, and persistently misread the significance of the self-identifying activity.

In addition to these classic statements, there is now much writing on the issue of self-labelling and deviance avowal (cf. Turner, 1972; Rock, 1973a; Rotenberg, 1974; Levitin, 1975); of neutralising deviance labels (e.g., Ball, 1966; Reiss, 1962; Rains, 1971; Warren, 1974b); of changing deviance labels (e.g., Lofland, 1969; Trice and Roman, 1970); and of labelling as a means of preventing as opposed to accelerating deviance (e.g., Cameron, 1964; Thorsell and Klemke, 1972; Tittle, 1975). Recently Rogers and Buffalo have furthered this kind of work by delineating nine possible adaptations of deviance to deviant labels — thereby reinforcing the view that people don't *have* to become deviant because of labelling, and furthering the sophistication of the labelling paradigm (Rogers and Buffalo, 1974).

THE LABELLING PERSPECTIVE AND
THE SEARCH FOR THEORETICAL PURITY

Labelling, then, should not be equated with a theory or a proposition but should be seen as a perspective in deviancy research. And because of this it can harbour several diverse theoretical positions. There is thus a great potential for the perspective to contain theoretical contradictions, and to be eligible for criticisms from all theoretical sides. Incompatible theories may get welded together. They may also be pitted against each other. Thus, as an illustration of the first point, interactional sociologists may use a drift-voluntaristic model to explain primary deviance, whilst succumbing occasionally to a deterministic, over-socialised conception of the actor in looking at secondary deviance (Broadbent: 1974); as illustration of the second, phenomenological sociologists can find much in labelling which violates the canons of their theoretical work. Seeking to take seriously the examination of 'meanings of morality and immorality as acted out in every day life' (Warren and Johnson, 1972, p. 70),[7] they argue that labellists have been too behaviourist and not taken these meanings seriously enough. Yet for critical criminologists it is precisely these concerns which are viewed disapprovingly. Thus, Taylor, Walton and Young wish to move away from the relativistic idealism of labelling into analyses which pay proper attention to 'structured inequality in power and interest which underpin the processes whereby the laws are created and enforced' (Taylor et al, 1973, p. 68). They wish to move away from a microscopic concern with those who are labelled and those who apply labels to build a fully social (and grand) theory of crime. They eschew microscopic ethnography in favour of global assertion (cf. Manders,

1975). Now, which is it to be? Is the labelling perspective voluntaristic or deterministic, behavioural or idealistic? Since it harbours within it diverse theories, it can, of course, be both. Putting the problem more generally, the labelling perspective generates some of the oldest dilemmas in sociological theory: how to weld analyses of the structural with those of the situational; how to reconcile phenomenonalism with essentialism, absolutism with relativism, idealism with materialism, formalism with *Verstehen*; and how to abstract and generalise without reification. Imbedded in the labelling perspective are the unresolved tensions of generations of social theorists. How they may be resolved, or at least how working resolutions may be obtained between them, remains a major issue for those working in the labelling perspective.

Illustrative of one kind of resolution is that provided by Rock, but it is a resolution which only a phenomenalism or interactionism-inclined sociologist could favour. Taking the intellectual claims of phenomenalism seriously, and seeing phenomenalism as a major motif of the new deviancy perspectives, he charts some of the tensions that I have located above. That is, he notes a tension between the *essentialism* found in the formalism of interactional sociologists, the deep rules of ethnomethodologists and the structural theories of Marxists, and the *phenomenalism* found in theories of *Verstehen* and the contextual analysis of interactional sociologists. The reconciliation of notions of structure with those of meaning is proposed through a focus on the actor's definition of structure:

> I shall argue that a systematic description of commonsense ideas of social structure affords the sociologist of deviance access to areas which have previously been denied him. This description will offer him the materials upon which a phenomenological analysis of social structure can be built. For instance, he will be able to explore the import of such phenomena as social class without committing himself to the belief that social class is an autonomous or 'real' entity. (Rock, 1973b, p. 19)

Such a solution hardly resolves the basic dilemma of whether there is a 'real world' out there, and it keeps Rock tottering on the brink of solipsism. Nevertheless, from his point of view it is a consistent way in which to cope with problems of structure and could give rise to one version of labelling theory fully grounded on phenomenalism. Alternative versions of labelling could also be constructed by those who seek a more essentialist and/or structural account, in which, presumably, some absolutist notion of deviancy will ultimately have to be imported. Since the labelling perspective contains a variety of theories, these need to be rendered explicit and consistent.

Symbolic interactionism and labelling theory: an aside

Although it is only one of several possible theories that could be applied to problems of labelling, symbolic interactionism has the closest affinity with labelling theory. Its central problem — the construction of meaning — is clearly closely allied to problems of labels. Indeed, many of the criticisms that are levied at labelling theory are in fact directed towards symbolic interactionism. Since Paul Rock has defended the symbolic interactionists' account of deviance at length elsewhere in this volume, it would serve no useful purpose to produce an extended discussion of the symbolic inter-actionists' enterprise here. I would, however, like to digress from my main arguments and make a few suggestions of my own.

The interactionist's distinctive view of the social world — a view which is quite unlike that of any other sociology or psychology — can be seen as a fusion of several intellectual (sometimes anti-intellectual) traditions, such as pragmatism, formalism, romanticism, mild libertarianism and humanism.[8] Taken collectively, such traditions focus upon the never-ending flow of emerging experience. The human being is both subject and object. The importance is stressed of the localised setting and context, the uncertainty of knowledge and the ambiguity and fragility of meaning — as well as the inexorable tension between the shapeless stream of human life and the shaping structures of the wider society. The intellectual traditions which have given rise to interactionism are important to understand as, without such comprehension, interactionism can easily be seen as a lightweight, passing, theoretical fad of the affluent sixties rather than as a well-established position flowing from strong philosophical arguments. Many of the criticisms made of interactionism in fact rest upon a misunderstanding of the interactionist problematic and a shallow comprehension of its philosophical background. They assume that because interactionism looks at certain theoretical problems while ignoring others, studies certain topics at the expense of others, and uses certain methodologies rather than others, it could only be doing this through ignorance and not reason. There are many criticisms of interactionism derived from postures which are radically different but from which it is assumed that the critics' position is unquestionably superior. Given adequate knowledge, we would all be structuralists or behaviourists, we would all study politics and the class structure and we would all use historical or quantitative methods. The intellectual enterprise is thus rendered closed and monolithic.

Yet the philosophical foundations of interactionism portray a world which is markedly at odds with the absolutism of structuralists, Marxists, positivistic criminologists and the like. Viewed collectively, pragmatism, formalism, romanticism, libertarianism and humanism have played an important formative role in the shaping of a distinctive interactive vision of the social world. Highlighting the endless flux of human experience, welded and shaped thorugh the transforming power of synthetic *a priori* categorisation, and focusing upon the dereified phenomenal world where knowledge is always limited and uncertain, the interactionists have come to portray an image that is at odds with most other academic theories. It is not, thus, a vision that many academics or sociologists can be content with, since it brings in its wake a strong anti-intellectual commitment, totters frequently on the brink of self-defeating arguments and seems to revel in a multitude of irresolvable paradoxes.

The anti-intellectualism is a product of the commitment that reality is inexhaustible, that the noumena can never be grasped and that the only firm flowing truth is that which emerges in the local situated experience: abstract, analytic reasoning and global theorising that attempts to grasp absolute transcendental truths, or vast classificatory edifices that are not firmly anchored in experienced life have no room in the interactionist scheme of things. Yet such a position — while cumulatively sponsored and often well argued — leads to a number of tottering paradoxes. It is difficult to conduct intellectual work on a foundation which denies its very possibility.

Thus interactionists might want to defend their position with abstract philosophical reasoning, but the very possibility of this is denied them by their pragmatist heritage. They may wish to produce systematic codified statements of their theory, but the very possibility of this is denied them by their phenomenalist heritage. They may wish to generalise, even produce universal statements, but the value of this is questioned by the romantic base of their position. They may wish to be messianic, absolute, imperial propagandists of an élite interactionist expertise, but their libertarianism forces them to a piecemeal eclecticism. They may wish to be objective external observers of the world, but their humanistic bent constantly hurls them towards the subject and the possibility of solipsism. The paradoxes of the interactionist heritage are great indeed. Interactionists have to live with contradiction and ambiguity, knowing that any argument they make could be self-defeating.

It is not surprising, given this, that interactionism has generally been seen as a marginal theory within sociology and that interactionists have often been 'marginal men'. For much of its history it has been submerged in an oral tradition, lacking the formalisation and proselytisation that accompanies most other theories. Only recently have texts and readers been spawned, but these have emerged alongside the tradition of pheno-menology which seems almost instantly to have superseded it. The Mullinses, in their admittedly curious study, 'Theory Groups in American Sociology', could actually say by 1973 that 'it is clear that the original ideas that developed within symbolic interactionism have run their course intellectually and socially. As a change maker and general orientation for sociology and as the loyal opposition to structural functionalism however it has come to an end' (Mullins and Mullins, 1973, p. 96).

Grounded in ambiguity and contradiction, floundering in irony and paradox, lacking a strong formal training ground, built by 'marginal men' and now given the death wish, it is amazing that interactionism has managed to survive at all. But it has, and I personally hope that it will continue to do so even in the face of criticisms from all sides and from within. Its view of the world may be quirky and its contradictions may be intellectually unsatisfying; it may find few sympathisers willing to stay with it for long — it is a phase one may pass through on the way to loftier enterprises. But — even in the face of all that — the interactionist does continue to provide an alternative vision of the world. It is a necessary and radical, though modest, counterbalance to most traditions of thought. Its final irony is that whilst it is consistently rejected as a valid approach to the world in academic writing, it is consistently acknowledged, most of the time, in our daily lives. The problematic meaning, ambiguity and flux which is the focal concern of interactionist thought is also the focal concern of many lives. It gels with empirical reality. Thus while inter-actionism may never be a dominant sociology, it has much to offer as a subversive tradition of thought within mainstream sociology (cf., Rock, forthcoming).

TWO GENERAL PROBLEMS IN LABELLING AND DEVIANCE THEORY

Before looking at some of the major limitations and biases which critics have levied at the labelling perspective, it would be useful to examine two objections which are not so much criticisms of labelling theory *per se* but problems to be found throughout the whole of the sociology of deviance. The two matters I refer to are, first, the problematic nature of defining deviance and, second, the problem of values. I will deal with each in turn.

The problem of definition

One major set of muddles occurs over the problem of defining deviance. The main source of these muddles is Becker's own classic statement (1963) where he starts his discussion of outsiders by first dispensing critically with definitions of deviance that evoke statistical, pathological or dysfunctional criteria before going on to suggest his own: 'Deviance is not a quality of the act a person commits, but rather a consequence of the application by others of rules and sanctions to an offender' (Becker, 1963, p. 9). That he does not see deviance as *solely* the manufactured product of societal responses is demonstrated a few pages later, when he introduces his equally famous typology of deviance, using the additional yardstick of rule violation. Thus, combining rule violation with society responses, the following typology is produced (ex Becker, 1963, p. 20):

	Obedient behaviour	Rule-breaking behaviour
Perceived as deviant	Falsely accused	Pure deviant
Not perceived as deviant	Conforming	Secret deviant

Now, locked within Becker's definition and typology are muddles indeed, some of which Becker himself addressed in a recent paper (Becker, 1974). What are the muddles, and how may they be resolved?

First, and most simple, it is argued that Becker has not provided a definition of deviance at all. As Sagarin noted:

Becker's statement is not a definition and should not be confused with one. It merely delineates the self-other process by which the placing of a person, or a group of persons, in the category of deviant is made, but it fails to note the characteristics that deviants have in common, and those which are utilised by oneself and others to give persons that label. (Sagarin, 1967, p. 9).[9]

Thus it is possible to say the same things as Becker about almost any other form of behaviour: conformity is behaviour that people so label, silliness is behaviour that people so label, and beauty is a state that people so label. Without specifying the criteria by which such labels can be recognised, the statement of Becker's remains a vacuous tautology.

This criticism is not so valid of other labelling theorists. For example, Lemert utilises a conception of deviance which straddles the statistical and the norm violation (Lemert, 1951, p. 27). Further, some work has devoted attention to the problem of the contents of deviant labels, the criteria used being such as (a) essentialist themes and (b) stigmatising or devalued meanings (Scott, 1970).

A second line of criticism suggests that labelling theory is 'relativistic in the extreme' (Gibbs, 1966, p. 10). Since nothing is intrinsically deviant, anything could be called deviant and nothing has to be. By this argument, child molesters, strippers, dwarfs or 'flat earthers' may be called normal if one so chooses, and routine marriage, hard work and average intelligence may be called deviant. Nothing is deviant but naming makes it so.

Now there are several real advantages of such an approach. It highlights the ambiguity of a world no longer divided into a series of neat types, the black and the white, the good and the bad, the normal and the mad: the continuity between normality and deviancy is stressed. It opens up the field of inquiry so that it is possible to discuss a range of areas hitherto neglected — blindness (Scott, 1969), subnormality (Mercer, 1973), fatness (Maddox, Back and Liedermann, 1968), and interpersonal relationships (Denzin, 1970) — thereby enabling both the foundations for a formal theory of deviance as a social property and a method for understanding the routine and the regular through the eyes of the ruptured and the irregular. And it provides the potential for a constant challenge to hitherto taken-for-granted categories and an impetus for a radical definition of those categories supported by master institution of power.

Yet this enlarging of the field has not been without difficulties. Most notably, it flies in the face of empirical reality, where we commonsensically know that some acts are more deviant than others. Deviance as a social category, and as opposed to a sociological category, is simply not as variable as the labelling theorists often seem to imply. As Taylor, Walton and Young say:

> Our objection to one assumption of the societal reaction position is this: we do not act in a world free of social meaning. With the exception of entirely new behaviour, it is clear to most people which actions are deviant and which are not deviant . . . We would assert that *most deviant behaviour is a quality of the act,* since the way we distinguish between *behaviour* and *action* is that behaviour is merely physical and action has meaning that is socially given. (Taylor et al, 1975a, p. 147)

What these writers assert is that behaviour is embedded in wider social contexts composed of systems of meaning which are pre-given: they cannot be neatly wished away. These contexts of meanings provide the resources out of which members fashion their interpretations of given behaviour, and are far from being capable of instant transformation. Thus, for example, in this culture 'everybody knows' that murder is illegal, that homosexuality is at least different and that blindness is a handicap. Our routine contexts simply do not permit us to say that murder, homosexuality or blindness are 'normal', and to argue such a case is to commit sociological mystification.

A second problem arising from the labelling theoreticians' relativism argues that their relativism notwithstanding, their work is directed at fields which are in fact commonly recognised as deviant: despite all disclaimers, it remains true that sociologists of deviance study strippers, drug users and criminals and not more mundane activities (Liazios, 1972). Their relativism is dishonest, since their work is informed by absolute categories commonly sensed as deviant. And closely allied to the above, the point is made that their work often serves to reinforce the apartness and 'deviantness' of certain groups (cf. Lofland, 1969). By studying the mentally ill as deviant, the sociologist tacitly concurs with public definitions of deviance. Further, when such categorisation is also combined with the sociologist's insistence on ambiguity or relativism, he may not only *reinforce* existing categories of deviance but also *create* new ones. Any work the sociologist of deviance performs is likely either to reinforce labels of deviance or to create new ones.

A third (now standard) definition muddle arises from Becker's typology cited earlier, in which there arise logically contradictory cells. More specifically, given Becker's relativistic, definitional approach to deviance, it is hard to see how two categories on his typology can exist. For if deviance is a matter of identifying and labelling, then clearly there can be no 'secret deviance' or 'falsely accused'. It is not possible to have people called 'deviant' who are not so identified, and it is not possible to have people called 'non-deviant' who are not so identified. There can only, therefore, be deviants and non-deviants.

Now all three of the criticisms outlined above pose problems (cf. Kitsuse, 1972; Becker, 1974; Gibbs, 1972; Pollner, 1974). Basically, the problems stem from a need to reconcile the irreconcilable: how to blend an absolutist conception of deviance with a relativist one. There are a number of ways in which such a tension might be partially resolved, depending upon one's theoretical posture. The solution that I feel most easy with is to define deviance as a conceptual field within sociology (not the social world) that is marked out by two criteria: that of rule violation and that of the imputation (by self or others) of stigma and devaluation. The issue of rule violation leads to the problems of which rules and whose rules —

which in turn leads to the analytic distinction between *societal* and *situational* deviance. By *societal deviance* I refer in a shorthand way to those categories that are either (a) commonly sensed by most of society's members to *be* deviant, or (b) lodged in some abstract meanings,[10] such as the law or reified norms, and not to be wished away by individual members. Such deviance implies a high degree of consensus over the *identification* of the deviance, even if there is subsequently much dissention about the *appropriateness* of such a label. Thus it would be hard for anyone to say that being blind, committing armed robbery or being a transvestite were publicly acknowledged as 'normal events', even though it is clear that many people may view their designation as deviant to be utterly inappropriate. By *situational deviance* I am referring not to abstract meaning systems (perceived or real), but rather to the actual manner in which members of society go about the task of creating rules and interpreting rule violations as 'deviance' (although, of course, they would hardly use such a word) in *context*. Clearly, much of this rule making and deviancy interpretation will be contingent upon the abstract societal system I have located above. But the point remains that in situations members are freer to (i) neutralise or reject the societal version of deviance and (ii) construct rules and definitions at odds with those commonly sensed to belong to 'society'. While, in one sense, societal deviance steers towards absolute categories of deviance, situational deviance steers towards a more relativistic stance. Two examples may help clarify some of these distinctions.

First, take the situation of routine, informal interaction on a production line (or any other conventional situation, such as routine marital interaction, peer interaction, or interaction in a club setting, etc.) (cf. Roy, 1954; Bryant, 1974, pt. 1). Such routinisation becomes possible through the co-ordination of conduct and the development of a network of tacit rules. Now, neither in society's minds nor in any dominant abstract system of values in society could such routine work be identified publicly as deviant. Routine work is not societal deviance. Yet it should also be clear that through the co-ordinated rule system, violation of such rules — or perception of violation — becomes a possibility. When such violation occurs — or is perceived as occurring — situational deviance emerges.

A second example can be drawn from the homosexual subculture (cf. Warren, 1974a). In this culture homosexuality must be viewed as societal deviance. All members of society must acknowledge (even if they strongly disagree) that homosexuality is commonly regarded as deviant; alternatively, it is hard to posit an objectified, abstract set of values in this society according to which homosexuality is not viewed as in some sense a marginal (sinful, sick, sad) state. Yet to acknowledge that homosexuality is societal deviance is not to acknowledge that it is situational deviance. Thus in situated contexts members of society or homosexuals themselves may create rules which normalise homosexuality. Homosexuality is no longer viewed as deviant. However, focusing, for example, on the rule systems of the homosexual subculture, the violation (or perceived violation) of this system becomes a possibility. Homosexuals themselves may create a category of deviance within their own ranks. For instance, homosexuals may come to view the 'too camp and swish' role, the 'too straight' role, or the 'too promiscuous' role of other homosexuals as deviant. Here we have compounded complexity: societal deviance becomes 'normal' situation becomes situational deviance.

The problem of values

A major issue with any sociology of deviance must be its explicit awareness of the problem of values and, concomitantly, its own value bias. At least superficially, the labelling perspective fares well here. Most of the writings of labelling theorists seem to lack the moral disapproval of sociologists of earlier decades, and many of their writings devote space to the value debate (e.g., Becker, 1963, 1964, 1967, 1974). However, while it may be unfair to accuse the labellists of lacking awareness of value problems, this by no means precludes criticism of their particular resolutions to the problems. Two issues may be raised here: the issue of bias and the issue of solipsism.

From all sides, Becker et al are accused of bias. To the Right, labelling theory is seen as deeply subversive of the *status quo* — challenging orthodox absolutist definitions of deviance and taking seriously the viewpoint of the deviant. It is biased in favour of the deviant. To the Left, labelling theory is seen as strongly supportive of the *status quo* — smuggling in taken-for-granted categories of deviance, focusing attention on lower-level functionaries while neglecting the oppressive power élites behind the dominant master institutions, and masking all these activities under a gentle radical guise. It is biased in favour of the oppressors, and provides a good example of the way in which the oppressive system of democratic capitalism is able to absorb potential academic threats. Now, these opposing criticisms may either simply be taken to represent the particular value positions of their proponents, or they may be taken as academic arguments about the nature of bias in scientific work.

In the former the critic has started out from a series of moral and political assumptions which the labelling theorist is shown not to support. Debates about these assumptions can ultimately only be conducted in the area of politics or philosophy, and while they must inform sociology, they are not coterminous with it.

The second issue is more germane to sociological (as opposed to purely political or moral) work. The issue here centres largely on what constitutes bias. Becker (1971) distinguishes two forms: (a) work is biased when it presents statements of fact that are demonstrably incorrect; (b) work is biased when its results favour or appear to favour one side or another in a controversy. Becker suggests that 'we cannot avoid being subjected to the charge of bias in the second sense', but that the former 'isn't in principle an unattainable goal and is worth striving for' (Becker, 1971, p. 13). Thus, taking Goffman's account of becoming a mental patient as an illustration, this work may be accused of bias because it gets the picture of what it is like to be a mentally ill person wrong, or because it tacitly sympathises with the patient, criticises the custodians and ignores the wider power structure. If the former is true, then the work is misleading and possibly dangerous — and should be rejected. But the latter could be true — until the unlikely day arrives when the sociologist is able to grasp the totality of 'all sides' in the situation at once (cf. Becker, 1967, p. 247). Those who make the charge of bias do so primarily in this second sense, which once again allows the sociologist to make clear on which side he perceives the bias to be generated.

Thus, assuming good 'objective' work is to be done, the problem becomes that of distinguishing how the work of labellists may be biased towards certain groups. In general, they do have an underdog bias: they do try to get the record straight on behalf of those groups who are conventionally perceived as troublesome, and hence challenge mainstream studies which view deviance through the eyes of the establishment and the correctionalist. Yet at the same time this 'unconventional sentimentality' is very often congruent with establishment definitions, because the very categories studied by the labellist remain those which are designated deviant by official groups. The labellist studies homosexuals not heterosexuals, criminals not law-abiders and prostitutes not heterosexual couples. In doing this the labellist tacitly confirms the establishment portrait of deviants. And in focusing — frequently — on the more exotic aspects of these deviant life styles, he also tends to emphasise the differentness of these groups. The bias of the labelling theorist to date, then, has been double-barrelled: supporting the deviant but not challenging the *status quo* (cf. Liazios, 1972; Warren and Johnson, 1972; Mankoff, 1971; Thio, 1973).[11]

Now this charge of bias — of seeming to 'take sides' — can often lead to a much more serious epistemological problem: that of solipsism. For in the work of some labelling theorists (notably those of an interactionist or ethnomethodological variety), there is a strong tendency to take seriously the persons, meanings or labels of the world and to ignore the possibility of any external referent. In the words of two extreme proponents of this view: 'Nothing in the social world has an inherent meaning. Meaning consists only of that which is imputed by people to persons and objects, as they go about their daily lives trying to make sense of the world' (Lyman and Scott, 1970, p. 26).

Thus, tacitly in some instances and explicitly in others, the sociological task becomes that of describing first one world view, then another and so on, through the entire social world. But there can be no way of reconciling these differing world views: each one has to be considered in its own terms. We study the delinquent as he experiences the world in his natural habitat and we document as accurately as possible this experience — taking very seriously the boy's own account and rejecting any concern for forces shaping his behaviour which are unperceived by the boy, or the possibility that the boy's account may not be 'right'.

In some ways this has been a most important development in sociology, for in the past sociologists have been trained *not* to take the individual's own accounts seriously but instead to go in pursuit of the causal factors unperceived by him. After listening to what the respondent says, the sociologist then sets about trying to find the *real* explanation for that behaviour, whether it lies in unconscious motivations, behavioural conditioning, the maintenance of needs or the consequence of economic forces. How the person defines his or her motives has been ignored in a pursuit of 'real' motives. And such 'real' motives are generally located in some absolutist metaphysic around which the entire world seems to revolve.

Now the beliefs upon which this 'orthodox' sociology have largely been built have all come under much fire recently. It can no longer pass unchallenged that there is surely a world of causation apart from actors' intentionality, that actors' meanings and talk can ultimately be translated through the medium of some universal constant, or that an absolutist metaphysic can be adhered to which explains the world by a few grand principles.

Yet a problem with much of this well-founded criticism is that it becomes guilty of 'rejection by reversal' and of what Sorokin has analysed as the 'fads and foibles' effect (Sorokin, 1956). By 'rejection by reversal' I mean the tendency to construct an alternative theory by simply reversing the major features of an opponent's theory. Thus absolutism turns into relativism, objectivism turns into subjectivism and value-free sociology becomes a value-committed sociology. By 'fad and foibles', Sorokin indicated the tendency of sociologists — in their hectic pursuit of new ideas and discoveries — to ignore what was good in past theories and to posit too radical a break with the past.

Now phenomenological labelling theory (in its preoccupation with actors' meanings) can be led to a defencelessly uncritical posture in which there are no external standards by which to appraise the individual's situation. When the homosexual tells us he or she is sick and needs treatment, when the poor tell us they are 'well off' and content, when the delinquent boy informs us that his delinquency is a product of a broken home, we can do nothing more than record this situation. A total solipsism emerges. Its rejection of absolutism reinforces this intellectual impotency.

Any work that fully espouses the principles of subjectivism and relativism must inevitably render its own findings, along with all others, incapable of possessing claims to be listened to or taken more seriously than anything else. While some of the phenomenological sociologists would go this far, interactionists walk a tightrope between social behaviourism and phenomenological idealism, and their intellectual origins in formalism and pragmatism certainly permits the incomplete grasping of localised truths. There is no inevitable connection between interactionism and 'mindless relativism' as some critics suggest (cf. Lewis, 1976). And, of course, for other — more structural or positivist versions of labelling theory — the relativist problem is bypassed.

THE BIASES AND LIMITATIONS OF LABELLING THEORY

A number of biases and limitations have been detected in labelling theory to date. It ignores the sources of deviant action; has too deterministic a conception of the labelling process; has relevance to only a limited range of deviant activities (cf. Reiss, 1970, pp. 80-2; Schur, 1971); ignores power; neglects structure; avoids history; focuses upon individuals to the detriment of interactional (Ward, 1971, p. 287) and organisational factors (Davis, 1972); has a 'methodological inhibition serving to limit the field to an ethnographic, descriptive, overly restrictive sociology' (Davis, 1972, p. 466), as well as a tendency to look only 'at the visible end of the selection process', ignoring 'those cases which do not develop into "career" deviants' (Bordua, 1967, p. 154). Because of restricted space, I will deal only with the first five here, but they can all be shown to be largely unfair.

The neglect of becoming deviant[12]

The first and most frequently cited limitation of labelling theory is that it fails to provide any account of the initial motivations towards deviance; it ignores the origins of deviant action and thereby frequently denudes the behaviour of meaning (Gibbs, 1966; Bordua, 1967; Mankoff, 1971; Taylor, Walton and Young, 1973a; Davis, 1972). These criticisms seem to be both fair and unfair. They are unfair in so far as they attack the perspective for not doing what it manifestly does not set out to do. A theory of labels does not have to be a theory of behaviour, although at those points where the theory suggests that the behaviour is shaped by the labels or the labels are shaped by the behaviour the two areas do interact.

However, a number of the criticisms are fairer, because while labelling theorists do not have to account for the initial deviance *in principle,* they very often do *in practice.* What critics are actually attacking is a tacit theory of primary deviance. Let me briefly give a few instances of how the problem of initial deviance has been dealt with in labelling theory (some are more successful than others).[13] In a number of studies the analysis picks up from the stage when the 'deviant' has been identified and follows the interactions from there on (e.g. Emerson, 1969; Sudnow, 1965); these simply ignore the problem. In others the analyst may provide a summary of extant eclectic work on deviant origins before embarking upon his own study of the impact of labelling (e.g. Schur, 1963). And in some an open-ended proposition is made about the sources of deviance, which acknowledges the importance of initiating forces other than labelling but elects to ignore them (e.g. Lemert, 1951, p. 67; Plummer, 1975). All of these seem to me to be reasonable positions: no theory explains everything and the analyst is entitled to set his boundaries. Yet there are some theorists, most notably Becker, who do tacitly produce theories of initial motivation. While they do not develop these, the theories lie dormant in their accounts awaiting explication. The two accounts most frequently criticised seem to be ones in which:

(1) the labels themselves are seen as the initiator of deviant behaviour; in other words, the deviance is created by societal reaction alone;

(2) the impulse towards deviant activities is regarded as ubiquitous and widespread in society; in other words, all people would be deviant if there were not good reasons to be otherwise.

The first proposition is one frequently used by critics for the purpose of attack, but I do not think any labelling theorist would endorse it (cf. Schur,

1971, p. 5; Rock, 1973a, p. 66). Yet despite the fact that no labelling theorist seems to espouse the 'label creates behaviour' view, it is very often developed by critics. Mankoff, for instance, has shown how in a number of empirical instances (including Becker's own marijuana smokers, and Lemert's own 'naive check forgers'), that 'societal reactions seem to be neither a necessary nor a sufficient condition for career-achieved deviance' (Mankoff, 1971, p. 211): there can be career deviance without societal reactions. Now, while in a few limited instances labelling theorists may argue that it is the societal reactions which sets a deviant off on his career, these are extremely untypical cases. Lemert, Becker and Schur have all denied that careers necessarily start with societal reactions, although it remains unclear where, according to their argument, careers do commence (cf. Stebbins, 1971).

It is, I think, a gross misreading of the interactionist version of labelling theory to impute the initiation of deviant careers to labelling. It is also a misreading to believe that labelling can only be evidenced by direct formal labelling. While, however, the critics' first attack on labelling theory's account of initial motivation can be faulted because no labellist would argue that position, the butt of the second criticism can certainly be evidenced in labellist writings.

This proposition is built right into the very heart of Becker's account. As Becker says: 'There is no reason to assume that only those who finally commit a deviant act actually show the impulse to do so. It is much more likely that most people experience deviant impulses frequently. At least in fantasy, people are much more deviant than they appear' (Becker, 1963, p. 26); or later: 'Instead of deviant motives leading to the deviant behaviour, it is the other way round; the deviant behaviour in time produces the deviant motivation. Vague impulses and desires — in this case — are transformed into definite patterns of action through the social interpretation of a physical experience which is in itself ambiguous' (Becker, 1963, p. 42). Becker's view has much in common with control theory. However, critics have pointed to the possibility that this theory can trivialise the actor's initial reasons for getting into deviant activities. As Young says: 'Thus human purpose and meaning are taken from the deviant; his project is not one of importance to him, rather, it is a product of experimentation and the "accident" of labelling' (Young, 1974, p. 165). Walton (1973) has exemplified this argument by providing a case study of a highly politicised deviant group — the Weathermen — in which the initial motivation for the acts can be seen as powerful. As he says: 'The aim of this paper has been to demonstrate that some deviants exhibit purposefulness, choice, and commitment in a very different manner from that allowed in the societal reaction approach' (Walton, 1973, p. 179).

Walton has successfully demonstrated that in some instances deviant choice may be much more wilful than that which is conventionally discussed by labelling theorists. But, in effect, both Young and Walton's critiques are rather one-sided. Labellists have generally played a major role in restoring choice and meaning to the deviant's activity (cf. Matza, 1969). And this they have done primarily by constructing processual models of becoming deviant, rather than static-state/causal snapshots. In the inter-actionist account of labelling, people do not become deviant 'all at once' but rather — through a series of shiftings and negotiations — gradually build up a deviant self. Minor but *meaningful* fantasies may gradually emerge in deviant action. Both Young and Walton seem to seek to close this processual model and return it to a picture of person who — at a certain moment in time — suddenly seeks a clear-headed, wilful, deviant activity (in Young's case it is the hedonism of the marijuana smoker and in Walton's it is the political commitment of the Weathermen). Yet a cumulative, sequential account of 'becoming' is largely incompatible with a model that postulates powerful initiating forces. At least in the inter-actionist variant of labelling, human life is constantly being pieced together through conjoint action and ambiguous interpretation: it is not hammered out by clear, unilateral motives.

It must be stressed, however, that to retain choice and process is not necessarily to see these processes as 'random' and 'accidental'. Processes may stem from different systems and choice may depend on different sets of contingencies. So while it may be true that in some parts of his writing Becker seems to imply a randomness of initial motivations towards deviance, I do not think this should be seen as a necessary feature of labelling theory. Indeed, at this point the most common postulate for explaining primary deviance may be evoked. This states simply that the early stages of deviant careers may be constructed from diverse sources. Thus for Scheff 'residual rule breaking' arises from 'fundamentally diverse sources' — 'organic, psychological, external stress, and volitional acts of innovation of defiance' (Scheff, 1966, p. 40), while for Lemert, 'differen-tiation' is accounted for by biology, demography, technology, groups, psychic processes and 'drift' (Lemert, 1951, ch. 2; Lemert, 1967, ch. 2). It is true that these amount to little more than open-minded confessions of ignorance, but as I have noted before it is basically unfair to criticise a theory for what it does not set out to do.

In sum, I do not find the criticisms of labelling theory, on the ground of its neglect of initial motivation, very convincing, since there is no reason of internal consistency why it should address itself to the problem of initial motives. However: (a) in practice, labelling theorists have often implicitly addressed themselves to these problems in the past, and these theories do need critical examination and elaboration; (b) some researchers (though not necessarily labelling theorists) need to focus more directly upon the possible range of links between initial motives and labels (cf. Turner, 1972).

The 'man on his back' bias: a determinism of societal reactions

Closely linked to the above is the argument that labelling theorists have rescued the deviant from the deterministic constraints of biological, psychological and social forces only to enchain him again in a new determinism of societal reactions. Thus Bordua suggests that labelling theory 'assumes an essentially empty organism or at least one with little or no autonomous capacity to determine conduct' (Bordua, 1967, p. 154), and Gouldner comments that it has 'the paradoxical consequence of inviting us to view the deviant as a passive nonentity who is responsible neither for his suffering nor its alleviation — who is more sinned against than sinning' (Gouldner, 1968, p. 106).

This argument has been most clearly documented by Schervish, who suggests that there is a philosophical bias in existing labelling studies which work from 'pessimistic and fatalistic assumptions that an imputed labelee is both *passive* and stands alone as an *individual*' (Schervish, 1973, p. 47). This has come about partly because it is methodologically easier to study relatively formal situations where the powerful label the weak, and partly because of the liberal assumptions of sociologists, as a consequence of which more aggressive political deviance tends to get ignored. Schervish is optimistic that although this bias has existed in the past, 'labelling theorists should now be able to move beyond their carefully drawn social psychological studies of individuals and begin to explore group, organizational, and societal levels of labelling conflict, (Schervish, 1973, p. 55).

Now while Schervish's optimism at least allows for a place for labelling theory in the future, I do not think that the 'man-on-his-back' criticism is particularly well founded.

First, even those studies which *seem* to provide the most crude model of labelling ('no deviance→slam label→deviance') are often firmly within a humanist tradition which sees the labelled person as sensitively playing a part under the weight of the deviant label. Goffman's mental patients are classic examples of people who have a label which is not internalised thrust upon them (Goffman, 1968). Secondly, there are a number of instances in the labelling literature of members working to fight off labels and neutralise their possible impact. Reiss's boy prostitutes, who develop normative systems which insulate them from homosexual self-conceptions, constitute one early instance of this tradition, and there have been many such accounts since that time (Reiss, 1962; McCaghy, 1968). Thirdly, studies are now developing of deviants who actively seek out the deviant label rather than having it cast upon them by others. The Braginskys' theory of mental illness centres on the idea that people seek out labels of madness in order to resolve problems of everyday life (Braginsky and Braginsky, 1969); and Rock has presented a discussion of expressive, politicised and entrepreneurial deviants, all of whom, for varying reasons, find it important to present themselves publicly as deviant (Rock, 1973a). In other words, although there may be instances of 'passive labelling' both in the literature and in the empirical world, there are also many instances where the passive picture of the man on his back simply does not apply.

I find this criticism an especially curious one when it is levied against the interactionists' account of labelling, for it is so clearly antithetical to some of the basic tenets of interactionist theory. To take a theory that is sensitive to self, consciousness and intentionality and render it as a new determinism of societal reaction could only be possible if the theory were totally misunderstood in the first place.

The irrelevance of labelling theory to certain problem areas

A third, and much less frequent, argument against labelling theory is raised by those who suggest that it is simply inapplicable to large areas of deviant behaviour. Thus the labelling model is not suitable for the analysis of impulsive crimes such as violence, physical deviance such as blindness or mild deviations which involve few overt labellers and low normative and physical visibility, such as premarital intercourse (cf. Reiss, 1970, pp. 80-2). These criticisms are generally based upon crude models of labelling, arguing either that the behaviour exists in the first place, before the application of a societal reaction (whereas presumably in areas where labelling theory is applicable, the behaviour has to be caused by labels), or that the non-existence of specific others to react to the deviance makes the model inappropriate (whereas presumably in areas where labelling theory is applicable, there have to exist specific others, like control agents, who respond to the deviance). These criticisms are based upon misconceptions of labelling theory. No labelling theorist argues that societal reactions bring about the behaviour: only that labels alter the nature, shape and incidence of the experience. And few labelling theorists believe that all the labelling has to flow from specific others: it may also stem from abstract rules and self-reactions. Labelling theory is, in principle, applicable to any area of social life, deviant or non-deviant, and key studies have already emerged in those areas often attacked as being irrelevant (e.g. Scott, 1969; Mercer, 1973; Edgerton, 1967; Rains, 1971; Christensen and Carpenter, 1962).

The neglect of power

The most serious objection to the labelling perspective which 'radical' or 'critical' criminologists have raised appears to be that it is insufficiently political. Their arguments, made forcefully in the early 1970s, take two major forms.

First, it is argued that labelling perspectives 'tend to incline sociologists toward focusing on deviance committed by the powerless rather than deviance committed by the powerful' (Thio, 1973, p. 8). Most notably, they concentrate upon the 'sociology of nuts, sluts and perverts' at the expense of 'covert institutional violence' (Liazios, 1972, p. 11). And as a result of the general acceptance of this criticism amongst 'radical' criminologists (certainly in England, though to a much lesser extent in America), there has been a drastic revision of the field in the past few years towards the study of the 'crimes of the powerful' (cf. Pearce, 1976) and offences against 'human rights' (cf. Schwendinger and Schwendinger, 1975).

Secondly, it is argued that while many labelling theorists 'mention the importance of power in labelling people deviant', 'this insight is not developed' (Liazios, 1972, pp. 114-15). In particular, labelling theorists focus upon interpersonal relationships and so-called 'caretaker institutions', but fail to look at the broader economic structures in which deviance emerges. Again, as a result of the general acceptance of this criticism among radical criminologists (in England), there has been a reorientation of the field towards 'the political economy of crime'.

The consequence of these criticisms can only be viewed positively. It is important that sociologists should study the crimes of the powerful and the political economy of deviance. But while the consequences of the criticisms are sound, the criticisms themselves are weak. Both of the criticisms mentioned above flow from an ignorantly insensitive and dog-matically assertive assumption of the rightness of an absolutist position. The criticisms come close to denying the rightness of any theoretical posture or problematic other than their own. They generally imply that sociologists who look at these 'powerless' areas do so out of blindness, stupidity, ignorance or plain conservatism rather than reason. I will consider these two objections in turn.

First, the issue of a focus on the powerless. At first sight this criticism would seem to have great force. Almost without exception sociologists have focused upon the deviance of the powerless. This granted, however, it still seems to me that 'radical' critics have failed to comprehend four things: the sociology of deviance is *not* criminology; the study of deviance *is* the study of the powerless; the symbolic interactionist problematic is *not* the Marxist problematic; and the politics of libertarianism *directs* one to work with the victims of state power. These four statements are inter-connected, but I will unpack each one separately.

First, the sociology of deviance is *not* criminology. This is a distinction that was much discussed during the mid-sixties, with the advent of the 'new deviance' theories. The rejection of so-called positivistic criminology ushered in the sociology of deviance; but this sociology not only changed the theoretical base for the study of criminals, it also brought in its wake a dramatic restructuring of empirical concerns. Sociologists turned their interests to the world of expressive deviance: to the twilight, marginal worlds of tramps, alcoholics, strippers, dwarfs, prostitutes, drug addicts, nudists; to taxi-cab drivers, the blind, the dying, the physically ill and handicapped, and even to a motley array of problems in everyday life. Whatever these studies had in common, it was very clear that it was not criminology. Of course, some of these same students continued to study crime, but only as one instance of deviance — an uneasy coexistence was established.

This uneasy coexistence has rarely been directly confronted, but it does serve as one root dividing point between the recent critical criminologists and the interactionist labelling theorists. The former gravitate towards criminological concerns; the latter gravitate away from them. Yet the former are unwilling to relinquish their affinities with deviance study. Thus even the title of their magnus opus *The New* Criminology — *For a Social Theory of* Deviance (my emphasis) captures the inherent confusion. For the book as a whole is about crime, criminals and the law; nowhere in the book is there to be found a concern for the blind, the stutterer, the subnormal, the physically handicapped, the physically ill, the religious deviant, the nudist or the interpersonal problems of families. It is essentially a book on criminology, but it is unwilling to relinquish its claim to be the study of deviance.

Now this is not nit-picking. Of course, I do not want to defend the arbitrary construction of academic boundaries and the creation of sterile demarcation disputes. But is it vital to recognise that the concerns of the sociology of deviance (and I am not here particularly concerned with what the concerns of criminology are — I am no criminologist) send one *necessarily* on a mission to study powerless groups. It is not capricious whimsy but theoretical necessity that leads the sociology of deviance to study powerlessness. And the reason should be so obvious that one wonders how the attacks could ever have been so seriously accepted. *For the study of deviance is the study of devalued groups, and devalued groups are groups which lack status and prestige.* Now, of course, it may be useful — for a full account of deviance — to study 'top dogs' who maintain their prestige in order to understand the mechanisms by which prestige and stigma gets allocated. It is theoretically relevant to understand why it was so long before Nixon was placed in a devalued role. But a sociology of deviance which does not focus centrally on powerless groups is likely to be a very odd sociology of deviance.

Given that deviance is concerned with devalued groups, it is also possible to suggest that there is an affinity between symbolic inter actionism and the study of deviance. That interactionists have readily studied deviance is apparent; that there are good theoretical grounds for doing so is perhaps less clear. Yet if it is agreed that the interactionists problematic is fundamentally the analysis of the ways in which members construct meanings — of self and of the social world — and of how such social constructions are pervaded with ambiguity, then it becomes clear that the topic of deviance provides an unusually complete set of illustrations for such analysis.

Thus the interactionists' persistent (though often tacit) concern with ambiguity may be greatly illuminated by an examination of those situations where incongruity and equivocations are central features. An ironic consequence is that such illumination may also serve to clarify the less ambiguous, more routine situations of the social world. In either case the study of deviant groups and deviant situations affords an unusually stimulating pathway to such understandings. Thus, for instance, to look at the world through the eyes of a hermaphrodite or a transvestite will tell us much about the ambiguity of gender roles and the way in which such precarious gender meaning becomes stabilised (Garfinkel 1967; Kando 1973; Feinbloom, 1976).

Further, the interactionists' desire to remove themselves from abstract generalities or reified theorising and to immerse themselves in the understanding of small, local contexts inevitably leads them to notice the diversity and plurality of small social worlds. All the world is not deviant, nor are there only limited realms which are consensually defined as deviant. It is not that the interactionist must select exotic groups, but that any group once studied closely will reveal a diversity of meanings and life styles, along with anomalies and problems that require studying. Most of the groups studied by interactionists are not really that quaint or exotic: they are you and I going about our daily tasks of walking and talking, living in families, visiting doctors and going to work, meeting friends and falling in love, making telephone calls, sleeping, dying and the like. This concern does not lead to the study of exotic groups but to the study of the commonplace situations of ordinary people. But once studied closely, the diversity and deviance of daily experience becomes more apparent.

Another affinity between interactionism and deviance stems from their direct concern with processes of identity construction. The building and negotiation of the self is, of course, a major focus of interactionist analysis and, again, it is clear that much can be learned from studying those situations where identities are changed, disrupted or put under severe stress. It is at those moments that the processes involved in the constitution of self may be most readily observed and studied. The study of deviance provides a host of such situations, while the study of covert institutional violence seems less well provided with such cases.

Understanding of why the powerless have frequently been the topic of labelling theory lies, finally, in recognition of the liberal-to-libertarian sympathies of many of its practitioners. They have been concerned with the excessive encroachment of technology, bureaucracy and the state upon the personal life — often in its grossest forms (the increasing criminalisation and medicalisation of deviance; the bureaucratisation of the control agencies and the concomitant dehumanisation of the lives of their victims'; and the direct application of technology in the service of control), but also in its more subtle forms — daily alienation, meaninglessness, despair and fragmentation (with the concomitant 'theory and practice of resistance to everyday life' (Cohen and Taylor, 1976)). Now, although critical criminologists deride such sympathies, they must at least agree that there is a political rationale behind the study of many powerless groups and that sometimes such concerns have had important practical, political pay-offs (decriminalisation, deinstitutionalisation, demedicalisation, deprofessionalisation and the creation of movements concerned with such activities).

112 *Deviant Interpretations*

In summary, then, the labelling perspective gravitates toward the powerless because (a) the sociology of deviance generally directs them to *devalued* groups; (b) symbolic interactionism directs them to areas where ambiguity, marginality and precarious identities are readily available for study; and (c) libertarianism directs them to work with groups who are seriously 'up against the state'. Theoretically, sociologically and practically there are good reasons for a concern with the powerless.

Aside from the criticism that the labelling perspective studies only powerless groups, there is the more general problem that it neglects political *analysis*. This attack takes a weak and a strong form. In its weak form it implies that labelling analysts ignore the study of power; in its stronger form, it asserts that their analysis is false.

The first — weak — criticism is simply wrong. One could well argue that the labelling perspective brought political analysis (back?) into deviancy study. It recognises that 'naming was a political act' (Goode, 1969, and that 'what rules are to be enforced, what behaviour regarded as deviant, and which people labelled as outsiders must . . . be regarded as political [questions]' (Becker, 1963, p. 7).

From this it went on to produce a series of empirical studies concerning the origins of deviancy definitions in political action, e.g. drug legislation (Becker, 1963; Dickson, 1968; Galliber and Walker, 1977); temperance legislation (Gusfield, 1963); delinquency definitions (Platt, 1969; Lemert, 1970); homosexuality (e.g. Spector, 1977); prostitution (Roby, 1969); pornography (Zurcher and Kirkpatrick, 1976); political bias in the apprehension and adjudication of deviants (cf. Box, 1971); and the distribution of power in the bargaining process (cf., Scheff, 1968; Emerson, 1969; Carlen, 1976). Masses and masses of work could be cited here which shows the concern with political factors in the labelling perspective.

The first attack — since it is false — leads to a consideration of the second: whilst power is present in the labelling perspective, the analysis is weak. This criticism is too vast to consider in detail here: it basically involves a reconsideration of classic debates in political science theory between pluralist, élitist and ruling-class models of power. For it is argued that labelling perspectives ultimately approach a pluralistic conception of power (albeit a 'radical pluralism — cf. Pearce, 1976) and that such analyses are discredited. Assuming that pluralism *has* been discredited (a gross assumption), the problem is then clear: does the labelling perspective really imply a pluralist conception of power? The answer should be equally clear: within the perspective, *any* theory can be applied (see the

ntroductory remarks to this paper), so there is clearly no endemic link
vith pluralism.

Whilst this solution may be satisfactory to a few, it actually bypasses the
asis of most of the criticism. This is the charge that interactionism is
quatable with labelling theory, and it is this theory which is pluralistic.
ome brief comments are necessary here, therefore, on the symbolic
nteractionism version of power.

The essence of the interactionists' notion of power highlights the
egotiated, ambiguous and *symbolic* issues in politics. It is a view which
hould capture the flow of the empirically observable political situations
hat people find themselves involved in daily. For the political acts that we
ll experience are shrouded in such issues — whether we confront them in
niversity senates, in radical committees, in political organisations, on the
hop floor, in church trustees' meetings or when working with (or against)
he media.

In all these situations, the empirically observable situations are those of
egotiation, disagreement and discussion, the selection of the right 'issue'
nd the right 'image', the behind-the-scenes canvassing. Interactionism
an be used to study and understand politics at this level (Edelman, 1964,
971; Gusfield, 1963; Hall, 1972). The objection that is voiced against
uch a view, of course, is that while it does show what goes on in
ituations, its astructural location of such situations neglects the real
ssues. The same model of power can be applied to a business corporation,
Boy Scout group, the IRA and the Women's Institute. Ultimately, as it
uilds up into a cumulative portrait of the society, the interactionist theory
as a close affinity with the pluralist model of power — with masses of
pparently equally weighted pressure groups vying and wrestling for
ontrol. In practice I think that this is precisely the conception of power
hat underpins much interactionist work — it is probably no mere
appenstance that Arnold Rose (a leading interactionist) is also the author
f a major book on pluralist politics (*The Power Structure,* 1967). But in
ny view — and given the largely discredited nature of the pluralist theory
- interactionism does not have to follow such a conception. In the same
vay as Scheff is ultimately able to weight the negotiation power of
sychiatrist and client, so, too, wider groups in society will not have equal
ower. Society may be seen as a vast negotiated order constantly
eproducing itself through a myriad of strategies and interpretive pro-
edures. Masses of historically produced, intended and unintended
ecisions with intended and unintended outcomes give rise to a highly
mbiguous and constantly shifting social order. To that one need only add

the hypothesis that the negotiations, decisions and outcomes are biased i
favour of specific economic groups. The negotiated order is a stratifie
one. Paul Rock captures this conception neatly:

> *In complex societies* there is a substantial fragmentation of rule-makin
> and rule-enforcing effort. There are innumerable legislating, definin
> and policing agencies which collectively make up the formal structur
> of a society's system of social control. Legislators, judges, magistrate:
> policemen, bailiffs, psychiatrists, prison officers and traffic warden
> form a loosely co-ordinated system with shifting internal boundaries;
> differentiation of power and function; and intricate linkages forged ou
> of internal conflict, exchange and co-operation. The overall structure i
> *hierarchical*; chains of command fashion the flow of power and decisio
> making. Each of the hierarchy's subsystems is shaped by its fellow:
> Each has the possibility of acquiring limited autonomy from the res1
> each tends to have a drive towards maximising its control over resource
> and problem areas; and each is concerned about defending it
> boundaries against outsiders. The *higher strata* have a greater capacit
> to exert influence over the whole but they are functionally dependent o
> and constrained by the lower strata. (Rock, 1973a: 123)

The Neglect of Structure

Although it is manifestly clear that in some accounts of labelling
structural matters are well represented (as, for example, in Erickson
Wayward Puritans, 1966), critics who (wrongly) equate labellin
processes with symbolic interactionism make the initially plausibl
complaint that the theory harbours an astructural bias. I say plausibl
because even sympathisers with the interactionist approach (such a
Reynolds, Petras and Meltzer, 1975) would find this criticism a valid one
Yet it is most surely ill-founded — like most of the other critiques.

To accuse symbolic interactionism of neglecting structural concerns i
to misread the interactionist enterprise. Every social science theory bring
with it its own distinctive problematic and set of concerns, and to accus
theories of failing to deal with what they do not intend to deal with i
unfair. A Marxist concern with the mode of production cannot be faulte
for failing to deal with an account of heart disease, any more than
Freudian account of the unconscious can be faulted for failing to explai
reinforcement contingencies. As Hewitt notes: 'It is not the task of soci
psychology, whether symbolic interactionist or some other perspective, t
account in great detail for the systematic and complex interrelationship
among institutions, organisations, social classes, large-scale social change

nd other "structural" phenomena' (Hewitt, 1976, p. 148). However, that
aid, Hewitt rightly notes:

> At the same time, such matters cannot go unremarked and unstudied:
> the basic social proceses [discussed by interactionism] take place within
> a larger context of social order and social change, and if it is not the job
> of the social psychologist to explain these macroscopic phenomena in
> their entirety, they must nevertheless be taken into account. (Hewitt,
> 1976, p. 148)

The central concern of symbolic interactionism is not with structural
matters; it does, however, need to acknowledge such concerns if it is to be
remotely adequate *social* psychology. And if one inspects the work of
many interactionists — including that of both Mead and Blumer — one
finds this is so. Thus, for instance, Mead comments: 'We are individuals
orn into a certain nationality, located at a certain spot geographically,
with such-and-such family relations, and such-and-such political relations.
All these represents a certain situation which constitutes the "me" . . .'
Mead, p. 182). And later in *Mind, Self and Society* (1934), Mead devotes
many pages to an (admittedly grossly inadequate) discussion of the
conomic and religious orders (cf. part 3). Any adequate interactionist
ccount will firmly acknowledge that the action of persons does not take
lace in a social limbo, although it is through the actions of persons that
ny wider social order becomes historically constituted. Further, it is also
rue that the interactionist generally has a conception of persons wrestling
with this wider order. Lichtman's argument that symbolic interactionism
ultimately abandons the sense of human beings in struggle with an alien
eality which they both master and to which they are subordinate'
Lichtman, 1970, p. 77) is (like much of his account) simply wrong. Most
f the interactionist accounts of deviance portray the labelled deviant as
omeone who employs multiple patterns of resistance (Goffman's mental
atients, Cohen and Taylor's prisoners, Matza's delinquents, Humphrey's
berated homosexuals, Scott's blind, etc., etc.), and the wider inter-
ctionist portrayals of everyday life in society are overwhelmingly full of
hemes of the self in struggle with a wider 'abstract', 'homeless',
aramount Reality' (Zijderveld, 1972; Berger et al, 1974; Cohen and
Taylor, 1976).

However, even given that the interactionists acknowledge the existence
f a wider social order and demonstrate the persistent struggles of
ndividuals with that wider order, it would be correct to say that they lack a
onception of this totality as a *structure*. But they do not neglect the
oncept of structure out of ignorance (they speak to many of the same

concerns as structuralists); rather they deny its importance and relevance
for the interactionist task. The notion of structure, they argue, is
reification which does not do justice to the central interactionist concern
of emergence, process and negotiation. At present I do not think the
interactionists have developed a wholly satisfactory method of dealing
with this denial of structures and simultaneous acknowledgement of
wider totality that is itself an emergent; but many attempts are now being
made to furnish such a solution, some of which may ultimately prove
effective.

Thus the wider social order may be approached through the concepts of
'the negotiated order' (Strauss et al, 1964; Day & Day, 1977), collective
action (Blumer, 1969), constraints (McCall and Simmons, 1966), the
'conglomerate' (Douglas, 1971; Rock, 1974), 'typifications' (Rock
1973a), 'co-ordinated activity' (Blumer, 1969; Hewitt, 1976), and the
'generalised other' (Mead, 1934) (cf. Laver and Handel, 1977). There is
no space in this article to deal with all these concepts but they all have in
common an awareness of wider social formations than the individual (and
the way they influence conduct) whilst managing to maintain a distance
from the notion of a reified structure.

THE EMPIRICAL VALIDITY OF LABELLING THEORY

One final group of objections suggest that labelling theory is simply
wrong: under the harsh light of research scrutiny, the ideas of labelling
theory are given little support. One noteworthy theory to receive critical
attack is Scheff's labelling theory of mental illness (1975). This is in part
because Scheff spells out his theory in proposition form and hence makes it
readily available for falsification. But it is also because Scheff's theory —
when dismantled from the riders and cautions that Scheff himself built
into the account — comes nearer than most to being a crude, deterministic
model of labelling; that is, it seems to suggest that without formal labelling
there would be no mental illness, and that formal labelling is an irrever-
sible stigma. Gove's empirical critique suggests that both of these
arguments do not hold (Gove, 1975). This same author has edited the
proceedings of a conference specifically designed to test the validity of
labelling theory over a wide range of areas — subnormality, alcoholism,
disability, heroin addiction, sexual deviance, crime and delinquency —
and has concluded: 'The evidence reviewed consistently indicates that it is

he behaviour or condition of the person that is the critical factor in causing someone to be labelled deviant' (Gove, 1975, p. 295).

Now, empirical critiques such as these may be answered in several ways. First, they may be answered on their own terms. Thus Scheff's analysis of Gove's critique reinterprets the evidence and concludes that of the eighteen systematic studies of labelling theory available, 'thirteen support the theory, and five fail to' (Scheff, 1975). But second, and more generally, my answer to this form of critique would stress that the 'testers' of labelling theory usually adopt a narrow, empirical and positivistic concept of labelling theory which can only focus upon a very few limited hypotheses dealing with a narrow range of questions drawn from the labelling perspective. The 'testers' ignore the idea that labelling is a perspective serving to reorientate research towards a vast array of new concerns and propositions, and prefer to focus instead upon a vulgarised and distorting version which, while making the theory testable, also renders it trivial (cf. Kitsuse, 1975; Schur, 1975).

This last form of defence is certainly not arguing that labelling theory should not be open to testing and falsification: it is simply stressing that the contribution of labelling theory is to open inquiry into an assortment of new, competing propositions which answer the full gamut of labelling questions. Given this, it becomes useful to distinguish two versions of an empirical labelling theory: one is *limited,* and contains a narrow (generally distorting) set of propositions, and the other is *wider* and contains an array of (often competing) propositions. The limited version only deals with questions associated with the issues of application and consequences, while the broader version deals with questions of the nature and origins of labels too. However, even the two areas which the narrow version considers are treated in a limited way, while the wide version sees a broader set of propositions emerging. Thus, for the first area — labelling is a dependent variable (Orcutt, 1973), or the problem of application — a narrow version suggests two key propositions:

(1) deviant labels are applied independently of the personality or behaviour of those labelled;

(2) deviant labels are applied *directly* by *formal* control agents.

In contrast, the wider perspective extends these propositions to acknowledge that:

(1a) deviants may contribute to their own labelling in many ways requiring specification;

(2a) deviant labels may be applied *indirectly,* by *informal* as well as formal control agents, and by self-labelling.

It is clear that the research directives of the narrow propositions are simple and manageable: look at the ways in which formal control agents define deviants through contingencies. The research directives of the wider version do not lend themselves to such simple testing; the interaction between deviant and definer has to be considered, and the possibility of (symbolic) self-labelling analysed in detail. Labelling may occur without any specific intervening definer (cf. Rotenberg, 1974, 1975; Farrell and Nelson, 1975).

For the second area — labelling as an independent variable; the consequences of labelling — the narrow version suggests propositions like:

(3) labelling initiates or amplifies deviance — it has negative consequences;

(4) labels are deterministically internalised by labelees;

(5) such labels are irrevocable.

In contrast, the wider perspective extends these propositions to acknowledge that:

(3a) labels may prevent (deter) or change deviance — they may also have 'positive' consequences;

(4a) labels may be voluntarily avowed and disavowed, and responded to in a variety of ways;

(5a) labels may be reversible and changeable: destigmatisation is possible.

Again, it is clear that the research directives for the latter are altogether more complex. Rather than assuming that there is only one negative response to labelling, the entire programme of possible responses has to be charted. Some important studies have made moves in these directions (e.g., Reiss, 1962; Scott, 1969; Turner, 1972; Warren, 1974b). In summary, although it is true that to date labelling theory has not usually fared well at the hands of empirical researchers, this is largely due to the narrow interpretation given to the theory by the researchers. When viewed as an orientating perspective, the approach becomes important as suggestive of a wide range of areas demanding empirical attack.

IN CONCLUSION: A PERSONAL COMMITMENT

I was first introduced to labelling theory during a criminology course in the mid-sixties. Naively I thought it was a 'new' theory and I found appealing. It switched attention away from the aetiology of deviant conduct and started to examine the definitional process and the ways in which this altered the shape of 'deviant' experiences. At that time there were few criticisms being made of the theory and — like an innocent — I was seduced.

Slowly its appeal spread through English sociology and it served, perhaps, as the central rallying flag at the establishment of the National Deviancy Conference in England in 1968. It began to emerge from the underground of theory to become a topic for books and theses, as well as enjoying widespread incorporation in newly developing sociology of deviance courses. And as it became more widely known, so — rightly — more and more problems with it were noticed. From one small anticipation of the weaknesses of the theory (Gibbs, 1966), there developed a major industry of criticism. Perhaps the watershed of this criticism was the publication of *The New Criminology* in 1973, for it served to divide the new British tradition of deviancy study into two groups: those who still found much to be gained from working within the approach of labelling (now the new orthodoxy), and those who had turned away from such matters towards a concern with a political economy of crime. From that time onwards, the content, nature and even frequency of the meetings of the National Deviance Conference changed. In America, too, the perspective increasingly came under fire — though usually on empirical grounds rather than ideological ones (Gove, 1975).

I have no doubt now that while some of the criticisms have been largely beside the point, many of them have served useful functions — forcing a clarification of key theoretical, methodological and ideological concerns, and properly redirecting much work to new and politically important arenas. But the critics drastically overstate their case if they believe they can announce the 'death' of labelling theory or claim paramountcy of perspective, theory or method! I have tried in this paper to defend the view that labelling is essentially a perspective: the questions it raises are ones a sociology of deviance has to consider. I have gone on to argue that symbolic interactionism is only one theory that need be used within the labelling perspective, but that it has an affinity with the study of marginality and deviance and is a useful corrective to grander, more general theories. It has a useful role to play. Most of the paper has then considered more specific issues; most notably the suggestion that the labelling perspective is over-limited in its sphere of application and empirically wrong when tested. I hope to have shown the weaknesses of such arguments.

Massive criticism and countercriticism can be extremely effective in sharpening perspectives and theories. It can also become sterile when the amount of 'theorising about theorising' outstrips empirical inquiry. Labelling perspectives, symbolic interactionism and political economies of crime do not have to rival each other. They each raise their important problems and they each deserve serious attention.

NOTES

1. The importance of Mead, Cooley and Tannenbaum is often acknowledged (for recent instance, see Finestone, 1976, p. 188-91), but its history can be traced back much further (see Pearson, 1975).
2. Although the pattern is broadly similar, England followed a few years behind America. The Society for the Study of Social Problems was formed in the early fifties, but the English counterpart — the National Deviancy Conference — was not formed till the late sixties. The former may have become much more traditional over time, though, than the latter. Likewise the major American publications date from Becker's books (1963 and 1964), but in England the first statements are Cohen's (1967) paper and Young's (1970) book. England came later to the theory and rejected it more speedily.
3. Outside of America and England, more specific versions of labelling theory have been developed (e.g. Muller, 1974; Shoham, 1970). For ease of management, I am excluding these theories from the above discussion.
4. The main theoretical omission from this list is Marxism. Labelling theorists have flowered into Marxists (e.g. Young, 1970, 1975; Quinney, 1970, 1974; Platt 1969, 1973), but Marxism does not seem to have facilitated the rise of the labelling problems.
5. Schur seems to be the most ardent contemporary defender of labelling theory (Schur, 1971), yet he is only occasionally mentioned as a labellist. Whilst sympathetic to interactionism, all his work is theoretically eclectic.
6. In a private communication. I am very grateful to him — along with Stan Cohen, Malcolm Davies and Jock Young — for helpful comments on various drafts of the paper.
7. Warren and Johnson, in an extremely lucid phenomenological critique, have amplified this basic point. They suggest that labelling theory fails on three grounds: first, in its desire to be an original 'new school', it has thrown out much from past deviancy theory that is of value; secondly, while it appears highly critical of much past theorising, it has in fact imported through the back door, in different guise, a number of the very items it purports to attack; and thirdly, it has grappled inadequately with certain existential problems. Each of these criticisms is derived from a phenomenological concern with meanings. Thus, under the first criticism, Warren and Johnson suggest that there has been a too easy dismissal by the labellists of notions of 'deviant conditions', of 'core values', of 'pathology' and 'aetiology', when all of these phenomena are often built into the meanings of deviance constructed by actors themselves. Thus the homosexual's own emergent set of meanings may be concerned with 'whether I'm sick or not', 'how I got to like this', 'why society casts me apart', and 'being a homosexual'. To ignore these is to do a disservice to the actors' meanings.

   Under the second criticism, Warren and Johnson point to the fact that when labellists rhetorically drop the notion of deviants as a special category, most of their work continues with unexplicated notions of conventional deviance. Instead of inquiring into how members categorise acts as deviant, labellists continue to function with the perspectives of officials in locating and studying deviance. They tacitly remain on the side of the officials.

Under the third criticism, the authors write:

> Perhaps the most fundamental existential problem with labelling theory is its abstracting of reality from the context of used and situations, and its neglect of empirical investigations into how typifications of deviance are used by, and what their use means to, social actors on the actual occasions of their use. (Warren and Johnson, 1972, p. 90)

Now, all these criticisms have in common a desire to get back to the situated activities of members of interpreting and making deviance, shunning any unexplicated assumptions, the existence of broader macro-structures or the validity of official data, in favour of a highly microscopic and relativistic approach.

8. Space does not permit an expansion on such links. For some basic sources, see Rock, forthcoming.
9. Sagarin also provides a most helpful general discussion of the meaning of deviance in his (1975) book (part one), and with Birenbaum (Birenbaum and Sagarin, 1976, ch. 2).
10. I cannot expand these distinctions here. But at the least it should be noted that these two societal definitions work from drastically differing phenomenological positions. The former (a) stays on the level of the actor's definitions of the world (cf. Rock, 1973a), whereas the latter (b) moves — with some difficulty — between situated meanings and abstract meanings, in a manner derived from Berger and Luckmann (1967), and — more problematically — Douglas (1971). What both these definitions have in common, though, is a concern with some form of seemingly objective, external standards of deviance.
11. While the interactional labelling theorist *is* often on the side of an underdog, there is no reason why he or she has to be. Rock — in a private communication — helpfully comments:

> I cannot imagine why it is necessary to take either stance during the process. If an account of public control exists, it should deal with social meanings as a mutually orchestrated process. The decision to give an interpretation priority, to either partner, simply distorts understanding in a discussion of an encounter between a policeman and a delinquent, for instance. The individuals' definition of this encounter and their conjoint definitions must both be incorporated.

12. This criticism occurs on both an individual motivation level and on a structural level. Labelling theory does not explain why people commit deviant acts (Sagarin, 1975), or why there exist different 'objective' rates of deviance (cf. Gibbs, 1972). The latter objection has the merit of being a sociological objection but the former is curiously misplaced. Why *should* a sociologist seek to explain individual motives? It is hard to imagine an industrial sociologist seeking the motives of a striker or a political sociologist those of a working-class voter. Yet sociologists of deviance are still supposed to seek such explanations. Paradoxically, the major attempt at a sociology of motivation has actually come from those who are broadly sympathetic to the labelling/interactional approach (cf. Taylor and Taylor, 1972).
13. For an even briefer 'list' of such accounts, see the introductory chapter in Gove (1975).

How to Retain Your Soul and be a Political Deviant [1]

Deryck Beyleveld and Paul Wiles

Gospel is ignored at our peril; thus evangelism merits attention. Fr
quently, however, under the guise of a new faith it demands a return to o
allegiances. The evangelists in latter-day criminology have proclaimed n
one but two radical breaks with received practice. We are exhorted
embrace non-deterministic theories and of necessity to realise progra
matic statements flowing from them. But beyond the boundaries
criminology neither demand is new. Any semblance of novelty on
emerged against a background of structural functionalism in sociolo
combined with logical positivism in philosophy. Before the period
dominance of these two perspectives, adherence to the positions canvasse
by the new criminologists was eminently respectable, though nev
conclusively established. By rejecting structural functionalism and logic
positivism the new criminologies have revoiced suppressed issues. But
attempting to resurrect old ghosts, have the new criminologists succes
fully countered the spells which were used to exorcise them? We w
suggest not. The new criminologies have not even begun to tackle th
issues involved systematically.

Though we share the evangelical faith, we will attempt to show that th
exhortations of the new criminologists are empty electioneering promise
We do not really know what it means to follow their banner. We wi
however, attempt to make good the deficiency. In the process, we w
argue that inasmuch as it is possible to glean any analytical sense fro
their writings, the model of man espoused by the new criminologies
incompatible with their vision of a criminological theory as a social theor
Since we share that vision we will try to present the necessary model
man.

'Man is both creature and creator of society!' This slogan is a rallyi

122

call for the new criminologists. Despite differences in intellectual aims, methods and content, all appear to be agreed that a prime failing of the 'old' criminology was that it portrayed man as a puppet of external circumstances, unable to exercise any degree of autonomous creativity. Man, it is agreed, is shaped by forces outside his control, but not so completely that all capacity for self-direction is negated. This agreement extends across American new conflict theorists, British neo-Marxists, American naturalists and phenomenologists.[2] Thus we find that the authors of the two works upon which we shall concentrate, *The New Criminology* (Taylor et al, 1973a) and *Becoming Deviant* (Matza, 1969), can concur that:

> . . . the existence of subjects is not quite exhausted by the arduous natural processes of reactivity and adaptation. Capable of creating and assigning meaning, able to contemplate his surroundings, and even his own condition, given to anticipation, planning and projecting man — the subject — stands in a different and more complex relation to circumstances. This distinctively human capacity in no way denies that human existence frequently displays itself in ways characteristic of lower levels. Frequently man is wholly adaptable, *as if* he were just organic being. And sometimes, though very rarely, he is wholly reactive, *as if* a mere object. But mere reactivity or adaptation should not be confused with the distinctively human condition. They are better seen as an alienation or exhaustion of that condition. A subject actively addresses or encounters his circumstances: accordingly, his distinctive capacity is to re-shape, strive towards creating, and actually transcend circumstances. Such a distinctly human project is not always feasible, but the capacity always exists. (Matza, 1969, p. 92)

This type of statement is entirely characteristic of the mode of argument used by Matza and Taylor, Walton and Young to establish the inadequacy of a deterministic model of man. We are repeatedly told that the fact that human beings make choices, have purposes, will outcomes, intend actions and in general attach meaning to their situations shows that determinism is false. We contend, however, that the meaning behind ordinary language is by no means obvious, and even if it were, this would not establish its truth. A fundamental point to realise is that some writers who by no means deny that actors attach meaning to their situations and do all the things that we are alerted to by the new criminologists contend, nevertheless, that it is not even meaningful for someone who wishes to account for human behaviour to deny determinism. The assertions of some degree of free will or some degree of indeterminism (the two basic strategies for denying determinism) are declared to be meaningless or, at best, mere articles of religious faith. This declaration, if it does nothing else, should awaken us to the possibility that weighty conceptual issues are involved in any attempt to deny determinism.

Thus witness an interesting alliance between Paul Q. Hirst and Hans J. Eysenck. Eysenck dismisses the attempt to espouse free will in the following manner:

> Essentially what the deterministic psychologist says is that human conduct is always determined by specific causes. What the opponent maintains amounts to saying that behaviour is, at least to some extent random, that it is not caused in any sense by motive, prior teaching or learning, or in any other way . . . To say that [James] has a freedom of will to decide between . . . alternatives means nothing if we are saying simply that there are certain motives, drives, and learned behaviour patterns pulling in one direction, while others pull in another, and that the strongest set of motives, behaviour patterns, and so on, will win. If this is what we mean then we are dealing with a completely deterministic event. If we are saying that there is genuine freedom involved in this then we are saying that the individual may act without regard to his motives and the learning and conditioning that has gone on throughout his life, and that the decision is completely undetermined, or random. It is impossible, of course, for science to prove a negative; for example, to show that such randomness never occurs. Some people have found support, in Heisenberg's principle of indeterminacy in physics, for a belief that random events of this kind may happen in the central nervous system and that, to that extent, conduct is not determined but is free. This possibility cannot logically be excluded; but I doubt if it would give much genuine support to the believers in free will. What they mean by free will is usually something entirely different from such random activity or 'white noise' in the central nervous system. (Eysenck, 1977, p. 197)

In a similar vein we may note Hirst's approving commentary on the work of Claude Bernard:

> Bernard's principle of scientific determinism states that if a phenomenon is produced under specified conditions then it must always necessarily appear in those conditions and in the same aspect, unless some immediate material cause intervenes to change those conditions .
>
> The instability and variability of a phenomenon is a function of the rudimentary nature of scientific practice and has nothing whatsoever to do with an essential variability or lack of causation of the phenomena (*sic*) itself. *Indeterminism characterises the nature of the means of knowledge and not the phenomena to which it is applied* . . . The concept of scientific determinism is a product of a philosophical practice which reflects on the operations of the experimental sciences . . . Scientific determinism, however, is not a universal determinism. It has nothing to say about the question of 'free will' for it is restricted to phenomena

whose conditions of existence can be vigorously determined in science. Scientific determinism in so far as it is not universal is not, however, a form of conciliation with voluntarism. It does not admit of indeterminacy in respect of thse things which lie within its limits. Scientific determinism rejects the doctrine of the freedom of the 'mind' or 'spirit' from material constraint, not from the standpoint of a fatalism but because it does not admit of the existence of real phenomena with an effectivity which are without conditions of existence, and which therefore have no cause. (Hirst, 1975, pp. 34-42)

We do not believe that the new criminologists present any defence beyond simple refutation of this case. They simply do not express their position at the required conceptual level.

Essentially the argument advanced by Hirst and Eysenck appears to be as follows:

(i)   All events which are scientifically understandable are (a) produced by material or mechanical causes, i.e. push-pull causality, (b) explainable only by such mechanical causes. (a) and (b) together constitute the *principle of determinism.*

(ii) Some indeterminism may exist, with the consequence that some events will be unexplainable. It is impossible to prove otherwise, but if we have scientific aims, and our intention is to explain events, then we must assume explainability.

(iii) The only coherent alternative to determinism is indeterminism.

(iv) If the free will position is distinguishable from determinism, then it asserts indeterminism.

(v)   This is not what advocates of free will wish to assert.

(vi) The free will position is thus, at best, unscientific, an article of blind, irrational faith, or, at worst, incoherent romanticism.

There are propositions in this argument with which we agree and others which we wish to question. Although (ii) and (v) seem unexceptionable, we contend that (iii) is by no means obvious, and as a result (i), (iv) and (vi) have not been established. The key to our denial of the exhaustive nature of the determinism/indeterminism dichotomy — (iii) — is the suggestion that it is by no means obvious, without presupposing determinism to be true, that to explain is necessarily to cite *material* causes. If we can show that some explanations do not cite material causes, then it will follow that the goal of providing explanations can be maintained without adhering to determinism.

It is necessary to be clear in our minds about the purely logical possibilities for denying determinism. Determinism can be denied either by claiming that some events have no explanation, or by claiming that whether or not all events have material causes, some events at least can be explained without citing material causes. Both forms of denial will yield at least a partial determinism, but only the former need be a partial indeterminism. Odd as it may seem at first sight, if the principle of determinism is defined as it is in (i) above, then it should be possible to deny total determinism while at the same time maintaining that all events have material causes.

Since we agree that indeterminism is not a possible presupposition for the scientific investigator, our defence against the Hirst/Eysenck argument will amount to a defence of the notion of free will, and in order to conform with the logic of possible denials of determinism, we will attempt to explicate a free-willed action as one which can be explained by non-material causes.

FREE WILL CHARACTERISED

We intend to examine the notion of free will in more detail so that we can say what role it could play in a sociology (criminology). In order to do so, we shall have to engage in a discussion which some of our readers may regard as unnecessarily philosophical. However, precisely what we are asserting is that the issue is a philosophical one, and that the form of its resolution determines different forms of sociology (criminology). Sociologists or criminologists cannot altogether escape their philosophical duties. We will, however, keep this discussion as brief as possible before returning to its implications for contemporary sociological (criminological) theory.

Eysenck tells us that advocates of free will do not generally intend to assert that free will entails undetermined action: i.e., unexplainable action. He is surely right in this. An action which has no explanation is clearly something which happens to the agent rather than something which the agent initiates. Historically, what free will proponents assert appears to be that a free-willed action (i) is caused by the self of the agent and (ii) this initiation by the self is self-caused, i.e., it is not to be explained by material causes impinging upon the self. These two conditions must be fulfilled by any characterisation we attempt to give of free will.[3] The question is whether it is capable of coherent characterisation. It should be noted that the first of these conditions alone is not sufficient. As we have already mentioned, some writers seem to think that the mere fact that agents have desires, beliefs and motives and cite reasons for their actions is sufficient to deny determinism, but this misses the whole point of the determinist's case. The determinist does not deny that agents have motives, etc. He claims that these items are material causes of the actions they produce, and that they themselves are produced by material causes. Actors' meanings or whatever are thus merely material causes in a chain of material causation.

It should be clear that in seeking a characterisation of free will we are seeking a concept of causality which is not material. There are many theories of material causality, but they all seem to share a specific criterion, namely, that explanation in terms of material causes is *indefinitely regressive.* What this means is that where A is the material cause of B, A itself has a material cause, and the cause of A is just as much the cause of B as is A. There is no way of logically excluding a request for a cause some way further back in the chain as part of the explanation of B. If we fail to ask for such causes, this betokens merely a lack of interest or a lack of time. It seems to us that if there is a type of explanation which is not indefinitely regressive, then determinism is false and, furthermore, that the notion of non-indefinitely regressive causality can be used to explicate the notion of self-causality (free will).

Is there, then, a type of explanation which is not indefinitely regressive and which applies to at least some human action? We think that there is, although it would take us far beyond the confines of this paper to construct anything like a proof of our contentions. Instead, we will merely indicate what we consider to be a promising line for the free will proponent to follow. We suggest that the line is at least coherent, that the issues are clear and that upon their resolution rests the resolution of the free will/determinism debate.[4]

It is not wholly implausible to argue that some reasons for actions are not material causes of action. The issue here is not so much whether or not reasons are causes of actions, but whether, supposing we grant that they are a type of cause, they are of such a nature as to be capable of explicating the notion of self-causality (see Davidson, 1963).

Suppose that an agent does B and cites A as the reason for that action. Can we not ask why A was the reason for B, or even what materially caused A to be held as the reason for B? Certainly if it is thought that A is not an adequate reason, that it manifests some degree of irrationality on the part of the agent, we might want to know what caused the agent to act irrationally and accept the explanation of this irrationality as the explanation of B. But suppose that the reason is adequate, that is, is effective in producing the action and justifies the action, is it then relevant to ask for an explanation of the reason? It seems that if we ask for such an explanation, then we might be doing one of two things: asking either (i) for the reason to be justified, or (ii) for a material cause of the agents having that reason. In the latter case, (ii), the request does not seem to be relevant as an explanation of B. It is necessary for A to explain B that it should justify B as well as being causally effective, and a material cause of A will not show why A justifies and thus explains B. The former case, (i), is more difficult to handle. Only if we can say that some reasons are self-justifying will we be able to claim that a reason, or set of reasons, requires no explanation outside itself. What we are suggesting is that a reason which is part of a set of beliefs that are self-justifying will provide a type of explanation which is not indefinitely regressive. But are there self-justifying beliefs? This is a fundamental epistemological issue.

A basic epistemological dilemma revolves around the question: 'Does knowledge require foundations?' Some philosophers believe that knowledge of any kind is only possible if some statements can be known to be true with certainty and without appeal to any evidence beyond that which a statement itself provides. The line of reasoning is that all knowledge claims are inferences, so that we can not claim to know that something is true except on the basis of statements from which it is inferred. If these statements are inferential too, then unless some statements in the chain of inference are not inferential (not self-evidencing), then it will be impossible to know anything in the chain. Rationalists, such as Spinoza, Descartes and Leibniz, transcendentalists such as Kant and the transcendental phenomenologist Husserl would claim that there are, and indeed must be, foundations if knowledge is to be possible. But this is not a popular view nowadays (cf. Collingwood, 1940; Quine, 1973b; Kühn, 1970; Popper, 1963). Nonetheless we espouse the unpopular view, but at this point claim only that the issue has by no means been settled. Our purpose is to outline the *meaning* of free will; it is not to establish it.

If it be granted that in some circumstances reasons for actions are not material causes of actions, then we can say that agents manifest free will in their actions to the extent that those actions are performed for adequate reasons. (At the same time we allow that other subjective items, such as motives, bad reasons, etc., *may be* material causes of action.) However, is it the case that explanations in these terms are scientific? Such explanations are clearly not determinist as Hirst and Eysenck define the term. It seems equally clear that they are also not indeterministic. A very strong requirement frequently suggested for scientific explanations is that a wholly adequate explanation must provide information which would enable the explained event to be predicted. A wholly adequate explanation shows why the explained event had to occur. It seems that reason explanations do not violate this criterion. It is, of course, true that simply to know that an agent has an adequate reason for acting does not imply that the agent will act in accordance with that reason. Before we can apply a reason explanation, we require a warrant for assuming that the agent will act rationally. But assuming that we do have such a warrant, it seems that we can predict what the rational agent will do on the basis of the reasons he possesses. The only circumstance in which this will not be the case is when the agent is presented with more than one equally rational course of action. But in such a case, by definition, the agent cannot have an adequate reason for preferring one course of action to another. Thus, whatever he does cannot be explained on the basis of his reasons; which shows only that not all actions can be explained by reasons, and not that reason explanations entail indeterminacy.

But might it not be objected that what we have done merely resurrects determinism in a slightly different guise? After all, determinism is sometimes characterised as the view that whatever an agent does, given the circumstances, he could not have acted differently. As we have characterised reason explanations, and thus free will, it is wholly compatible with this viewpoint. We do not wish to deny this. We do, however, claim that it is important to distinguish what might be called the principle of 'determinatism' (or the principle of universal explainability) from the principle of determinism.

The thesis that the scientific investigator must assume that every event has an explanation ('determinatism') does not entail, without considerable argument, that we must assume that all events have material causes and that to explain them is to cite these causes (determinism). 'Determinatism' would appear to be a necessary presupposition in the scientific enterprise. Its opposite is indeterminism. As Hirst and Eysenck both claim, we can never rule out the possibility that some events have no explanation. At the same time, we can never identify an event as having no explanation. The only evidence relevant to establish that an event has no explanation is the failure to find an explanation, but this may only mean that we haven't looked hard enough. Furthermore, if we were to assume that the event indeed has no explanation, we would remove any meaning from the notion of indeterminism, for this notion rests upon the evidence of failing to find an explanation. It is not possible to fail to find what you do not seek, and you can only seek what you presuppose is findable.

The same considerations will not, however, establish a determinism as a necessary presupposition for doing science. Independent arguments are required to establish that a 'determinatism' entails determinism. It must be shown that all explanation cites material causes. Unless this can be shown, 'determinatism' and determinism must be held to be distinct. The viewpoint that the assertion of free will is in some sense nonsensical may be attributed to failing to recognise such a distinction.

We conclude at this point that the enterprise of the new criminologists to construct a partially determinist criminology can, therefore, be given an intellectually respectable defence against the onslaught of the likes of Hirst and Eysenck. But this can only be done if the meaning which is attached to partial determinism is compatible with 'determinatism'.

FREE WILL IN A SOCIOLOGICAL CONTEXT

Thus far our considerations have been very abstract. What we will now attempt to do is to give some sociological flesh to the concept of free will, guided by adherence to the principle of 'determinatism'.

For the purposes of our discussion it is convenient to divide theories of human action into four types according to the property space illustrated in the figure below.

This property space has two dimensions: determinism-free will, which we have already discussed, and the role which norms play in human action. The determinist position is not challenged by pointing out that agents make choices and endow their world with meaning. The real issue concerns the way in which we explain those beliefs, norms, etc., which the agent uses in making his choices. If what an agent wants is determined by forces outside his control, then we can hardly say that the agent's choice in terms of these wants is a free one. A genuine free will position has to find a coherent way of explicating the notion that the bases for decisions, choice, meaning, endowment, etc., are not determined by material causes.

	Social norms essential	Social norms inessential
Determinism	Normative structuralism	Non-normative structuralism
Free will	Normative actionism	Non-normative actionism

These boxes are ideal-types. While it is true that some sociological theories can be fitted neatly into one box, in other cases it is very difficult to decide in which box to locate a theory, or even whether all the propositions which characterise a theory will allow it to be located in a single box. However, these boxes are dictated by what we might call organising assumptions, and to the extent that a theory cannot be placed unequivocally in a single box it must be held to be inconsistent.

In normative structuralism the social world is composed of interrelated parts which are not individual actors as such, but social positions or statuses with their attendant roles, the roles being defined by norms which specify the conduct appropriate to the occupant of a status. In order to explain the behaviour and functioning of social groups and institutions, we need only appeal to the properties of social positions or statuses which constitute a social reality *sui generis*. Those properties of individuals which are independent of the properties of this social reality are irrelevant to its functioning. Nevertheless, it is individuals who are the incumbents of social positions. The sociologically relevant actions of an individual are performed in accordance with the norms which an individual, as an incumbent, adheres to. Different individuals may occupy different sets of social positions, may perform different roles and act in acordance with different norms. In this sense, the individual's identity is defined by his roles; he is the sum of his roles. The type of explanation appropriate to an individual's behaviour is normative explanation. In it reference to social norms occurs essentially and cannot be eliminated. Furthermore, this kind of normative explanation is distinctive. The individual does not autonomously choose his norms, but receives them in the course of a deterministic socialisation process. The roles of an individual determine his behaviour; they are not chosen by the individual. In sociology the historical position which would seem to have the closest fit with normative structuralism is the position of Talcott Parsons in *The Social System* (1970). What is usually known as 'role theory' would seem to be a parallel position. In criminology the differential association theory of Edwin Sutherland (in its more deterministic formulations) and perhaps some subcultural theories which have been developed from it, such as the work of Walter Miller, would seem to be located here. In essence, Merton's theory would also seem to be normatively structuralist, though less obviously so.

In non-normative structuralism the social world is composed of interrelated parts made up of the non-symbolic environment of individuals. The focus is upon the conditions of action, on natural and non-normative factors, external to and constraining individuals. Norms may guide individual action, and action may be defined as behaviour in accordance with norms, but here the norms are not societal givens. They are aspects of a superstructure, epiphenomena of a non-normative structure and determined by it. Normative terms, social positions and so on are not essentially involved in the explanation of action, as they may be written out by reducing them to their non-normative causes. Behaviourism charac- terises non-normative structuralism's model of man. In the final analysis, action is a response to non-normative stimuli upon the human organism. In this process individual human characteristics play no part. To be human is defined not as the ability to act on the basis of norms, beliefs, etc., but as the ability to produce human-species responses to stimuli. Varieties of non-normative structuralism may be distinguished by the particular elements which are seen to constitute the substructure. In sociological theory economism (whether vulgar Marxism or otherwise) exemplified this position. Two examples come immediately to mind in criminology: 'ecologism', which is exemplified by the tendency of some Chicagoans to portray deviant norms and life styles as epiphenomena of the structure of the inner city, and 'biologism' as, for example, the XYY chromosome theory of criminality.

For actionism, whether normative or non-normative, the social world is made up of interrelated acts of individuals rather than structures. The social world is not something wholly external to individuals which explains action and defines personal identity. To some extent individuals are capable of choosing thier own identities and of acting independently of natural and social determination. The degree of autonomy which the individual has is not autonomy in relation to the social world alone. The autonomous self is not the result of biological and pysical determination independent of social factors. If it were, there would be no real autonomy and we would be dealing with a version of structuralism. Actionism accords the individual a degree of free will, whereas structuralism is wholly deterministic. As in normative structuralism, norms and other symbolic elements are the keys to the explanation of action, but the relevant norms are not primarily properties of social groups and structures but of individuals. Individuals are capable of playing roles which they do not merely receive in a socialisation process but which they autonomously choose and even, perhaps, create. To some extent, properties of individuals explain properties of the social world. Inasmuch as actionism involves an essential reference to norms, meanings, etc., the type of explanation involved is different from that which characterises normative structuralism. Norms are not given to the individual in ways which he is unable to alter or resist.

Actionism is not, however, the view that individuals are never deter- mined or constrained. It is merely the view that there is some behaviour to which the actionist scheme applies. Because actionism is defined by a principle of *partial* determinism, it may appeal to structuralist models in certain circumstances. Structuralism, however, characterised as it is by a principle of total determinism, can find no room for actionist modes of explanation.

The difference between normative actionism and non-normative actionism is fairly easy to state but rather difficult to explain, and the difference will occupy us in the next section. Briefly, non-normative actionism regards norms and symbols as products of meaning-endowing acts of individuals, acts which themselves are not, in the final analysis, governed by norms or symbols. On the other hand, normative actionism regards those norms which are involved in adequate reasons for action, i.e. those norms adherence to which endows action with free will, as being in some sense independent of individuals, social structures or indeed anything with a spatio-temporal location. These norms define the individuals who possess them as individuals of the class of members possessing free will. The norms themselves are defined by an abstract calculus of rationality.

Before we turn to making sense of this rather epigrammatic formulation, we must briefly consider who are the actionists. Clear examples in sociological theory are Max Weber, Herbert Blumer and Erving Goffman. George Herbert Mead's position is more ambivalent; it is not at all clear that his work is not subject to a behaviourist interpretation. In criminology some of the new criminologists will be located here and, in addition to Goffman, most other interactionists. However, interactionism is such an umbrella description that non-actionist formulations seem possible.[5]

NORMATIVE ACTIONISM AND NON-NORMATIVE ACTIONISM

We have suggested that the acceptance of non-materially causal reason explanations is what differentiates actionists from structuralists. The actionist maintains that agents have free will to the extent that they act in accordance with their autonomous reasons for action. What, however, is a rational action? Weber distinguished two classes of rational action *Wertrationalität* (substantive rationality) and *Zweckrationalität* (instrumental rationality). A substantively rational action is one which is performed because the action itself represents a desirable end, and instrumentally rational action is one in which the actor adopts means to achieve desired ends. Initially we may accept a definition of rational action as instrumentally rational action, although it should be clear that if an objective concept of rationality is adopted (see below) then instrumental rationality may depend upon substantive rationality.

What basis does an actor have for acting in an instrumentally rational manner? Obviously the beliefs he has about the situation he is in, about the situation he wishes to achieve and about the means by which he can translate one set of circumstances into another. Within the framework of instrumentally rational action we can construct different definitions of rational action by placing different epistemic requirements upon this set of beliefs. Least stringently we may require no more than that the actor believes that he is in a situation, and believes that the means he will adopt will achieve a situation which he desires. We require that none of his beliefs, whether normative or non-normative, be either true or rational. In other words, his beliefs about his situation and proposed means may be false and crazy, and the question of whether the ends he desires are in some sense objectively desirable never arises. (The problem of how we may decide whether a belief is true or rational need not concern us here.) In brief, we place no more restrictions on the concept of a rational action than upon that of an instrumental action. If we were to do this, we would be adopting what we shall call the 'subjective concept of rational action'. Those deviancy theorists who claim that an action is rational if it is reasonable from the deviant's point of view, and who would resist any suggestion that the investigator may challenge this presumption, adopt this subjective concept.

On the other hand, we may require one or more of the actors' beliefs to be true or rational, additionally requiring that truth and rationality be independent of what actors happen to regard as true or rational; and, in the extreme case, that all beliefs, both normative and non-normative, be both true and rational. The different requirements we impose within this range will selectively distinguish different concepts of objectively rational action.

It will transpire that a non-normative actionist must adopt the subjective concept of rationality, and that a normative actionist must adopt some objective concept of rationality, most plausibly the requirement that all beliefs be rational without having to be true as well.

The difference between normative and non-normative actionism can be explicated by attending more carefully to the notion of autonomy from social determination which the idea of free will requires.

It is important to note that there is no logical necessity for the actionist to hold that actions, or the norms which prescribe them, cannot be materially caused. Although a norm which has been materially caused can be given a materially causal explanation, it does not automatically follow that it cannot be given some other kind of explanation as well. However, some people may find the notion that their actions can be materially caused, and yet they may perform these actions with a free will, rather hard to accept. Such persons will require that agents who act with free will are not materially caused (by their social positions or whatever) to hold the norms or to perform the consequential actions which they do. They will claim that the norms of a rational action cannot be given in a materially causal manner. But let us suppose that an actor is brought up in a 'rational' society (i.e. a society which has social positions which prescribe only 'rational' norms). No sociologist would deny that agents very often internalise norms from their social positions whilst at the same time not rationally choosing to accept them. Thus we must allow the possibility that in a 'rational' society, as described, some people may internalise norms which they have been materially caused to have. However, it follows from this that if we hold that norms of a 'rational' action cannot be given materially causally, then we must hold that in order to act with a free will an agent must reject norms which society 'pressures' him to hold, even if they are 'rational' norms. It begins to look as if the free man can only assert his freedom by acting 'irrationally' when society requires him to act 'rationally'. But such a position threatens to be fatal to the determinating status of reason explanation. In some circumstances we will not be able to predict what the rational man will do, since to do the 'rational' thing is simply to do what the 'rational' society does not require, and whereas there is only one way of being rational, there are any number of ways of being irrational. The free man will cease to be a fit subject for science. More obviously still, by implying that free will requires 'irrationality', this position seems to abdicate its intention to explicate free will in terms of rationality.

However, there is a first line of defence for those who hold this position. We can imagine the reply: 'This whole *coup de grâce* rests on importing into the argument an authoritarian, external concept of rationality. It is simply not true that the free man may be driven to being irrational, since the only proper description of a rational action is what the free man decides to do in terms of his *own* criteria of rationality. It is simply improper in the above paragraphs to have assumed that a society which could conflict with the free agent was a rational society.' This reply shows that if autonomy requires the absence of material causes, then a subjective concept of rational action must be adopted. This characterisation of autonomy we ascribe to non-normative actionism. Non-normative actionism uses the

source of norms as the criterion of autonomy. If norms come from th
agent, and only from the agent, then those norms are freely chosen. If the
come from anywhere else, then they are not.

Suppose, however, that we find this relativism too high a price to pay.
there any other way in which we can conceive of autonomy in order t
remain actionists? If we are prepared to assert that there are objectiv
criteria of rationality, then provided that we substitute a validation
criterion for a source of norm criterion, there does appear to be a way.

Let us return to our hypothetical supposition of a person growing up in
rational society. This time, however, we will not only suppose that all th
norms which people are encouraged to have are rational, but also th.
during the process of socialisation society's norms have a 100 per cen
infection rate. In such a society we could say that all persons who act i
accordance with their norms do the rational thing. However, it would ne
follow that they were rational actors, or that they were acting with fre
will. Their norms are rational, but their adherence to them is not. Wha
would be required to convert an actor who merely has rational norms int
a rational actor is that he carry out a critique of his norms (using th
correct epistemology). Since the norms are rational, the carrying out c
such a critique would lead the critic to the conclusion that his norms wer
rational. His behaviour would not alter, but in the process of his critica
activity he would have converted a determined acceptance into a free
willed acceptance. The fact that he would continue to adhere to hi
previous norms is a contingent feature of the rationality of the norms. Ha
they not been rational, the critical process would have led to their reje
tion. The critical process gives the agent free will because he could an
would have rejected the norms had they not been rational.

In this account the meaning given to autonomy rests upon the rational
ty or epistemic status of the norms, and upon an actor's ability to carr
out a critique on the basis of criteria which simply are *the* criteria c
critique. As a result, reference to these norms must occur essentially in th
explanation of rational action, and cannot be reduced by claiming that th
norms and criteria are creations of actors. This is why we designate thi
option as characterising normative actionism. Whereas non-normativ
actionism reduces norms of the free agent to spontaneous acts of the fre
ego, normative actionism characterises the free ego as the possessor c
rational norms and the correct criteria for assessing them, regardless c
how the free ego may have acquired these norms and this ability.[6]

*

THE PARTIAL DETERMINISM IN *BECOMING DEVIANT* AND *THE NEW CRIMINOLOGY*

We have explicated the options for a denial of determinism as being three; namely, some form of partial indeterminism, normative actionism and non-normative actionism. We have concentrated upon the latter two quite simply because we wish to retain a scientific status for criminology (or any study of human behaviour). We must now decide which option is preferred by Matza and Taylor, Walton and Young. Our implicit claim is that if there is any substance to their repudiation of determinism, then they must adopt some form of the three positions we have mentioned.

In the case of Matza classification is exceptionally difficult. At several points in *Becoming Deviant* Matza suggests that he wishes to be a partial indeterminist. Indeed, it is one of the main themes of his book that explanation, in a sense which implies predictability, is incompatible with 'appreciation', and only by adopting a stance of 'appreciation' can we be faithful to man's nature. Furthermore, Matza quite explicitly repudiates both determinism and a free will position. We can see no other option but indeterminism.

> To recognise and appreciate the meaning of being willing is by no means to assert the existence of a free will. Indeed, it is the very opposite. The logic of one's past, the human agencies in one's situation are certainly real. They are the grounding for the conduct of will. Free will, as the phrase itself implies, takes will out of context, converting it inexorably into an abstraction of as little use as any other. (Matza, 1969, p. 116)
>
> The misconception of man as object oscillated between two major forms: the first radical, the second heuristic. In the first, man *was* object. In the second, scientists deemed it heuristic merely to act *as if* man were object. In both views, however, a similar consequence appeared. Irrespective of whether man was object or merely heuristically treated as object, the terms of analysis were set in a fashion that minimised man's causal capacity, his activity, his tendency to reflect on himself and his setting, and his periodic struggles to transcend rather than succumb to the circumstances that allegedly shaped and constrained him . . . (For a distinction between these different versions of determinism, hard and soft, see my *Delinquency and Drift* (New York: John Wiley & Sons, Inc., 1964), Chapter 1, pp. 1-32). In that discussion I more or less settled on a position of soft determinism. I suppose the present discussion moves even further away from an acceptance of any sort of determinism.) (Matza, 1969, p. 7)

But, as we have argued elsewhere (Beyleveld and Wiles, 1975),[7] Matza's

positions are rarely unambivalent. At times he would appear to accept t
explanatory endeavour:

> Given the understandable dominance of the correctional perspective
> the study of deviation, concern with the nuances and character of t
> phenomenon itself seemed idle, literary or even romantic. But whatev
> the reasons for the prominence of etiology and however we judge th
> expenditure of ingenuity, few would challenge its intrinsic legitimacy
> worth. Certainly I would not, though I do think that we have given it to
> much emphasis. (Matza, 1969, p. 87)

We do not want to labour an exegesis of Matza too far. But whatev
position Matza does espouse, it is not at all clear what it is, and indeed v
would challenge anyone exegetically to provide a coherent analytic
position. What we can be sure of is that such a position will not I
normatively actionist.

We can find no evidence for attributing indeterminism to Taylo
Walton and Young. Their position is fairly clearly actionist:

> An adequate social theory of deviance would need to be able to expla
> the relationship between beliefs and action, between the optimu
> 'rationality' that men have chosen and the behaviour they actually car
> through. . . . The formal requirement at this level . . . is for a
> explanation of the ways in which the actual acts of men are explicable i
> terms of the rationality of choice or the constraints on choice at th
> point of precipitation into action. (Taylor et al, 1973a, pp. 271-2)

Such a statement, however, is neutral as between normative and no
normative actionism. Whether it is the one or the other depends upo
whether an objective or subjective concept of rationality is adopted. N
explicit treatment of this matter is to be found in *The New Criminolog*
The best indication of a choice which is to be found is the acceptance c
Thomas Kühn's thesis of the incommensurability of paradigms (Taylor e
al, 1973a, p. 26). This thesis is extremely difficult to reconcile with a
objective concept of rationality. Thus, if an attribution must be made, w
would suggest that Taylor, Walton and Young are committed to a no
normative actionism.[8]

We are suggesting that if a specification of the partial determinist
involved in *Becoming Deviant* or *The New Criminology* is requested, w
are in a much better position to say what it is not than to say what it is. It i
clear to us only that neither book adopts an unequivocal normativ
actionism and, furthermore, that the semblance of agreement between th
two which we highlighted at the beginning of our essay is only superficia
Our most informed guess is that Matza wishes to be an indeterminist

whereas Taylor, Walton and Young wish to be non-normative actionists, but it is only a guess.[9]

ACTIONISM AND PROGRAMMATIC SOCIOLOGY

New criminologists not only want to assert partial determinism, they also wish to claim that a sociological theory entails political commitments. The link between sociological theory and political action is effected by a model of man. The task of sociological theory is to portray accurately the nature of man, to describe human needs and potentials and to analyse those conditions which obstruct their realisation. Conceptually related to a view of human needs and potentials is a view of the society in which these are capable of realisation. Descriptions of man's nature are not neutral, and acceptance of any description entails a commitment to bringing about those conditions which will enable man's essential nature to become empirical reality.

If this is the structure of the logic of sociological theory as social praxis, we must ask which vision of the Good Society is dictated by different forms of partial determinism. Indeed, we must also ask whether any partial determinism is compatible with such a logic.

It should be fairly clear that indeterminism, at least, is incompatible with the logic. If analysis of the social structure is to guide praxis, then we must surely be able to predict the consequences of our actions on the basis of our analysis. A rational praxis is not merely a Utopian ideal, it is activity, the end of which has a realistic chance of achievement. Whatever the details of the relationship between the individual and society, it can hardly be denied that what individuals do has an impact upon the social structure. If, in the final analysis, actions of individuals are indeterminate, there can be no warrant for assuming that a praxis based upon social analysis will have an intended outcome. Any expectation that it will is sheer romanticism.

Actionism assigns human beings an essence. What distinguishes man from other animals and constitutes the distinctively human potential is man's capacity to act with free will. Since the Good Society is the society which maximises the realisation of human potentials, the Good Society is that society which maximises the realisation of free will. The Good Society for the non-normative actionist would have to place no constraints whatsoever on the free ego's capacity to act as it wishes. Any aspect of a society which presented norms of any kind would carry with it the danger of these norms acting causally on the actor through socialisation — and to the extent that this occurred, the actor's freedom would be curtailed. Law would not so much be unnecessary: its very existence would be dangerous to freedom. Education would certainly be subversive of freedom. The free ego's demands and satisfactions must be without constraint: no principle or criterion can stand over and above them. The rational society is the society of utterly free egos. The political promise of non-normative actionism is anarchism.

In its analysis of the present, unfree society, non-normative actionism commits the man who would seek the Good Society to permanent deviance against all and every rule and norm. The political actor for the non-normative actionist must be deviant, and all deviant acts, if the actor has acted in accordance with his beliefs (regardless of the status of those beliefs), are the acts of a free and rational man. But what would be the implications, assuming it to be possible, of constructing a society which would enable men to act in this manner? There would seem to be two possibilities. We may either assume, with Hobbes, that a 'war of all against all' would ensue or, with Rousseau, that, freed from all constraints, men would realise an essentially uncorrupted nature. We doubt that the Hobbesian assumption represents anyone's picture of the Good Society. Thus the non-normative actionist must share Rousseau's faith. But is it anything more than merely a faith? Can it be said to be an implication of non-normative actionism's model of man? It might just be possible that, left to their own devices, men would arrange themselves into an anarchic consensus. But there can be no reason for expecting it, and we need to be able to predict it if non-normative actionism is to conform to the logic of sociological theory as social praxis.

The political vision displayed at the end of *The New Criminology* seems to depend on exactly this kind of faith.

> Crime is ever and always that behaviour seen to be problematic within the framework of those (existing) social arrangements: for crime to be abolished, then, those social arrangements themselves must also be subject to fundamental social change ... The task is to create a society in which the facts of human diversity, whether personal, organic or social, are not subject to the power to criminalise. (Taylor et al, 1973a, p. 282)

The Good Society for the normative actionist is very different. For the normative actionist freedom consists in the actor doing what he rationally wants. It is still correct to say that a man is free when he does what he wants to do, but the sense of the concept 'man' does not have the sense it carries in everyday discourse, namely, the desires of the empirical ego given to us by our senses. A man only really wants what he rationally wants. When he does not want something rationally, the ground of his want is not the self, but whatever determines the self. In fact, in such a case the *man* is not doing any wanting at all. The concept of a 'man' for the normative actionist is the concept of a transcendental ego. Men have selves only to the extent that they are rational, and free action is rational action. In the Good Society structural norms are rational norms. Structures impose only rational wants and options and so there should be no conflict between determined action and rational action.

The political promise of normative actionism, therefore, is the Utopia of collective responsibility guided by reason.

For the normative actionist the present society is unfree to the extent that it is irrational. The man who wishes to be free is committed to accepting law and norms in the degree that they are rational. His search for freedom commits him to deviance only against laws or norms which are irrational. In the irrational society the political actor will be deviant in certain situations. The deviant, therefore, is a political actor (one whose deviance is directed to creating or maintaining the Good Society) to the extent that he can give good reasons for his deviance which satisfy objective criteria of rationality.

We would suggest that if the new criminologists really want to construct a programmatic sociology, then they will have to overcome their distaste for objective or 'absolutist' conceptions of truth and rationality. Their first task must be to provide an elaborate description of the good and rational society which can be seen to be good and rational by all because it *is* the rational society. They will need to espouse an epistemology which makes such a conception possible.

CONCLUSIONS

We have attempted to show that a coherent denial of determinism which has programmatic implications for social praxis is possible, but that the new criminologies have conducted their critiques in too shallow a manner. If they have had difficulty in specifying their vision of the Good Society, we should not find this too surprising. An unclear conception of the nature of human potentials is unlikely to yield a clear conception of the type of society capable of realising them.

Lest our task be misunderstood, it is perhaps wise to specify what we have not attempted and the questions we have sidestepped.

We have assumed throughout that metaphysics is respectable and th positivism, logical or otherwise, has not laid it to rest. We have a assumed that although it may be true that evaluative assertions can not derived from factual ones, it is nevertheless the case that if it is accept that it is permissible to make evaluation, then the acceptance of a model man will dictate which evaluations should be made. Given the facts, need not do anything, but once it is accepted that we are going to something, i.e. attempt to make programmatic statements about the Go Society, then not any vision of the Good Society will be compatible wi those facts. In the context of this paper we can do no more than declare o predilections.

We have provided no account of the way in which to establish tho beliefs and actions which are objectively rational. We do, however, belie that it is possible to do so, and that the necessary criteria are implicit with a rationalist epistemology (cf. Hollis, 1977; Beyleveld, 1975). Neith have we provided a list of human needs and potentials. Finally, we have n attempted to use our explicit or implicit analysis to conduct a critiqu within the concrete social context in which actual choices and decisio are made, and in which actors grow into rational beings or find the rationality hampered, destroyed or thwarted.

If the line which we have pursued is accepted, then there are battles to waged on several fronts. The epistemological task is to secure a strate against empiricist and pragmatist invasions.[10] The ontological task is develop an account of human potentials and a detailed vision of the Go Society. The sociologist's role is to perform the critique of existing socie which will specify means for the attainment of Utopia. Everyman's du will be to use this analysis for social praxis.

NOTES

1. An earlier version of this paper was presented at the Cambridge Criminolog Conference in July 1977. We are grateful for comments from John Paley, Stanle Cohen, Paul Rock and John Wood. Some parts owe much to the influence of Brya Hedding and Martin Hollis. Our treatment of theories as actionist or structuralis derives in part from Alan Dawe's article, 'The Two Sociologies' (1970). Howeve none of the above-mentioned is responsible for the use we have made of the guidance.
2. Respectively, e.g. Richard Quinney, Austin Turk and W. J. Chambliss; Ian Taylo Paul Walton and Jock Young; David Matza, Jack Douglas; Mike Phillipson an Maurice Roche. No doubt the reader can supply his own favourite examples.
3. In order to avoid confusion it must be emphasised that throughout this discussio when we refer to 'free action' or 'the expression of a free will', we do not mea

simply to refer to action which is what an agent merely wants to do, that is, to unconstrained action. We do not regard action in accordance with an agent's contingent wants as genuinely free action if the agent has not chosen those wants or what has led up to the having of them.

4. For further discussion of this, see Hollis (1977) and Beyleveld (1975), ch. 7.

5. For example, if we consider labelling theory, then depending on how we interpret it, we may regard it as either actionist or structuralist. If labelling theory is not regarded as a global perspective or theory, but instead as referring to a process which may or may not occur as a result of societal reaction to deviance (namely, the process of deviance amplification or secondary deviation), then it would seem to be compatible with actionism. This will be so whether or not the actual process is a deterministic or non-deterministic one. Actionism, to reiterate, can allow some processes to be determined by material causes. On the other hand, if the process is treated as a global theory, as it is when labelling theory is held to be incompatible with deterrence theory, then labelling theory is clearly structuralist. Gibbs (1976) claims that labelling theory predicts that sanctions will lead to more deviance, whereas deterrence theory predicts the opposite. However, this will only be so if the outcomes of sanctions are independent of any individual self-determination.

6. The normative actionist really conceives of the human ego in two ways. To the extent that a human being does not act rationally, this behaviour indicates an empirical ego, i.e. an ego which can be explained in a wholly deterministic manner. But to the extent that a human being acts in a rational manner, this behaviour indicates a transcendental ego. Only in so far as a human being possesses (is) a transcendental ego would we say that that human being is a free self or *person*. Being a person (transcendental ego) is distinct from having a personality (possessing individualising characteristics within the class *homo sapiens*). It should further be noted that we envisage no necessary connection between the concept of a transcendental ego and the concept of an immortal soul. It is also not clear that a transcendental ego, or better, the possession of a transcendental consciousness, entails the existence of a mind 'stuff' or substance. Furthermore, the idea of a transcendental ego is wholly compatible with a developmental psychology: one in which the transcendental ego is viewed as emergent upon, or within, purely physical being. What we do envisage, however, is that between the polar contingencies of emergence and total destruction, the transcendental ego is impervious to physical events except in so far as it views these events as determining the context within which it must make choices. The concept of such a limited enclosure may seem alien to social or human science. We suggest, however, that it is shared by Piaget's concept of a stage of cognitive development.

7. We neglected the possibility that Matza might wish to be an indeterminist in our discussion of *Becoming Deviant* in our article 'Man and Method in David Matza's *Becoming Deviant*' (1975). We are grateful to John Paley of the University of Lancaster for pointing this deficiency out to us in private correspondence.

8. This attribution becomes more plausible if we examine Ian Taylor and Paul Walton's 'Values in Deviancy Theory and Society' (1970), pp. 362-4. There we are quite explicitly told that what it means to be rational is what it is rational to do from the agent's point of view.

9. Without providing any evidence here we would suggest that the other new criminologies, whatever their form of partial determinism, are least plausibly to be treated as normatively actionist.

10. One of us has argued (see Beyleveld, 1975) that there are basically only three strategies within the theory of knowledge — rationalism, empiricism and pragmatism. Although many epistemological works display propositions which cut across these divides, this only shows that most epistemological works are internally

inconsistent. Some writers, notably Marxists such as Jürgen Habermas and Paul Q. Hirst, object to this sort of trichotomy and claim that Marxism presents a fourth option. We consider, however, that the vaunted fourth option is merely an inconsistent mix of the elements of the trichotomy. It might be objected that this is an inevitable conclusion within 'bourgeois modes of thought': Marxism can only be adequately comprehended by transcending non-dialectical thinking. This line of attack has been extended to the point at which the need for epistemology has been totally denied (e.g. in the later work of Hirst). Our reply to all this is quite simple. If Marxism has incommensurable relations with 'bourgeois epistemologies', then it cannot conflict with them. If it does conflict with them, it must be possible to state the conflict fairly in both languages. As for denying the necessity for epistemology, it should be obvious that because of the nature of an epistemological thesis, the very denial of one must itself be an epistemological thesis. It makes one realise why Marx himself was once forced to exclaim:'*Je ne suis pas un Marxist.*' Actually, we are not aware that Marx presented any systematic epistemological theory. But this does not mean that epistemology is irrelevant to Marxism. Marx did make systematic ontological, sociological and social claims. Whether he was right or not will depend upon whether these assertions survive epistemological critique. Some of the attempts to construct a Marxist epistemology seem to us to manifest a strategy not uncommon among mystics — claim that your faith is incommensurable with anything which might attack it and, of course, you won't need to defend it. Never mind that the result is mysticism, which risks confronting all the problems of meaning which attach to it. Ironically, such strategies will run counter to any socialist attempt to construct the Good Society.

Vocabularies, Rhetorics and Grammar: Problems in the Sociology of Motivation [1]

Laurie Taylor

The role of the sociology of motivation within deviance theory has been to provide a social psychological perspective which reduces analytic dependence upon psychologistic constructs (drives, instincts, internal states) and inhibits recourse to dubiously grounded notions of 'value systems' and 'ideologies'. It is far from being an autonomous approach and it is certainly not intended that this critical review of the topic should do anything to extend its claims or increase its isolation from closely related works. It is best regarded as an ethnographic technique, a set of suggestions for the treatment of the 'motivational elements' which regularly appear within the verbalisations of specific groups and individuals. The 'vocabularies of motive' which are assembled from such discrete verbalisations are viewed as valuable cultural resources, in that they are seen as critically involved in inducing action and in remedying its effects upon self and others. They are also valuable resources in that their differential distribution within society means that certain groups will be able to draw upon a wide range of 'reasons' to justify their behaviour, while others will either have to negotiate in order to be allowed 'reasons', or passively accept their own behaviour as being without proper reason (irrational, determined) and therefore as indicative of some form of moral unworthiness (madness, psychopathy).

This paper will not concentrate, however, entirely upon the field of deviance. The sociology of motivation was not initially developed in relation to this topic and, indeed, it will be argued that its contemporary restriction to this area may serve to obscure some of its strengths. However, most of the examples will necessarily come from the field and also primarily from sociologists of deviance working within this country — for it seems to be in Britain in recent years that this perspective has received its most explicit (and arguably its most sophisticated) treatment.

There were a number of ways in which this review might have been structured, but it was eventually decided to use C. Wright Mills's original papers (1940 and 1954) as a framework for discussion, in that these not only articulated the field most precisely, but also contained the seeds of many of the ambiguities and contradictions which emerged in later work.

INTERNAL MOTIVES AND LINGUAL FORMS

One of the first things that Mills sets out to achieve is a clear distinction between a sociology of motivation and the traditional psychological and biological search for a set of distinctive 'internal' motives. This distinction initially appears to rest upon an analytical dismissal of the whole psycho-biological endeavour, upon the claim that there are no such elements as internal motives and that therefore a sociological approach to motivation is not an alternative perspective on the subject, but the only valid way in which the subject can be comprehended. In his 1940 paper, for example, he addresses the idea that 'real' motives are in some way biological, and that therefore the 'lingual forms' with which the sociology of motivation must work are only rationalisations:

> The quest for 'real motives' suppositiously set over against 'mere rationalisations' is often informed by a metaphysical view that the 'real' motives are in some way biological. Accompanying such quests for something more real and back of rationalisation is the view held by many sociologists that language is an external manifestation or concomitant of something prior, more genuine, and 'deep in the individual' (Mills, 1940, p. 908)

Sociologists who take this view are likely, he argues, to claim that human statements about their motives provide us at best with an opportunity to 'infer' their real motives. Mills dismisses any such attempts to discover inner springs to action from an examination of the actors' verbalisations:

> . . . What *could we possibly* so infer. Of precisely *what* is verbalisation symptomatic? We cannot *infer* physiological processes from lingual phenomena. *All we can infer and empirically check is another verbalisation of the agent's which we believe was orienting and controlling behaviour at the time the act was performed.* The only social items that can 'lie deeper' are other lingual forms. The 'Real Attitude or Motive' is not something different in kind from the verbalisation or the 'opinion'.

They turn out to be only relatively and temporally different (my emphasis). (Mills, 1940, p. 908)

This clear statement about the limits or inference is important. For although Mills concentrates upon our inability to infer 'physiological processes from lingual phenomena', the emphasised passage also makes it evident that we can have no other motivational concern than the actual verbalisations made by the agent. In other words, this is a rejection of any attempt to impose particular mentalistic constructs upon the actor on the basis of his statements. The only alternative to the verbalisation under examination is another verbalisation which might have been more closely connected with the activity. This does not mean, however, that there is nothing that can be 'inferred' from the verbalised motive: 'Within the perspective under consideration, the verbalised motive is not used as an index of something in the individual but as *a basis of inference for a typical vocabulary of motives of a situated action*' (emphasis in original) (Mills, 1940, p. 910).

The proper research task, then, is the gradual establishment of the set of verbalised motives which typically accompany actions occurring in specified situations. Unfortunately, Mills, at this critical point, becomes somewhat unhelpful about the ways in which such situations might be characterised. At times, for example, he starts to assemble typical constellations of motives for entire historical periods; for capitalism, for feudalism. But at others he concentrates more narrowly upon the sets of motives which might inform business activity within two phases of capitalism: 'The "profits motive" of classical economics may be treated as an ideal-typical vocabulary of motives for delimited economic situations and behaviours. For late phases of monopolistic and regulated capitalism, this type requires modification; the profit and commercial vocabularies have acquired other ingredients' (Mills, 1940, p. 908).

There are even more specific references to the vocabularies which might typically characterise certain class and status groups, and finally to the motives which might inform such discrete activities as marriage in contemporary society. Now, it is probably unreasonable to expect Mills to provide clear-cut examples of distinctive situated actions together with their ideal-typical vocabularies of motives at this early theoretical stage. Nevertheless, his somewhat sweeping and rather unilluminating references to historical and institutional vocabularies of motives may have led later researchers to ignore such matters and turn their attention instead to less formal structures, to the interactional and 'causal' features of his formulation which promised more immediate empirical pay-off.[1]

Certainly some of the more general typifications resemble the rather unhelpful lists of 'dominant societal values' which occasionally decorate certain functionalist texts. Some analytic purchase only seems to be regained within these sections when Mills discusses the articulation and ironic overlap of different sets of motives within capitalist society.

REAL MOTIVES

It does seem, then, that Mills's stress upon the research task of producing ideal-typical vocabularies of motives for situated actions is incompatible with any search for 'real motives'. There *are* only lingual forms and whether some of these are to be regarded as 'more real' than others appears to depend not upon their relationship to inner states but rather upon their situational typicality. If large numbers of people within a specified group produce particular motivational accounts in particular situations, then we may presumably refer to these as the 'real' motives, for they are the verbalisations which actually influence conduct, which persuade people to act or not to act.

This situational pragmatism allows no place for any considerations of truth or sincerity. Verbalisations are real because they are socially efficacious: they are not, therefore, less real if they happen to be untrue: 'Of course, since motives are communicated, they may be lies; but, this must be proved. Verbalisations are not lies merely because they are socially efficacious. I am here concerned more with the social function of pronounced motives, than with the sincerity of those pronouncing them' (Mills, 1940, p. 908). As long as we concentrate on these features of Mills's work — that is, upon the external, observable features of vocabularies of motive, their typicality and their relative social efficaciousness — then we can regard Mills as working along within a very similar tradition to that of Kenneth Burke.[2] He is, that is to say, treating the verbalisation of motives as an aspect of rhetoric, as a part of public attempts to persuade oneself or others to act in a particular manner. Undoubtedly Burke's approach is much less specific than Mills's. He is seeking to write 'a philosophy of rhetoric', and therefore examines other matters than the explicit public verbalisation of motives as a means of inducing action. He is not just interested, for example, in those situations where actions are urged upon us by reference to such obvious motives as patriotism and economic self-interest, but also in subtler attempts at attitude change. 'All told, persuasion ranges from the bluntest quest of advantage, as in sales promotion or propaganda, through courtship, social etiquette, education, and the sermon, to a "pure form" that delights in the process of appeal for itself alone, without ulterior purpose' (Burke, 1950, p. xiv).[3]

Attempts to arouse particular human motives, argues Burke, may not always appear in an obviously 'motivational' form. There are so many forms of persuasion that we need a 'version of human motives equal to the depths at which the ways of persuasion (appeal, communication, "justification") . . . really operate' (Burke, 1950, p. 127).

But, overall, this elaboration of the linguistic (or rhetorical) approach to motives in no way represents an analytic shift from the Mills position as we have so far described it. Indeed, at times there is an almost complete overlap between their concerns. Mills, for example, in his quest for typical vocabularies of motive which are historically and societally specific, attempts to describe the nature of pecuniary motives in the American social structure:

> Due to the great weight which the economic order has in the American social structure, pecuniary motives tend to form a sort of common denominator of many other roles and motives. Other vocabularies are treated as shams, facades and 'rationalisation', and the 'wise guy' knows that *the real* motive is the desire for money which, as is commonly said, may not be everything but is almost everything. (Gerth and Mills, 1954, p. 123)

Whereas Burke (in the course of commenting upon Bentham's discussion of rhetoric) complements Mills by providing a sophisticated elaboration of the rhetoric of this 'common economic denominator' by pointing to the way in which the apparently 'neutral vocabulary' of the economic world (for example, the terminology of investment) may nevertheless serve as a powerful inducement to action:

> . . . since purposes indigenous to the monetary rationale are so thoroughly built into the productive and distributive system as in ours, a relatively high proportion of interest in purely 'neutral' terminologies of motives can be consistent with equally intense ambition. For however 'neutral' a terminology may be, it can function as rhetorical inducement to action in so far as it can in any way by used for monetary advantage.
> In fact 'neutralisation' may often serve but to eliminate, as far as it is humanly possible, the various censorial weightings that go with the many different philosophic, religious, social, political and personal outlooks extrinsic to the monetary motive. (Burke, 1950, p. 96)

Although Burke and Mills share a common concern with characterising the motivational rhetoric of different institutional orders, it is often Burke who is more sensitive to the ironic, multi-layered aspects of the problem. Mills, for example, is inclined to sweep aside certain rhetorical appeals on the simple grounds that they are dissonant with contemporary motivational constructs: '. . . individuals are sceptical of Rockefeller's avowed religious motives for his business conduct because such motives are not *now* terms of the vocabulary conventionally and prominently accompanying situations of business enterprise' (Mills, 1940, p. 910); and 'A medieval monk writes that he gave food to a poor but pretty woman because it was "for the glory of God and the eternal salvation of his soul". Why do we tend to question him and impute sexual motives? Because sex is an influential and widespread motive in our society and time' (Mills, 1940, p. 910).

Burke, on the other hand, has a more sophisticated awareness that religious, philosophical, patriotic, etc., motives are still powerful means of persuasion within society, and can be rhetorically effective even when embedded within quite dissonant settings:

> The same newspapers that are run for money, that get their income by advertising goods sold for money, that are read by people on their way to and from the place where they work for money, and that distribute accounts of political, economic and social events bearing upon money (high among them, news of the crimes against property) — these same papers, in their more edified moments, will talk rather of 'liberty', 'dignity of the individual', 'Western man', 'Christian civilisation', 'democracy' and the like, as the motives impelling at least *our* people and *our* government, and to a lesser extent the 'nations' that 'we' want as allies, but not the small ruling class, or clique, that dominates countries with which 'we' are at odds. (Burke, 1950, p. 108)

Burke provides, then, a welcome extension to Mills's rhetorical concerns. He introduces a wider range of possible motives and does much to establish their specific interplay and overlap within various rhetorics. And although his concern with attitudinal change as well as with the inducement of activity means that he is less concerned than Mills with specifying precise verbalisations as the basis for constructing typical rhetorics, his emphasis upon rhetoric as active persuasion allows him to avoid any simplistic 'inventorising' of possible motives.[4] (Indeed, he actually categorises such an activity as an example of psychological rhetoric!) His emphasis upon the range of motives which may be employed and upon the ways in which these are articulated with other rhetorics is also directly in line with Mills's recommendations for the construction of typical constellations by inference from specific verbalisations.[5]

It is not just Burke's sensitivity to the available range of rhetorical inducements, not just his subtle elaboration of the range of many motives which might be aroused, which makes him a welcome complement to Mills. It is also his continual emphasis upon the actual activity of rhetorical persuasion, upon the variety of strategies and tactics which can be employed in different settings: '. . . an act of persuasion is affected by the character of the scene in which it takes place and of the agents to whom it is addressed. The same rhetorical act could vary in its effectiveness according to shifts in the situation or in the attitude of audiences' (Burke, 1950, p. 62).

Neither is his account of motivational rhetoric limited to mere verbalisations; it extends to other persuasive settings: '. . . we could observe that even the medical equipment of a doctor's office is not to be judged purely for its diagnostic usefulness, but also has a function in the rhetoric of medicine. Whatever it is as apparatus, it also appeals as imagery' (Burke, 1950, p. 171).[6]

PSYCHOLOGICAL REGRESSION IN MILLS

Examples of Burke's analysis of rhetoric have been given here to add some resonance to Mills's formulations, to show the way in which his original insights might have been developed. Of course, Burke was involved in creating a philosophy of rhetoric, with elucidating its range and traditional principles, with establishing its particular presence within philosophy, art and religion, while Mills was more concerned with sociological problems about the relationship of particular vocabularies of motives to typical social-historical situations and institutions. And although Mills's examples of motivational inducement are often attitudinal, he explicitly directs his analysis far more towards 'action' than does Burke. But both share a recognition of 'motivational rhetoric' as a fundamental feature of social life, a realisation that particular collectivities of motives do not just characterise specific situations, groups and institutions but actually propel them[7] and legitimate their activity, and an awareness that there are distinctive strategies and tactics which allow the manipulation of such motivational elements.

Unfortunately the development of Mills's concerns along these promising rhetorical lines was inhibited by the presence of other elements within his original papers. For although he declared his emancipation from conventional motivational concerns there were certain issues which tended to pull his analysis back in that direction.

The most critical of these (in that others may be seen to stem from it)
was the problem of the 'realness' of motive verbalisations. It will be
recalled that Mills was anxious to deny the validity of this question on the
empirical grounds that there was no way in which a real psycho-biological
motive which lay within an individual could possibly be inferred from a
lingual form, and also on the more analytic grounds that social efficaciousness was a more significant criterion for the sociological differentiation
and aggregation of typical vocabularies of motive than any question of the
actor's truth or sincerity.

But Mills was less consistent over this matter. For although he sought
to steer clear of the 'motive-mongering' which he regarded as the preserve
(or perhaps the collective delusion) of psychologists and psychoanalysts,
and tried to produce an account of motive which was situationally rather
than individually located, he nevertheless fell back at points into the
conventional view of motive as an account of someone's state of mind.

This retreat is more evident in the later than in the earlier paper.[8] In
fact, the only reference to the possible theoretical significance of 'internal'
considerations in the 1940 article is a grudging acknowledgement in a
footnote to the possibility of making inferences about an individual's
constructs from his verbalised motives: 'Of course, we could infer or
interpret constructs posited in the individual, but these are not easily
checked and they are not explanatory' (p. 909).

However, in the later paper, which is cast in a more functionalist mode,
we find a clear-cut attempt to define 'real' motives, not in terms of their
social efficaciousness, but by reference to their degree of integration with
the psyche of the individual: 'We may assume that the more deeply
internalised in the person, and the more closely integrated with the psychic
structure, a vocabulary of motives is, the greater is the chance that it
contains "the real motives". In fact, that is what "real motives" may be
assumed to mean' (Gerth and Mills, 1954, p. 120). And although Mills
then tries to wriggle back to a slightly more relativistic position by arguing
that such deeply integrated motives are just those which will have been
most used by the person in public, it is clear that we are close to a
conventional 'inner state' view of motivation. The later discussion of the
actor's awareness of his motives — 'sometimes in. . . intimate conversations. . . a person will suddenly become aware of motives which he
did not know as his own' (p. 127), only confirms the extent of the retreat.

Some of the debate over motives within the sociology of deviance in
recent years has displayed a similar tendency to shift from an analysis of
situational rhetoric towards a psychologistic concern with real motives

Thus, the authors of *The New Criminology*, who show a more sophisticated awareness of situational factors than many writers, declare, with reference to David Matza:

> ... the naturalistic perspective can lead... into a position where the only *true* account of how the deviant phenomena come into being, and what its real nature is, can be given by the deviants themselves. This position is paradoxically . . . both true and untrue. It is clearly true that what deviants believe must be the motor force behind their actions, since beliefs and actions are not separate phenomena. But it is also the case that what they believe may be false, even when it is regarded by them as true. (Taylor et al, 1973a, p. 173)

This is too simple. Those who work from what deviants say do not regard the remarks they collect and typify as constituting some essential truth:[9] they are rather impelling rhetorical statements which, when collectively evaluated, can be seen to derive their persuasive potency — that is, their situational truth — from their context, from the often complex, over-lapping, ironic relationships which they bear to other culturally 'true' vocabularies of motive.

Matza, for example (particularly in Sykes and Matza, 1957), by carefully tracing the relationship between delinquents' situational rhetoric and other established constellations of motives, is able to show not only how the delinquents in question are able to produce such accounts of their behaviours, but also why they are able to believe them to be true. His opponents, by contrast, feel able to bypass such relativistic rhetorical analysis by directly inferring 'real motives': '*There is no warrant* for assuming, with Matza, that because these codes enable only a non-critical and inarticulate response therefore their "implicit critique" is not a critique at all but a neutralisation' (my emphasis) (Taylor et al, 1973a, p. 184): and 'Matza's sociology . . . tends to be pitched at the level of describing false-consciousness' (Taylor et al, 1973a, p. 186); and again 'Matza's delinquent, moreover, is largely concerned to negate his society in a neutral fashion: a peculiar observation to make about delinquency in societies where the mass of delinquents are literally involved in the practice of redistributing private property' (Taylor et al, 1973a, p. 187).

This sort of argument does seem to rest upon just the type of 'motive-mongering' which Mills deprecated and at which anyone can play. (Is it not just as credible, for example, to observe that 'the mass of delinquents are literally involved in a demonstration of their thorough-going commitment to the acquisitive ethic of contemporary capitalism'?) This is not to claim that an analysis of rhetoric is the only route to the explication of ideology.

As Donald Ball observes, 'It is quite conceivable that individual actors will utilise a rhetoric without any ideological convictions as regards its validity, but with a recognition of its pragmatic efficacy; and similarly, that ideological dedication does not automatically assume any developed rhetoric to attempt its maintenance or furtherance' (Ball, 1967, p. 296). The objection is to that type of argument which postulates an ideological state which somehow gives rise to action while being in apparent conflict with the rhetorical resources which make such action possible.

New causes

The psychologistic backtracking which Mills reveals in his quest for a definition of 'real' as distinct from 'socially efficacious' motives reappears in his treatment of the *explanatory* role to be accorded to vocabularies of motive, to the verbalisations which actually induce action in oneself and others. He is not happy that these should simply be described as 'reasons': 'The vocalised expectations of an act, its 'reason', is not only a mediating condition of the act *but it is a proximate and controlling condition for which the term "cause" is not inappropriate*' (my italics) (Mills, 1940, p. 906). This 'discovery' of a new 'cause' of action was to prove one of the most influential aspects of Mills's work on the sociology of motivation, but it is difficult now to see the logic of the distinction that is being made in this sentence between 'reason' and 'cause'. The phrase 'a proximate and controlling condition' certainly has a firm positivistic smack, but it is not clear why the term 'reason' should be replaced by 'cause' on the basis that 'the vocalised expectation of an act' contains such attributes. It would seem that the word 'cause' is being invoked because Mills wishes to give some additional significance to 'vocalised expectations': he is anxious to stress the *antecedent* and not just the justificatory character of verbalised motives. But in his anxiety to gain such emphasis he is forced into adopting a positivistic tone which is eventually in conflict with his own concern for rhetorical analysis. Thus the fact that we seek to persuade ourselves and others about the reasons for acting in this or that way *before* such action occurs degenerates into a discrete chronological paradigm in which 'vocalised expectations' play a rather similar part to that which is traditionally accorded to 'antecedent variables' in orthodox psychological learning theory (indeed, at times Mills's language is uncomfortably reminiscent of the behaviourist Edward Tolman; see Tolman, 1958, especially ch. 5): 'Stable vocabularies of motive link anticipated consequences and specific actions . . . Anticipation is a subvocal or overt naming of terminal phases and/or social consequences of conduct' (Mills, 1940, p. 906).

In recent years there have been a number of attempts to correct Mills's unnecessarily positivistic emphasis upon a precisely placed, causally efficacious 'vocalisation'. There has been a recognition that 'motivational rhetoric' can serve several functions — not only propelling oneself or others to action but also remedying any possible damage to self-images which may be consequent upon the activity. Jason Ditton, for example, usefully distinguishes between a 'rhetoric of self-adjustment' which constitutes a 'prior' denial of responsibility, and a 'rhetoric of self-reconciliation' which serves as a 'posterior' denial. He insists, however, that 'before-and-after-ness is an existential rather than a temporal issue. Importantly the adjustment rhetoric may, in fact, be formulated or conceptualised by the actor *after* an act takes place, but is *seen* by him as being causally antecedent' (Ditton, 1977, P. 164).

This abandonment of temporal specificity does nothing to reduce the significance of motivational verbalisations. We may be able to suggest the likely stages at which certain rhetorical elements occur — as we may be able to distinguish between different types of imaginative fantasies according to their chronological functions (Rock, 1973a; Cohen and Taylor, 1976) — but this does mean that we are describing the concrete temporal allocation of such matters for any specific actor. Nevertheless, the ability to establish distinctions of before-and-after-ness remains analytically useful, as Stuart Henry's summary of the role of language constructs in the context of trading in stolen property nicely indicates:

> Language constructs . . . may be used as self-defence mechanisms or rationalisations, given after a criminal act in order to protect the person's conscience against culpability for the act (though they might stem from the person's overall social philosophy). They may feature as verbalisations used prior to the commission of a criminal act, but after its contemplation, in order to allow the person to act guiltlessly. Finally they may operate as a process of neutralisation occurring to the actor prior to both contemplation and decision to act. (Henry, 1976, p. 100)

'NON-MOTIVATED' VOCABULARIES OF MOTIVE

The somewhat positivistic role which is assigned to sub-vocalisations or overt naming within Mills is closely related to another reason for his failure to develop a comprehensive sociological theory of motivation: his insistent emphasis on the fact that verbalisations of motive occur at critical or unexpected moments in our lives and primarily in response to questions:

> . . . men live in immediate acts of experience and their attentions are directed outside themselves until acts are in some way frustrated. It is then that awareness of self and of motive occur. The 'question' is a lingual index of such conditions. The avowal and imputations of motives are features of such conversations as arise in 'question' situations. (Mills, 1940, p. 905)

This formulation obscures a most significant feature of motivational rhetoric, namely its actual absence from large stretches of private and public discourse. This is not because such discourse is unconcerned with the avowal and imputation of motives, but rather because it is characterised by that particular form of persuasion which depends for its effect upon appearing to be unconcerned with motives. It is, in other words, an example of that type of 'neutralised' rhetoric to which Burke referred, a rhetoric which eschews obvious evaluations, which avoids the 'censorial weightings' which usually accompany 'philosophic, religious, social, political and personal outlooks' (Burke, 1950, p. 96), and which would be pleased to be called 'official', 'business', 'technical', 'objective', 'judicious' — even 'bureaucratic'. Appropriately enough, the type of action which is frequently induced by such rhetoric is literally 'inaction'. A most interesting account of this type of implicit motivational rhetoric is provided by Burton and Carlen in two recent papers, 'Official Discourse' (1977) and 'Judicial Discourse' (1978).

Both papers analyse official reports on law and order. There is not space to do justice to the subtlety of much of this work, but in terms of our present argument about 'absent motives' it is enough to consider their 1977 discussion of the manner in which two official reports (the Devlin Report on identification and the Scarman Report on Northern Ireland) attempt to convince their audience that the only motive with which they operate is one of distributive justice. The existing 'material conditions', argue Burton and Carlen, make such an ideal impossible, so that a rhetorical style must be developed which rules out the possibility of any subversive questioning:

> The main problem for Official Discourses on law and order is that all problems have to be discussed in terms of an ideal of distributive justice which cannot admit to the material conditions which render that ideal impossible. A discourse has to be developed which will both pre-empt

and foreclose any theory within which questions could be posed which might destroy the pre-givens of that discourse. (Burton and Carlen, 1977, p. 385)

The strategies by which the ideal is realised and the threat to state legitimacy absolved are perfect examples of the type of rhetorical devices discussed by Burke: they involve the systematic omission of explicit motivational accounts and the substitution of a series of implicit but persuasive appeals to such justifications as 'common sense', 'what everyone might feel in the situation', 'natural reason' and 'historical necessity'. The simplest way in which to illustrate the appearance of such 'invisible' motivational inducements is to reproduce a section from an early chapter of the Scarman Report, with Burton and Carlen's italicised references to the rhetorical strategies which are being employed.[10]

We are satisfied that the great majority of the members of the RUC was concerned to do his duty . . . Inevitably, (*common sense*) however, this meant confrontation and on occasions conflict with disorderly mobs. Moreover since most of the rioting developed from action on the streets started by Catholic crowds, the RUC were more often than not facing Catholics who, as a result, came to feel that the police were always going for them, baton-charging them — never 'the others' (*empiricist subjectivism*). In fact the RUC faced and, if necessary, charged those who appeared to them to be challenging, defying or attacking them. We are satisfied that, though they did not expect to be challenged by Protestants they were ready to deal with them in the same way, if it became necessary. The Shankill riots of the 2nd/4th August establish beyond doubt (*positivist empiricism*) the readiness of the police to do their duty against Protestant mobs . . . But it is painfully clear from the evidence adduced before us that by July the Catholic minority no longer (*apposite history*) believed the RUC was impartial and that Catholic and civil rights activists were publicly asserting the loss of confidence. Understandably (*natural reason, common sense*) these resentments affected the thinking and feeling of the young and irresponsible and induced the jeering and throwing of stones which were the beginnings of most of the disturbances. The effect of this hostility on the RUC themselves was unfortunate (*natural reason*). They came to treat as their enemies, and accordingly also the enemies of the public peace, those who persisted in displaying hostility and distrust towards them (*common sense*). Thus, (*argument through temporal neutrality*) there developed the fateful split between the Catholic community and the police. (Burton and Carlen, 1977, pp. 404-5)

Crises and Motivational Avowal

There is one final aspect of Mills's original formulation which must be examined. This is the assertion that the imputation and avowal of motives occurs in response to questions which arise at particular moments of crisis or frustration. The Burton and Carlen work upon the way in which awkward questions about motives are avoided by the use of implicit justifications for a certain style of discourse already makes this formulation seem suspect. But an examination of the function of motives in everyday usage also reveals the over-specialised nature of this characterisation.

For as Blum and McHugh maintain in their 1971 paper, motive may be regarded as a 'collective procedure for accomplishing social interaction' (p. 98): in other words we bring a notion of motive and motivated behaviour to bear upon the world, not just in puzzling or frustrating situations, or when we are asked or ask others why this or that was done, but in order to formulate behaviour as intelligible, to conceive of persons as rule-guided, and to provide the resources by which we typically connect persons and events.

Blum and McHugh argue that 'to talk motives is to talk grammar' (Blum and McHugh, 1971, p. 100), for they are concerned not with the factual status of the motive (with its rightness or wrongness, for example) but with what must be known by everyone in order that they can produce such motive talk, with the assumptions which make such talk possible. Whether members know these assumptions is 'analytically irrelevant'; what is interesting is the description of the understandings and conventions which they must employ if they are to 'invoke motive as a method for making a social environment orderly and sensible' (Blum and McHugh, 1971, p. 103). Without such a method:

> . . . . . . observers would be unable to organise the current and flow of socially intelligible events, nor could they observe the products of biography; i.e. they could not see interaction as a course of history. They would be without a temporal method . . . They are a grammar in that they methodically collect these disparate phenomena. And they are social in that they transform what would otherwise be fragmentary series of unconnected immediate events into generally intelligible social courses of behaviour. (Blum and McHugh, 1971, p. 106)

It is clear that Blum and McHugh regard their own approach to motive as different in kind to that proposed by Mills. After a reference to the fallacious conception of motive as a concrete report on a state of mind, they go on to associate such conventional concerns explicitly with the Gerth and Mills chapter and declare that questions about such matters are 'not the questions of those who have grasped the analytic character of motive' (p. 102).

Kenneth Burke fares only slightly better. He also 'confuses analytic and concrete conditions', and fails to 'explicate the grammar of motive in more than a metaphoric sense' (p. 102). Now it is certainly true that Blum and McHugh do perform the important task of emphasising the notion of motive as a procedure for collecting and formulating objects and events in the world. Indeed, their later postulation (in an addendum to the article) of the type of world in which motive talk is intelligible and interesting, one in which 'there is a continual process of clarifying the things one is with by making reference to things outside of them . . . [where] one knows what one is with only by assimilating it to what is different from what one is with', (McHugh et al, 1974, p. 45) produces an even more fundamentalist frisson about the methods by which our familiar world is rendered familiar.

Nevertheless, it is difficult to see how such epistemological form-ulations vitiate attempts to explain the particular employment of motiv-ational rhetoric by those members of a causal world who wish to persuade others (or themselves) to believe or to act in a particular fashion. Blum and McHugh's own demonstration of the 'truly' analytic character of their enterprise depends, for example, upon the employment of a sociological rhetoric which, like all other rhetorics, aims to persuade us that there are 'good reasons' for believing their reasoning.

We may agree with their delineation of what is implied in 'motivating the world', but still seek explanations of the manner in which various types of rhetorical appeal allow the eventual ascription to oneself or others of 'good reasons' or 'motives' for acting in this or that way. Our cognitive commitment to formulating the world according to motivational pro-cedures is actually a prerequisite for our amenability to rhetorical appeals which attempt to persuade us, by recourse to a range of tactics, that this institution, practice, group is more adequately and more appropriately motivated than another — that it is, therefore, more intelligible, more natural and more socially and morally legitimate.

But although Blum and McHugh may not be allowed to appropriate the term 'analytic' for their own approach to motivation, their emphasis upon the grammar of motives (as distinct from 'vocabulary' or 'rhetoric') is an important reminder that motivational ascription is not a specialised task to be performed at crisis points or in answer to questions, but is rather a routine procedure for actually producing a 'coherent' notion of 'people', 'events' and their interconnections.[11]

CONCLUSION

As was observed earlier, this brief review has no pretensions to comprehensiveness. Many significant contributions to ethnographic analysis which have depended upon a Millsian analysis of talk and the delineation of constellations of 'reasons' and 'motives' have been excluded, as have many which aimed at the more Burkean task of explicating the rhetoric of motives within various kinds of discourse. Neither has there been any imperialist intention of demarcating a specific 'area of sociology'. It is simply hoped that the paper has drawn attention to the affinities, discontinuities and ambiguities within the field, in a way which will be of some value to future researchers.

NOTES

1. The present author did contribute to an historical survey of motivational constructions of deviance: this, like some of Mills's attempts, was somewhat impaired (at least in this author's view) by its tendency to rely upon ideal-typical constructions which were inadequately based upon empirical evidence (see Taylor and Taylor, 1972).
2. Mills does cite Burke in both articles, but the reference is necessarily to the earlier *Permanence and Change* (1935) and not to *A Grammar of Motives* (1945) or *A Rhetoric of Motives* (1950).
3. Burke goes on to discuss the relationship between identification and persuasion: Nelson Foote (1951) develops this theme with reference to C. Wright Mills.
4. Burke's concern with the presence of rhetorical motives in poetry is an illustration of his interest in attitudinal change rather than inducement to action. An interesting contrast in this context is provided by Brian Taylor (1977). In an original and subtle article the author draws upon Mills in order to examine the literary output of a group of pederast poets and to show how such work 'enabled the *enactment of pederast activity* through a dilution of the component of guilt' (my emphasis).
5. There are some recent examples of attempts to link verbalisations with broader cultural patterns. The present author, for example, attempted to relate sex offenders' verbalisations with a number of ideological, aesthetic and behaviouristic constellations (1972b). For a critical discussion of the inferences which are made from sex offenders' verbalisations in this article, see Wooton (1975), pp. 86-92. Ditton (1977) draws upon David Matza's work in order to suggest that 'fiddling' is

a 'subterranean version of business', which derives its rhetorical persuasiveness from a 'simplistic extraction and undue emphasis of some of [business's] minor values and minor imperatives' (p. 174). Henry (1976) also attempts to assemble a 'social philosophy' from the verbalisations of purchasers of stolen property, but is careful to observe: 'It is arguable that members choose the components that they speak from their total social philosophy as and when they deem them relevant to the job at hand, that is in the face of questioning by others. This does not, however, preclude them from reflecting deeper-held beliefs' (p. 96).

6. A particularly useful example of this type of rhetorical analysis can be found in Ball (1967). Ball, who describes his approach as 'similar' to that of Kenneth Burke, is concerned to characterise the strategies by which the clinic develops a 'rhetoric of legitimatisation' such that conventional views of abortion are subverted and more legitimate ones instilled in both staff and patrons.

7. Mills declares that the problem of motivation is one of 'steered conduct' (Gerth and Mills, 1954, p. 113).

8. I am grateful to John Newman for this observation.

9. See, for example, Ditton (1977), p. 148: 'When I talk of the salesmen's "motives" I shall not attempt somehow to look behind their verbal and symbolic restructuring of events to elucidate the so-called 'real' motives of fiddling.'

10. There is an important distinction to be made between the type of 'non-motivated' discourse analysed by Burton and Carlen and what we might call the 'unmotivated' rhetoric used by such persons as 'compulsive' offenders (arsonists, kleptomaniacs, sex offenders). For early work in this area within the Mills tradition, see Cressey (1962); see also Taylor, L. and Walton (1971) and Taylor, L. (1972).

    David Oldman's recent (1977) paper on compulsive gamblers is particularly valuable here for its analysis of the way in which gamblers' 'non-motive' talk about their behaviour becomes talk of 'compulsion'.

11. The Blum and McHugh exercise needs to be distinguished from that form of analysis which concentrates upon the procedures by which breakdowns or disjunctions within interaction are remedied by the participants (Goffman, 1971).

    There is also some interesting and related work on the manner in which blame allocation is handled within conversation, and on the ways in which justification and excuses are employed in order to reduce such allocation (Atkinson and Drew, forthcoming).

Bibliography

The page numbers in italic after each entry give the text pages where reference to the author is made.

ABRAMS, P. and McCULLOCH, A. (1976), *Communes, Sociology and Society:* Cambridge, Cambridge University Press. *p. 47*

AKERS, R.L. (1973), *Deviant Behaviour: A Social Learning Approach;* California, Wadsworth. *p. 89*

ANDERSON, P. (1968), ,Components of the National Culture', *New Left Review,* 50 (July-August). *pp. 14-15*

ANDERSON, P. and BLACKBURN, R. eds (1965), *Towards Socialism;* London, Fontana Library. *p. 11*

ARENDT, H. (1965), *Eichmann in Jerusalem;* New York, Random House. *p. 50*

ATKINSON, M. and DREW, P. (forthcoming), *Order in Court: Aspects of Interaction and Cross-Examination in Courts;* Macmillan. *p. 161*

BAILEY, R. and BRAKE, M., eds (1975), *Radical Social Work,* London, Edward Arnold. *pp. 7, 15-16, 39, 50*

BALL, D. (1967), 'An Abortion Clinic Ethnography', *Social Problems,* 14 (3), 293-301. *pp. 154, 161*

BALL, R. A. (1966), 'Empirical Explanation of Neutralization Theory', *Criminologica,* 4, (2). *pp. 22-32 and 90*

BECKER, H. S. (1963), *Outsiders: Studies in the Sociology of Deviance;* New York, Free Press. *pp. 3, 87, 89, 95, 97, 99-100, 104-5, 112, 120*

BECKER, H. S. (1964), *The Other Side: Perspectives on Deviance;* New York, Free Press. *pp. 88, 99-100, 120*

BECKER, H. S. (1967), 'Whose Side Are We On?', *Social Problems,* vol 14, No 3, 239-47. *pp. 5, 17, 99-100*

BECKER, H. S. (1971), 'Reply to Riley', *American Sociologist,* 6, 1. *p. 13*

BECKER, H. S. (1974), 'Labelling Theory Reconsidered', in P. Rock and M. McIntosh, eds, *Deviance and Social Control,* op. cit. *pp. 87-8, 95, 97, 99-100*

BERGER, P., BERGER, B. and KELLNER, H. (1974), *The Homeless Mind;* Harmondsworth, Penguin. *p. 115*

BERGER, P. and LUCKMANN, T. (1967), *The Social Construction of Reality;* London, Allen Lane. *p. 121*

BEYLEVELD, D. (1975), 'Epistemological Foundations of Sociological Theory; (Ph.D. dissertation), University of East Anglia. *pp. 142-4*

BEYLEVELD, D. and WILES, P. (1975), 'Man and Method' in David Matza's *Becoming Deviant*, *British Journal of Criminology*, vol 15, No 2, 111-27. *pp. 137, 143*

BIANCHI, H., SIMONDI, M. and TAYLOR, I., eds (1975), *Deviance and Control in Europe;* London, John Wiley. *p. 58*

BIRENBAUM, A. and SAGARIN, E. (1976), *Norms and Human Behaviour;* New York, Praeger. *p. 121*

BLUM, A. and McHUGH, P. (1971), 'The Social Ascription of Motives', 36, No 1, 98-109. *p. 158*

BLUMER, H. (1969), *Symbolic Interactionism;* Englewood Cliffs, N. J., Prentice-Hall. *p. 116*

BORDUA, D. J. (1967), 'Recent Trends: Deviant Behavior and Social Control;, *The Annals of the American Academy of Political and Social Science*, 57, 149-63. *p. 102-3, 106*

BOX, S. (1971), *Deviance, Reality and Society;* London, Holt, Rinehart and . Winston. *p. 112*

BRAGINSKY, B. M. and BRAGINSKY, D. D. (1969), *Methods of Madness: The Mental Hospitals as Last Resort;* London, Holt, Rinehart and Winston. *p. 107*

BROADBENT, R. S. (1974), 'A Theoretical Critique of the Societal Reaction Approach to Deviance', *Pacific Sociological Review*, 17 (3), 287-312. *p. 90*

BRYANT, C. D., ed. (1974), *Deviant Behavior: Occupational and Organizational Bases;* Chicago, Rand McNally. *p. 98*

BURKE, K. (1935), *Permanence and Change;* Indianapolis, Bobbs-Merrill. *p. 160*

BURKE, K. (1945), *A Grammar of Motives;* New York, Prentice-Hall. *p. 160*

BURKE, K. (1950), *A Rhetoric of Motives;* Englewood Cliffs, N.J., Prentice-Hall. *p. 148 et seq.*

BURTON, F. and CARLEN, P. (1977), 'Official Discourse', *Economy and Society*, 6 (4), 377-407. *p. 156-7, 158*

BURTON, F. and CARLEN, P. (1978), 'Judicial Discourse' (mimeo), University of Keele. *p. 156, 158*

CAMERON, M. (1964), *The Booster and the Snitch;* New York, Free Press. *p. 90*

CARLEN, P. (1976), *Magistrates' Justice;* London, Martin Robertson. *p. 112*

CHRISTENSEN, H. T. and CARPENTER, G. R. (1962), 'Value Behavior Discrepancies Regarding Pre-Marital Coitus in Three Western Cultures', *American Sociological Review*, 27, No 1. 66-79. *p. 108*

CHRISTIE, N. (1976), 'Conflicts as Property', Foundation Lecture, Centre for Criminological Studies, University of Sheffield. *p. 47, 49*

CLOWARD, R. A. and OHLIN, L. E. (1960), *Delinquency and Opportunity;* Chicago: Free Press. *p. 60*

COATES, K. (1965), 'Democracy and Workers' Control', in P. Anderson and R. Blackburn, eds, *Towards Socialism*, op. cit. *p. 11*

COHEN, A. K. (1955), *Delinquent Boys;* Chicago: Free Press. *p. 60*

COHEN, S. (1967), 'Mods, Rockers and the Rest', *Howard Journal*, 12, No 2, 121-30. *p. 120*

COHEN, S., ed. (1971), *Images of Deviance;* Harmondsworth, Penguin. *p. 161*

COHEN, S. (1975), 'It's All Right For You to Talk: Political and Sociological Manifestoes for Social Work Action', in R. Bailey and M. Brake, eds, *Radical Social Work,* op. cit. *pp. 7, 15-16, 39, 50*

COHEN, S. and TAYLOR, L. (1975), 'From Psychopaths to Outsiders: British Criminology and the National Deviancy Conference', in H. Bianchi, M. Simondi and I. Taylor, eds, *Deviance and Control in Europe,* op. cit. *p. 58*

COHEN, S. and TAYLOR, L. (1976), *Escape Attempts: The Theory and Practice of Resistance to Everyday Life;* London, Allen Lane. *pp. 110, 115, 155*

COHEN, S. (1977), 'Prisons and the Future of Control Systems: From Concentration to Dispersal', in M. Fitzgerald *et al,* eds, *Welfare in Action,* op. cit. *p. 51*

COLE, S. (1975), 'The Growth of Scientific Knowledge: Theories of Deviance as a Case Study', in L. Coser, ed., *The Idea of Social Structure,* op. cit. *p. 85*

COLLINGWOOD, R. G. (1940), *An Essay on Metaphysics;* Oxford, Clarendon Press. *p. 128*

CONN, S. and HIPLER, A. E. (1974), 'Conciliation and Arbitration in the Native Village and the Urban Ghetto', *Judicature,* 58, 228-35. *p. 46*

CONNOR, W. (1972), 'Deviance in Soviet Society', New York, Columbia University Press. *p. 9*

CONOVER, P. W. (1976), 'A Reassessment of Labelling Theory: A Constructive Response to Criticism', in L. A. Coser and O. Larsen, eds, *The Uses of Controversy in Sociology,* op. cit. *p. 85*

COSER, L., ed. (1975), *The Idea of Social Structure: Papers in Honour of R. K. Merton;* New York, Harcourt Brace Jovanovich. *p. 85*

COSER, L. A. and LARSEN, O., eds (1976), *The Uses of Controversy in Sociology;* New York, Free Press. *p. 85*

CRESSEY, D. (1962), 'Role Theory, Differential Association and Compulsive Crimes', in A. Rose, ed., *Human Behavior and Social Processes,* op. cit. *p. 161*

DANZIG, R. (1973), 'Toward the Creation of a Complementary Decentralised System of Criminal Justice', *Stanford Law Review,* 26, 1-54. *p. 46*

DAVIDSON, D. (1963), 'Actions, Reasons and Causes', *Journal of Philosophy,* 60, No 23, 685-700. *p. 127*

DAVIS, N. J. (1972), 'Labelling Theory in Deviance Research', *Sociological Quarterly,* 13, 4, 447-74. *pp. 89, 102-3*

DAWE, A. (1970), 'The Two Sociologies', *British Journal of Sociology,* 21, No 2, 207-18. *p. 142*

DAY, J. and DAY, R. (1977), 'A Review of the Current State of Negotiated Order Theory', *Sociological Quarterly,* 18 (Winter), 126-142. *p. 116*

DENZIN, N. (1970), 'Rules of Conduct and the Study of Deviant Behaviour', in J. Douglas, *Deviance and Respectability,* op. cit. *p. 96*

DICKSON, D. T. (1968), 'Bureaucracy and Morality', *Social Problems,* 16, No 2, 143-56. *p. 112*

DITTON, J. (1974), 'On the Motives of Naughty Bread Salesmen', Working Paper 9, University of Durham. *p. 161*

DITTON, J. (1977), *Part-Time Crime: An Ethnography of Fiddling and Pilferage;* London, Macmillan. *pp. 51, 155, 160-61*

DOUGLAS, J., ed., (1970), *Deviance and Respectability;* London, Basic Books. p. 96

DOUGLAS, J. (1971), *American Social Order;* New York, Free Press. pp. 116, 121

DOWNES, D. M. (1966), *The Delinquent Solution;* London: Routledge & Kegan Paul. p. 60

EDELMAN, M. (1964), *The Symbolic Uses of Politics;* Urbana, Ill., University of Illinois Press. p. 113

EDELMAN, M. (1971), *Politics as Symbolic Action;* Chicago, Markham Books. p. 113

EDGERTON, R. (1967), *The Cloak of Competence;* Berkeley, Calif., University of California Press. p. 108

EMERSON, R. (1969), *Judging Delinquents;* Chicago, Aldine. pp. 103, 112

ENNIS, P. H. (1967), *Criminal Victimisation in the United States: A Report of a National Survey,* Washington D.C.: U.S. Government Printing Office. p. 13

ERICKSON, K. T. (1966), *Wayward Puritans;* London, John Wiley. p. 87, 114

EYSENCK, H. J. (1977), *Crime and Personality* (rev. edn); London, Paladin. pp. 124-6

FARRELL, R. and NELSON, J. F. (1975), 'A Causal Model of Secondary Deviance: The Case of Homosexuality', *Sociological Quarterly,* 17, 109-21. p. 118

FEINBERG, J. (1970), *Doing and Deserving;* Princeton, N.J. Princeton University Press. p. 51

FEINBLOOM, D. H. (1976), *Transvestism and Transsexualism: Mixed Views;* New York, Delacorte Press. p. 110

FILSTEAD, W., ed. (1972), *An Introduction to Deviance;* Chicago, Markham Books. pp. 87, 97

FINESTONE, H. (1976), *Victims of Change: Juvenile Delinquents in American Society;* London, Greenwood Press. pp. 30-31, 120

FISHER, E.A. (1975), 'Community Courts: An Alternative to Conventional Adjudication', *American University Law Review,* 24, 4-5, 1253-91, 46

FITZGERALD, M., HALMOS, P., MUNCIE, J. and ZELDIN, D. (1977) *Welfare in Action;* London, Routledge and Kegan Paul. p. 51

FOOTE, N. (1951), 'Identification as the Basis for a Theory of Motivations', *American Sociological Review,* 16, 1. pp. 14-21, 160

FOUCAULT, H., ed. (1975), *I, Pierre Riviere, having slaughtered my mother, my sister, and my brother . . .: A Case of Parricide in the Nineteenth Century;* New York, Random House. p. 32

FOUCAULT, M. (1977), *Discipline and Punish;* London, Allen Lane. pp. 39, 44-5

FRIEDSON, E. ed. (1964), *The Hospital in Modern Society;* New York, Free Press. p. 116

GALLIBER, J. and WALKER, A. (1977), 'The Puzzle of the Social Origins of the Marijuana Tax Act of 1937', *Social Problems,* 24, No 3, 367-77. p. 112

GARFINKEL, H. (1967), *Studies in Ethnomethodology;* Englewood Cliffs, N.J., Prentice-Hall. p. 110

GERTH, H. and MILLS, C. Wright (1954), *Character and Social Structure;* London, Routledge and Kegan Paul. pp. 149, 152, 161

GIBBS, J. (1966), 'Conception of Deviant Behavior: The Old and the New', *Pacific Sociological Review,* 8, 1, 9-14. *pp. 96, 103, 119*

GIBBS, J. (1972), 'Issues in Defining Deviant Behaviour', in R. A. Scott and J. Douglas, eds, *Theoretical Perspectives on Deviance,* op. cit. *pp. 97, 121*

GIBBS, J. (1976), *Crime, Punishment and Deterrence;* New York, Elsevier. *p. 143*

GIDDENS, A. (1973), *The Class Structure of the Advanced Societies;* London, Hutchinson. *pp. 15, 16*

GIDDENS, A. (1976), *New Rules of Sociological Method;* London, Hutchinson. *p. 13-14*

GOFFMAN, E. (1968), *Asylums;* Harmondsworth, Penguin. *p. 107*

GOFFMAN, E. (1971), *Relations in Public;* London, Allen Lane. *p. 161*

GOODE, E. (1969), 'Marijuana and the Politics of Reality', *Journal of Health and Social Behaviour,* 10, 83-94; (1970), *The Marijuana Smokers,* New York, Basic Books, Ch. 3. *p. 112*

GOODE, E. (1975), 'On Behalf of Labelling Theory', Social Probelms, 22, 570-83. *p. 87*

GORZ, A. (1965), 'Work and Consumption', in P. Anderson and R. Blackburn, eds, *Towards Socialism,* op. cit. *p. 11*

GOULDNER, A. (1968), 'The Sociologist as Partisan: Sociology and the Welfare State', *American Sociologist,* 103-16. *pp. 4, 5, 59, 89, 106*

GOULDNER, A. (1971), The Coming Crisis of Western Sociology, London, Heinemann. *pp. 1-2, 15*

GOVE, W. ed. (1975), *The Labelling of Deviance;* London, John Wiley. *pp. 85, 89, 116-7, 119, 121*

GREENWOOD, V. and YOUNG, J. (1976), *Abortion on Demand;* London, Pluto Press. *pp. 8, 50, 83*

GUSFIELD, J. (1963), *Symbolic Crusade: Status Politics and the American Temperance Movement:* Urbana, Ill., University of Illinois Press. *p. 112-3*

HALL, P.H. (1972), 'A Symbolic Interactionist Analysis of Politics', *Sociological Inquiry,* 42, 3-4, 35-75. *p. 113*

HART, H. L. A. (1968), *Punishment and Responsibility,* Oxford University Press. *p. 51*

HARVEY, D. (1973), *Social Justice and the City;* London, Edward Arnold. *pp. 5, 15*

HAWTHORNE, G. (1976), *Enlightenment and Despair;* Cambridge, Cambridge University Press. *p. 84*

HENRY, S. (1976), 'Fencing with Accounts: The Language of Moral Bridging', *British Journal of Law and Society,* 3 (1), 91-100. *pp. 155, 161*

HENRY, S. and MARS, G. (forthcoming), 'Crime at Work: The Social Construction of Amateur Property Crime', *Sociology. p. 51*

HEWITT, J. P. (1976), *Self and Society: A Symbolic Interactionist Social Psychology;* London, Allyn and Bacon. *pp. 114-6*

HIRSCH, F. (1977), *The Social Limits to Growth;* London, Routledge, Kegan Paul. *p. 10-11*

HIRST, P. (1975a), 'Marx and Engels on Law, Crime and Morality', in I. Taylor, P. Walton and J. Young, eds, *Critical Criminology,* op. cit. *p. 77*

168   *Deviant Interpretations*

HIRST, P. (1975b), *Durkheim, Bernard and Epistemology;* London, Routledge and Kegan Paul. *p. 124-6*

HOLLIS, M. (1977), *Models of Man;* Cambridge, Cambridge University Press. *p. 142-3*

HOMANS, G. (1964), 'Bringing Men Back In', *American Sociological Review,* Vol 29, No 6, 809-18. *pp. 1, 3*

HONDERICH, T. (1976), *Punishment: The Supposed Justifications;* Harmondsworth, Penguin. *p. 51*

HUGHES, E. (1963), 'Race Relations and the Sociological Imagination', *American Sociological Review,* Vol 28, No 6, 879-90. *p. 1, 3*

KANDO, T. (1973), *Sex Change: The Achievement of Gender Identity Among Feminine Transsexuals;* Springfield, Ill., C. E. Thomas. *p. 110*

KITSUSE, J. (1972), 'Deviance, Deviant Behavior, and Deviants: Some Conceptual Issues', in W. J. Filstead, *An Introduction to Deviance;* op. cit. *pp. 87, 97*

KITSUSE, J. (1975), 'The New Conception of Deviance and its Critics', in W. Gove, ed., *The Labelling of Deviance,* op. cit. *p. 117*

KITSUSE, J. and CICOUREL, A. V. (1963), 'A Note on the Use of Official Statistics', *Social Problems,* 11, p. 131-9. *p. 54-5*

KONRAD, G. (1975), *The Case Worker;* London, Hutchinson, *pp. 7, 15*

KUHN, T. S. (1970), *The Structure of Scientific Revolution;* Chicago, University of Chicago Press. *p. 128*

LAUER, R. H. and HANDEL, W. H. (1977), *Social Psychology: The Theory and Application of Symbolic Interaction;* London, Houghton, Mifflin. *p. 116*

LEMERT, E. (1951), *Social Pathology;* New York, McGraw Hill. *pp. 95-6, 103, 105*

LEMERT, E. (1967), *Human Deviance, Social Problems and Social Control;* Englewood Cliffs, N. J., Prentice-Hall. *pp. 87, 105*

LEMERT, E. (1970), *Social Action and Legal Change;* Chicago, Aldine. *p. 112*

LEMERT, E. (1972), *Human Deviance, Social Problems and Social Control* (2nd edn); Englewood Cliffs, N. J., Prentice-Hall. *pp. 87-8*

LEMERT, E. (1974), 'Beyond Mead: The Societal Reaction to Deviance', *Social Problems,* 21, No 4, 457-68. *p. 87-8*

LEVITIN, T. E. (1975), 'Deviants as Active Participants in the Labelling Process: The Mentally Handicapped', *Social Problems,* 22, No 4, 548-57. *p. 90*

LEWIS, J. D. (1976), 'The Classic American Pragmatists as Forerunners to Symbolic Interactionism', *Sociological Quarterly,* 17 (1), 347-60. *p. 102*

LIAZIOS, A. (1972), 'The Poverty of the Sociology of Deviance: Nuts, Sluts and Perverts', *Social Problems,* 20, No 1, 103-19. *pp. 97, 100, 108*

LICHTMAN, R. (1970), 'Symbolic Interactionism and Social Reality: Some Marxist Queries', *Berkeley Journal of Sociology,* 15, 75-94. *p. 115*

LOFLAND, J. (1969), *Deviance and Identity;* Englewood Cliffs, N. J., Prentice-Hall. *pp. 90, 97*

LOVEJOY, A. (1960), *The Great Chain of Being;* New York, Harper and Row. *p. 72*

LUKACS, G. (1963), *The Meaning of Contemporary Realism;* London, Merlin Press, *p. 27*

LYMAN, S. M. and SCOTT, M. B. (1970), *A Sociology of the Absurd;* New York, Appleton-Century-Crofts. *p. 101*

McCAGHY, C. M. (1968), 'Drinking and Deviance Disavowal: The Case of Child Molesters', *Social Problems,* 16, No 1, 43-9. *p. 107*

McCALL, G. H. and SIMMONS, J. L. (1966), *Identities and Interactions;* London, Collier-Macmillan. *p. 116*

McCARTHY, M. (1972), *Medina;* London, Wildwood House. *pp. 29-30, 50-1*

McHUGH, P., RAFFEL, S., FOSS, D. and BLUM, A. (1974), *On the Beginning of Social Inquiry;* London, Routledge and Kegan Paul. *p. 159*

MADDOX, G., BACK and LIEDERMANN (1968), 'Overweight as Social Deviance', *Journal of Health and Social Behaviour,* 9. *pp. 4, 96*

MALINOWSKI, B. (1926), *Crime and Custom in Savage Society,* London, Kegan Paul, Trench, Trubner and Co. *pp. 54, 89*

MANDERS, D. (1975), 'Labelling Theory and Social Reality: A Marxist Critique', *Insurgent Sociologist,* 6 (1). *pp. 53-66, 85, 90*

MANKOFF, M. (1971), 'Societal Reaction and Career Deviance: A Critical Analysis', *Sociological Quarterly,* 12, Spring, 204-18. *pp. 89, 100, 103-4*

MATHIESEN, T. (1974), *The Politics of Abolition;* London, Martin Robertson. *pp. 15-16, 49, 84*

MATZA, D. (1964) *Delinquency and Drift;* New York, John Wiley. *pp. 50, 137*

MATZA, D. (1969) *Becoming Deviant;* Englewood Cliffs, N.J., Prentice-Hall, *pp. 15, 17-18, 20, 23, 25-6, 31, 87, 105, 123, 137-9, 143*

MEAD, G. H. (1934), *Mind, Self and Society;* Chicago, University of Chicago Press. *pp. 115-6*

MEADOWS, D. H., MEADOWS, D. L., RANDERS, J. and BEHRENS, W. W. (1972), *The Limits to Growth;* London, Earth Island Ltd. *p. 10-11*

MERCER, J. R. (1973), *Labelling the Mentally Retarded;* Berkeley, University of California Press. *pp. 96, 108*

MILLS, C. Wright (1940), 'Situated Actions and Vocabularies of Motive', *American Sociological Review,* 5, 4, 904-13. *p. 146 et seq*

MILLS, C. Wright (1954), 'A Sociology of Motivation', in H. Gerth and C. Wright Mills, *Character and Social Structure,* op. cit. *p. 146 et seq*

MILLS, C. Wright (1959), *The Sociological Imagination;* Oxford, Oxford University Press. *pp. 1, 15*

MORRIS, H. (1976), *On Guilt and Innocence: Essays in Legal Philosophy and Moral Psychology;* Berkeley, University of California Press. *p. 51*

MORRIS, N. and HAWKINS, G. (1970), *The Honest Politician's Guide to Crime Control;* Chicago, Chicago University Press. *p. 50*

MULLER, R. (1974), 'The Labelling Theory in the version of F. Sack', *International Journal of Criminology and Penology,* 2, 1, 11-22. *p. 120*

MULLINS, C. J. and MULLINS, N. (1973), *Theories and Theory Groups in Contemporary American Sociology;* New York, Harper and Row. *p. 94*

MURPHY, J. G. (1973), 'Marxism and Retribution', *Philosophy and Public Affairs,* 2, 3, 217243. *p. 37-8*

NEWMAN, O. (1974), *Defensible Space;* London, Architectural Press. *p. 46*

NOZICK, R. (1974), *Anarchy, State and Utopia;* New York, Basic Books. *p. 48*

OLDMAN, D. (1977), 'Compulsive Gamblers' (mimeo), University of Aberdeen. *p. 161*

ORCUTT, J. D. (1973), 'Societal Reaction and the Response to Deviation in Small Groups', *Social Forces,* 52, 259-67. *p. 117*

PARKIN, F. (1972), *Class Inequality and Political Order;* London, Paladin. *pp. 15, 16*

PARSONS, T. (1970), *The Social System;* London, Routledge and Kegan Paul. *p. 131*

PASSMORE, J. A. (1970), *The Perfectibility of Man;* London, Duckworth. *p. 15*

PEARCE, F. (1973), 'Crime, Corporations and the American Social Order', in I. Taylor and L. Taylor, *Politics and Deviance,* op. cit. *p. 78*

PEARCE, F. (1976), *Crimes of the Powerful* (Foreword by Jock Young); London, Pluto Press. *pp. 4, 8, 9, 108, 112*

PEARSON, G. (1975), *The Deviant Imagination;* London, Macmillan. *pp. 21-23, 32, 45, 50, 120*

PILIAVIN, I, and BRIAR, S. (1968), 'Police Encounters with Juveniles: in Rubington, E., and Weinberg, M., (eds.), *Deviance,* New York, Macmillan. *p.87*

PLATT, A. (1969), *The Child Savers: The Invention of Delinquency;* Chicago, University of Chicago Press. *pp. 87, 112, 120*

PLATT, A. (1973a), 'Features Review Symposium', *Sociological Quarterly,* 14, 597-599. *pp. 79-80, 120*

PLATT, A. (1973b), 'Interview with Platt', *Issues in Criminology,* 8 (1), 11-22. *pp. 79, 120*

PLATT, A. (1975), 'Prospects for a Radical Criminology in the U.S.A.', in I. Taylor, P. Walton and J. Young, eds, *Critical Criminology,* op. cit. *pp. 23, 78-9*

PLUMMER, K. (1975), *Sexual Stigma: An Interactionist Account;* London, Routledge and Kegan Paul. *p. 103*

POLLNER, M. (1974), 'Sociological and Common Sense Models for the Labelling Process', in R. Turner, (ed.) *Ethnomethodology,* op. cit. *p. 97*

POPPER, K. R. (1963), *Conjectures and Refutations;* London, Routledge and Kegan Paul. *p. 128*

QUINE, W. V. O. (1973a), *From a Logical Point of View;* New York, Harper and Row. *p. 128*

QUINE, W. V. O. (1973b), 'Two Dogmas of Empiricism', in W. V. O. Quine, ed., *From a Logical Point of View,* op. cit. *p. 128*

QUINNEY, R. (1970), *The Social Reality of Crime;* Boston, Little, Brown. *p. 120*

QUINNEY, R. (1972a), 'The Ideology of Law: Notes for a Radical Alternative to Legal Repression', *Issues in Criminology,* 7, 1, 1-35. *p. 24*

QUINNEY, R. (1972b), 'From Repression to Liberation: Social Theory in a Radical Age', in R. Scott and J. Douglas, eds, *Theoretical Perspectives on Deviance,* op. cit. *p. 76-80*

QUINNEY, R. (1973), 'Feature Review Symposium', *Sociological Quarterly,* 14, 589-594. *pp. 52, 74-5, 80*

QUINNEY, R. (1974), *Critique of Legal Order;* Boston, Little, Brown. *p. 120*

QUINNEY, R. (1975), 'Crime Control in Capitalist Society: A Critical Philosophy

of Legal Order', in I. Taylor, P. Walton and J. Young, eds, *Critical Criminology,* op. cit. *pp. 74-5, 79*
QUINNEY, R. and WILDEMAN, J. (1977), *The Problem of Crime: A Critical Introduction to Criminology:* New York, Harper and Row. *pp. 39, 45, 50*

RAINS, P. (1971), *Becoming an Unwed Mother;* Chicago, Aldine. *pp. 90, 108*
RAINS, P. (1976), 'Imputations of Deviance: A Retrospective Essay on the Labelling Perspective', *Social Problems,* 23 (1), 1-11. *p. 87*
RAWLS, J. (1971), *A Theory of Justice;* Cambridge, Mass., Harvard University Press. *p. 48*
REISS, A. (1962), 'The Social Integration of Queers and Peers', in H. S. Becker, *The Other Side: Perspectives on Deviance,* op. cit. *pp. 90, 107, 118*
REISS, I. L. (1970), 'Premarital Sex as Deviant Behavior', *American Sociological Review,* 35, 1, 78-87. *pp. 102, 107*
REX, J., ed. (1974), *Approaches to Sociology;* London, Routledge and Kegan Paul. *p. 104-5*
REYNOLDS, J., PETRAS, J. and MELTZER, B. (1975), *Symbolic Interactionism: Origins, Variables and Critique;* London, Routledge and Kegan Paul. *p. 114*
ROBY, P. A. (1969), 'Politics and Criminal Law', *Social Problems,* 17, (1), 83-109. *p. 112*
ROCK, P. (1973a), *Deviant Behaviour;* London, Hutchinson. *pp. 90, 103-4, 107, 114, 116, 121, 155*
ROCK, P. (1973b), 'Phenomenalism and Essentialism in Deviancy Theory', *Sociology,* 7, 1, 12-129. *p. 91*
ROCK, P. (1974), 'Conceptions of Moral Order', *British Journal of Criminology,* 14 (2), 139-49. *p. 116*
ROCK, P. (forthcoming), *The Making of Symbolic Interactionism;* London, Macmillan. *pp. 94, 121*
ROCK, P. and McINTOSH, M., eds (1974), *Deviance and Social Control;* London, Tavistock. *p. 87-8*
ROGERS, J. W. and BUFFALO, M. D. (1974), 'Fighting Back: Nine Modes of Adaptation to a Deviant Label', *Social Problems,* 22 (1), 101-18. *p. 90*
ROSE, A., ed. (1962), *Human Behavior and Social Processes;* New York, Houghton Mifflin. *p. 113*
ROSE, A. (1967), *The Power Structure: Political Process in American Society;* New York, Oxford University Press. *p. 113*
ROSS, A. (1975), *On Guilt, Responsibility and Punishment;* London, Stevens. *p. 51*
ROTENBERG, M. (1974), 'Self Labelling: A Missing Link in the Societal Reaction Theory of Deviance', *Sociological Review,* 22, 3, 335-54. *pp, 90, 118*
ROTENBERG, M. (1975), 'Self Labelling Theory: Preliminary Findings Among Mental Patients', *British Journal of Criminology,* 15 (4), 360-75. *p. 118*
ROY, D. (1954), 'Efficiency and the Fix: Informal Intergroup Relations in a Piece-work Machine Shop', *American Journal of Sociology,* 60 (3), 255-66. *p. 98*

SAGARIN, E. (1967), 'Voluntary Associations Among Sexual Deviants', *Criminologica,* 5, 1, 8-22. *p. 95*

SAGARIN, E. (1975), *Deviance and Deviants: An Introduction to Devalued People;* New York, Praeger. *p. 121*

SCHEFF, T. J. (1966), *Being Mentally Ill;* London, Weidenfeld and Nicolson. *pp. 89, 105*

SCHEFF, T. J. (1968), 'Negotiating Reality', *Social Problems,* 16 (1), 3-17. *p. 112*

SCHEFF, T. J., ed. (1975), *Labelling Madness;* London, Spectrum Books. *p. 116-7*

SCHERVISH, P. G. (1973), 'The Labelling Perspective', *American Sociologist,* 8, 2, 47-56. *p. 106*

SCHUR, E. (1963), *Crimes Without Victims: Deviant Behavior and Public Policy;* Englewood Cliffs, N. J., Prentice-Hall. *pp. 87, 103*

SCHUR, E. (1971), *Labelling Deviant Behaviour: Its Sociological Implications;* London, Harper and Row. *pp. 102-4, 120*

SCHUR, E. (1973), *Radical Non-Intervention: Rethinking the Delinquency Problem;* Englewood Cliffs, N. J., Prentice-Hall. *p. 50*

SCHUR, E. (1975), 'Comments', in W. Gove, ed., *The Labelling of Deviance,* op. cit. *p. 50*

SCHWENDINGER, H. and SCHWENDINGER, J. (1975), 'Defenders of Order or Guardians of Human Rights', in I. Taylor, P. Walton and J. Young, *Critical Criminology,* op. cit. *pp. 23, 78, 108*

SCOTT, R. (1969), *The Making of Blind Men;* New York, Russell and Sage. *pp. 96, 108, 118*

SCOTT, R. (1970), 'Construction of Conception of Stigma by Professional Experts', in J. Douglas, ed., *Deviance and Respectability,* op. cit. *p. 96*

SCOTT, R. and DOUGLAS, J., eds (1972), *Theoretical Perspectives on Deviance;* New York, Basic Books. *pp. 97, 121*

SCULL, A. (1977), *Decarceration: Community Treatment and the Deviant,* Englewood Cliffs, N. J., Prentice-Hall. *pp. 16, 51*

SHOHAM, S. (1970), *The Mark of Cain: The Stigma Theory of Crime and Deviation;* Jerusalem, Israel University Press. *p. 120*

SKLAIR, L. (1970), 'The Fate of the "Functional Requisites" in Parsonian Sociology', *British Journal of Sociology,* 21 (March), 30-42. *p. 8*

SOROKIN, P., (1956) *Fads and Foibles in Modern Sociology,* New York, Regnery. *p. 101*

SPECTOR, M. (1976), 'Labelling Theory in *Social Problems:* A Young Journal Launches a New Theory', *Social Problems,* 24 (1), 69-75. *p. 85*

SPECTOR, M. (1977), 'Legitimating Homosexuality', *Society* 14, 5, 52-59. *p. 112*

SPERGEL, I. (1964), *Rackerville, Slumtown, Haulberg;* Chicago University Press. *p. 60*

STEBBINS, R. (1971), *Commitment to Deviance: The Non-Professional Criminal in the Community;* Westport, Conn., Greenwood Press. *p. 104*

STRAUSS, A. (1964), 'The Hospital as a Negotiated Order', in E. Friedson, ed., *The Hospital in Modern Society,* op. cit. *p. 116*

SUDNOW, D. (1965), 'Normal Crimes: Sociological Features of the Penal Code', *Social Problems,* 12 (Winter), 255-76. *p. 103*

SYKES, G. and MATZA, D. (1957), 'Techniques of Neutralisation: A Theory of Delinquency', *American Sociological Review,* 22, December, 664-70. *pp. 34, 153*

TAYLOR, B. (1976), 'Motives for Guilt-Free Pederasty: Some Literary Considerations', *Sociological Review,* 24, 1, 97-114. *p. 160*

TAYLOR, I. (1973a), Review of Walter Connor's "Deviance in Soviet Society", *British Journal of Criminology,* 13, 1, 66-70. *p. 9*

TAYLOR, I. (1973b), 'Prospects for Radical Criminological Theory and Practice: Some Thoughts on the British Experience', paper presented to the First Conference of the European Group for the Study of Deviance and Social Control, September 1973. *p. 84*

TAYLOR, I. and TAYLOR, L. (1972), 'Changes in the Motivational Construction of Deviance', *Catalyst,* 7. *pp. 121, 160*

TAYLOR, I. and TAYLOR, L., eds (1973), *Politics and Deviance;* Harmondsworth, Penguin.

TAYLOR, I. and WALTON, P. (1970), 'Values in Deviancy Theory and Society', *British Journal of Sociology,* 21 (4), 362-74. *p. 143*

TAYLOR, I., WALTON, P. and YOUNG, J. (1973a), *The New Criminology: For a Social Theory of Deviance;* London, Routledge and Kegan Paul. *pp. 4, 15, 16, 20-21, 25, 27, 41 et seq, 58 et seq, 89, 90, 103, 109-110, 119, 123, 137-142, 153*

TAYLOR, I., WALTON, P. and YOUNG, J. (1973b), 'Rejoinder to the Reviewers', *British Journal of Criminology,* 13 (4), 400-403. *p. 10*

TAYLOR, I., WALTON, P. and YOUNG, J., eds (1975a), *Critical Criminology;* London, Routledge and Kegan Paul. *pp 4-5 and Ch. 1,* passim, *41 et seq, 58 et seq, 96-7*

TAYLOR, I., WALTON, P. and YOUNG, J. (1975b), 'Critical Criminology in Britain: Review and Prospects', in I. Taylor, P. Walton and J. Young, eds, *Critical Criminology,* op. cit. *pp. 12, 73, 76*

TAYLOR, I. and YOUNG, J. (1977), untitled, unpublished paper given at the Fifth Conference of European Groups for the Study of Deviance and Social Control, Barcelona, September 1977. *pp. 38-40, 51*

TAYLOR, L. (1972), 'The Significance and Interpretation of Replies to Motivational Questions: The Case of Sex Offenders', *Sociology,* 6 (1), 23-39. *pp. 34, 160, 162*

TAYLOR, L. and WALTON, P. (1971), 'Industrial Sabotage: Motives and Meanings', in S. Cohen, ed., *Images of Deviance,* op. cit. *p. 161*

THIO, A. (1973), 'Class Bias in the Sociology of Deviance', *American Sociologist,* 8, 1, 1-12. *pp. 100, 108*

THORSELL, B.A. and KLEMPE, L.W. (1972), 'Labelling: Reinforcement and Deterrent?', *Law and Society Review,* 6, 3, 393-403. *p. 90*

TITMUSS, R. (1971), *The Gift Relationship: From Human Blood to Social Policy;* London, Allen and Unwin. *p. 11*

TITTLE, C. R. (1975), 'Deterrents or Labelling?', *Social Forces,* 53, 3, 399-410. *p. 90*

TOLMAN, E. (1958), *Behavior and Psychological Man;* Berkeley, University of California Press. *p. 154-5*

TRICE, H. and ROMAN, P. (1970), 'Delabelling, Relabelling and Alcoholics Anonymous', *Social Problems,* 17 (4), 538-46. *p. 90*

TURNER, R. (1972), 'Deviance Avowal as Neutralisation of Commitment', *Social Problems,* 19 (3), 308-21. *pp. 90, 106, 118*

TURNER, R., (ed.) (1974), *Ethnomethodology;* Harmondsworth, Penguin.

VON HIRSCH, A. (1976), *Doing Justice: The Choice of Punishments (Report o* *the Committee for the Study of Incarceration);* New York, Hill and Wang *pp. 36-39*

WALTON, P. (1973), 'The Case of the Weathermen', in I. Taylor and L. Taylor eds, *Politics and Deviance,* op. cit. *pp. 77, 104-5*

WARD, R. (1971), 'Labelling Theory: A Critical Analysis', *Criminology,* 9, 2 an 3, 268-90. *p. 102*

WARREN, C. A. B. (1974a), *Identity and Community in the Gay World;* London John Wiley. *p. 98-9*

WARREN, C. A. B. (1974b), 'The Use of Stigmatising Social Labels in Conven tionalizing Deviant Behaviour', *Sociology and Social Research,* 58, 3, 303-11 *pp. 90, 118*

WARREN, C. A. B. and JOHNSON, J. M. (1972), 'A Critique of Labelling Theor from the Phenomenological Perspective', in R. Scott and J. Douglas, eds *Theoretical Perspectives on Deviance,* op. cit. *pp. 89, 90, 100, 120-1*

WILKINS, L. (1964), *Social Deviance;* London, Tavistock. *pp. 47 87*

WILLIAMS, C. and WEINBERG, M. (1971), *Homosexuals and the Military: A* *Study of Less than Honourable Discharge;* New York, Harper and Row. *p. 89*

WILSON, J. (1975), *Thinking About Crime;* New York, Basic Books. *p. 50*

WOOTTON, A. (1975), *Dilemmas of Discourse;* London, Allen and Unwin *p. 160*

WRONG, D. (1961), 'The Over-Socialised Conception of Man', *American* *Sociological Review,* 26, (April), 183-91. *pp. 1, 3*

YOUNG, J. (1970), *The Drugtakers;* London, McGibbon and Kee. *p. 120*

YOUNG, J. (1974), 'New Directions in Subcultural Theory', in J. Rex, ed. *Approaches to Sociology,* op. cit. *pp. 104-5*

YOUNG, J. (1975), 'Working-Class Criminology', in I. Taylor, P. Walton an J. Young, eds, *Critical Criminology,* op. cit. *pp. 6, 11-12, 19, 22, 24-5, 27, 33 43-45, 120*

ZIJDERVELD, A. C. (1972), *The Abstract Society: A Cultural Analysis of Ou* *Time;* Harmondsworth, Penguin.

ZURCHER, L. and KIRKPATRICK, R. G. (1976), *Citizens for Decency: Anti* *Pornography Crusades as Status Crusades;* Austin and London, University o Texas Press. *p. 112*

Index